DotNetNuke® Websites

D1430459

DotNetNuke® Websites
Problem — Design — Solution

Tracy Wittenkeller

WILEY

Wiley Publishing, Inc.

DotNetNuke® Websites

Published by
Wiley Publishing, Inc.
10475 Crosspoint Boulevard
Indianapolis, IN 46256
www.wiley.com

Published simultaneously in Canada

ISBN: 978-0-470-19064-7

Manufactured in the United States of America

10 9 8 7 6 5 4 3 2 1

Library of Congress Cataloging-in-Publication Data

Wittenkeller, Tracy, 1965-
    DotNetNuke websites : problem, design, solution/Tracy Wittenkeller.
     p. cm.
    Includes index.
    ISBN 978-0-470-19064-7 (paper/website)
     1. DotNetNuke (Electronic resource)   2. Active server pages.   3. Web sites—Design.   4. Web site
development. I. Title.
    TK5105.8885.A26W62   2008
    006.7'6—dc22
                                        2008022845

To my beautiful wife, Allison — Your undying love, patience, friendship, strength, and support mean more to me than I can possibly ever express or repay. I don't know how you do it. I'm the luckiest man on earth.

To my beautiful daughters, Miette (mommie) and Brielle (bwells), and to my son, Remy (bo-DEE) — Your boundless joy makes me laugh and cry at the same time. You mean more to me than anything in the world.

I love you all with my heart and soul.

About the Author

Tracy Wittenkeller is the president and founder of T-WORX, INC, a leading provider of professional DotNetNuke skins and website solutions. He has been working with DotNetNuke since its inception over five years ago and has successfully offered skins commercially since November 2004 through his company's website (`www.t-worx.com`), snowcovered (`www.snowcovered.com`), and the DotNetNuke Marketplace (`http://marketplace.dotnetnuke.com`).

As a result of his company's success in the commercial skin market, Tracy has developed custom DNN skin packages and custom website solutions for a large variety of companies all over the world. He works with many DotNetNuke core members and has also donated his time to different aspects of the DotNetNuke open source project. He has been a professional designer for web, print, and electronic presentation media for over 17 years. He also does a lot of public speaking at important .NET conferences in person and online.

If you want to contact Tracy to talk about this book, please use the Contact t-worx form or blog on his website (`www.t-worx.com`).

Credits

Acknowledgments

I almost can't believe the time has finally come for me to take the opportunity to thank all the people that have had a role, at some level or another, in helping me to write my first book because it means that I am actually almost done . . . WooHoo!

First, I would like to thank Jim Minatel, the Wrox acquisitions editor, for accepting my idea for this book. When I learned that Wrox might be looking for someone to write a skinning book for DNN, I was referred to Jim, and I was really excited . . . but only for a moment. After introducing myself to Jim via e-mail, I quickly learned that Wrox had already committed to another "skinner" for a book just one week prior! So my hopes were dashed right? Wrong! Although Wrox had already committed to an author for a skinning book, Jim told me he was open to additional possibilities. Well, as soon as I suggested my idea, Jim agreed that it would be helpful to the DNN community . . . and the rest is history. Thanks Jim!

Next, I would like to thank the two editors that kept in touch with me throughout the writing of the book and did their best to keep me on schedule: Rosanne Koneval and Chris Webb. Unfortunately, I did not make it easy for them (in fact, I'm behind my schedule even as I write this). However, I can't thank them enough for their patience, positivity, and understanding throughout this entire process. You guys have been great!

In addition to the Wrox folks, there are several people who deserve many thanks. First, I have to start with Darrell Hardy for a number of reasons. Darrell originally introduced me to DNN in its early years as IBuy Spy Portal after many months of prodding (and more than my share of two-by-fours from him to the side of my head). I'm glad I finally listened because now, just a few short years later, my entire business is built around DNN, and my company, T-WORX, has worldwide recognition for the products and services we deliver — how cool is that? Darrell is a really good friend and colleague. And I'm happy to say that we still work together on almost a daily basis. I'm also amazed at the fact that he still has the patience to field stupid questions from me so regularly, which alone is pretty impressive. But, even more impressive, is the fact that he seems to have the answer to just about any technical question I can throw at him because he is a very good Microsoft developer. (In fact, without his help, I could not have made it though Chapter 2 of this book.) For all these reasons (and more) . . . thanks Darrell for being my go-to-guy when I need answers or just need someone to listen. Your friendship means a lot.

Next, I would like to thank a few members of the DNN core team, in particular, Chris Paterra, Nik Kalyani, and Scott Willhite. Thanks for answering my IMs, even when you wanted to stay hidden. It's almost like having a live Q&A at my fingertips. Actually, it's even better than that. Your knowledge is vast and so much appreciated!

I would also like to thank all the DNN developers that I collaborate with who are paving their own way using this wonderful framework. Developers like Alex del Real of Adcuent Consulting and Technology (www.adcuent.com), Chad Nash of Datasprings (www.datasprings.com), Peter Donker of Bring2Mind (www.bring2mind.net), Will Morgenwick of ActiveModules (www.activemodules.com), Malik Kahn of PointClick Technologies (www.pointclick.net), Kevin Schreiner and Chris Chodnicki

Acknowledgements

of R2integrated (`www.r2integrated.com`), Lee Sykes of DNN Creative Magazine (`www.dnncreative.com`), and many others. These world-class developers offer great products and services and add a ton of value with their DNN expertise and forward thinking. I attribute part of my own success to the relationships I have with these guys, and other DNN wizards, whom I have not mentioned.

Finally, I want to thank my readers for discovering and using this book. Over the course of the last five years, I have found a true passion for DotNetNuke and achieved a level of success that would not have been possible without my own discovery of the framework. I sincerely hope DotNetNuke does the same for you!

Contents

Contents

Contents

Foreword

Over the past ten years we have witnessed a fundamental shift in terms of how a new phenomenon known as the Internet has affected our everyday lives. From humble beginnings as a part-time hobby for the technically inclined, the web has evolved to an essential consumer service, and we find ourselves increasingly more dependent on online tools for communication, collaboration, education, and commerce.

Nowhere is this change more profound than in the professional world, as we observe the disruptive effect of technology on every market sector and industry around the globe. And with broader acceptance comes even greater innovation, which will continue to push the economic, social, and political boundaries in the coming years. For organizations of all sizes, the web represents an exciting new frontier. But like any new frontier, there is plenty of uncharted territory to navigate, which can definitely prove to be challenging as the landscape continues to change and evolve. In today's highly competitive world, your online presence represents a critical extension of your business. As more consumers get online, your website is fast becoming the first point of contact, regardless of whether you are serving a local or global market. As a result, it is essential that this first impression conveys the core identity, values, and goals of your organization. And in addition to meeting your ongoing brand and marketing objectives, you really need to be leveraging your site as an interactive communication channel for cultivating and strengthening customer relationships and emerging business opportunities.

In the early stages of the Internet, there was a massive land rush for domain names and great pressure for business owners to establish an online presence for their brick and mortar operations. The problem in these early stages was that the tools were so immature that the actual opportunity offered by the Internet could not be capitalized upon by the majority of its users. In fact, more often than not, a company's website ended up becoming more of a balance sheet liability than an asset, as even the seemingly simple task of keeping basic content up-to-date proved to be non-trivial. This frustration resulted in many "first-movers" abandoning the web altogether for a period of time, as they could not see the return on the investment. The only exceptions were large enterprise organizations, who could afford to invest, substantial sums of money into full-time content editors or sophisticated content management solutions.

Over the years, a variety of solutions have been developed in order to address the online needs of business owners. So many solutions in fact, that we are now approaching the opposite extreme of having too many options to choose from when it comes to content management. From basic website builders to highly sophisticated web platforms, it has become increasingly more difficult to understand the advantages and disadvantages of each approach, and make educated decisions for the long term benefit and economic viability of your organization. The one thing which has remained constant, however, is the exponential growth of digital assets within the enterprise and the critical need to manage them effectively, using established information architecture techniques and advanced software solutions.

The DotNetNuke® project is a collaborative, software development effort aimed at creating a robust, enterprise-grade, full-featured, and freely available open source implementation of a web content management system for the Microsoft platform. The goal of the project is to provide a secure, extensible, high performance web application framework, which provides content management services focused on addressing the broadest set of online business requirements and the most innovative web trends.

Foreword

In this book, Tracy has done an exceptional job of explaining the various facets of content management from a serious business perspective. The Problem, Design, Solution approach provides unparalleled insight into the decision-making criteria you will face each step of the way. And the focus on how to apply the DotNetNuke web application framework to solve real business problems provides greater value and insight than any high level tutorial. His in-depth experience and product knowledge provide the reader with a potent combination of fundamental content management principles, as well as guidance on how to use the DotNetNuke software platform productively and effectively. This makes *DotNetNuke Websites* a must-have book, not only for users of the DNN® platform, but also for professionals who need to understand how a web site can be used to fill a vital role in their organization.

Shaun Walker
President/Chief Architect
DotNetNuke Corporation
DotNetNuke®, DNN®, and the DotNetNuke® logo are trademarks of DotNetNuke Corporation.

Introduction

Dear Reader, Thank you for choosing this book, and welcome to *DotNetNuke Websites Problem — Design — Solution*. You have taken the first step to understanding the many benefits of the DotNetNuke framework and harnessing its power to create truly professional website solutions. The idea of this book was born from the overwhelming need of the many DNN users who require help with creating real-world websites. Because DotNetNuke is in its infancy, very few books have been written to date about using DNN's flexible, powerful framework. Many people are using DNN because of its excellent functions as a Content Management System (CMS), and because it is open source. However, many users don't understand how to utilize the many features and functions of DNN to their fullest. I thought a book like this would be helpful to DNN users who are having difficulty implementing DNN for their website(s) on a day-to-day basis, or for users who are not taking full advantage of DNN's built-in feature set because they lack the necessary experience, or because they are simply not aware of the possibilities.

About four years ago, a colleague introduced me to DNN (thanks Darrell!). At the time, DNN was in its early stages as "IBuy Spy Portal," and I was a Mac guru with a professional design background spanning 17 years. At first glance, IBuy Spy Portal was just another PC application that I had no interest in whatsoever. After all, I was a hardcore Mac user and to me the only good use for a PC was as a paperweight. After months of prodding, I decided the only way to silence my colleague was to experience IBuy Spy Portal in all its splendor, so I could tell him how right I was about my initial reluctance to give it the time of day. Needless to say, it didn't take me long to see the light. I was immediately taken by what I experienced, and the opportunities that were apparent to me were seemingly endless. It literally changed my life overnight. Strange as it may seem, I've gone from being a well-traveled Mac guru to becoming a true DNN evangelist. And now that I have achieved my own level of success with DNN, I decided the best way for me to show my appreciation and give something back to the DNN community was to write this book in an effort to help others who have traveled their own paths to DNN. My hope is that this book does at least two things: raises your level of excitement and understanding of DNN and what can be achieved with it, and gives you the knowledge to take your DNN website(s) to a truly professional level.

The objective of this book is to enlighten you in the ways of DNN by showing you how to design and implement a professional, real-world DNN website solution, while taking the opportunity to outline and detail many of the terrific features of the DNN framework. While describing in detail how to take full advantage of just some of DNN's feature set, I'll try to explain most of the problems you'll face when building your website, and offer one or more solutions for solving them. In the end, the result will be a great deal of knowledge surrounding a key set of features that includes a myriad of functions you may not have thought were possible from an open source application framework. Many beginning to intermediate users will be surprised, as I was, by the depth and power of DNN and the ease at which professional-level, modern functionality can be implemented. More advanced users may already be utilizing DNN in similar ways but should also find the information contained in this book to be helpful and insightful. I hope you enjoy reading this book and, I hope it helps you create more complete, functional, professional, and profitable website solutions.

You can browse the website online at www.wrox.com.

> The author's blog is available at www.t-worx.com/blog/twittenkeller. Please keep an eye on it to read about further development and explanation of the sample project.

What This Book Covers

This book is basically a large case study that starts with a foundation and works its way through to completion with a series of designs and solutions for each incremental step along the way. What sets the Problem-Design-Solution series apart from other Wrox series is the structure of the book and the start-to-finish approach to many aspects of a completed project. Specifically, this book leads the reader through the development of a complete modern, sophisticated, highly functional, and professional DNN business website solution including many of DNN's key built-in modules/functionality:

- ❑ Account login/registration, roles, and permissions
- ❑ Announcements
- ❑ FAQ
- ❑ Media
- ❑ Links
- ❑ Survey
- ❑ Text/HTML

From an administrative point of view, the following features and problems are also covered:

- ❑ Full DNN Administration to manage many aspects of the website solution
- ❑ Skin deployment
- ❑ Content deployment

The implementation of each of these features provides the opportunity to present various processes of creating, designing, and developing our DNN website solution such as the following:

- ❑ Skin and containers/site layout
- ❑ CSS customizations
- ❑ Security: site membership, roles, and profile management
- ❑ Detailed content implementation: working with pages and modules

This book covers DNN's key built-in features and demonstrates how to get the most out of them to create a complete, professional website solution. All of the features are explained and presented in detail to make you aware of all of the options that are possible. At the end of the book you will have learned many of the best practices for using DNN and will have acquired a well-rounded foundation to use it comfortably on a day-to-day basis, allowing you to gain proficiency and efficiency in developing more professional and profitable DNN website solutions.

How This Book Is Structured

This book provides the foundation to build a complete, professional DNN website solution based on a key set of built-in features. All chapters are self-contained components within the overall solution, build on the chapters before it, and are structured in three sections:

❑ **Problem:** This section defines the problem or problems to be addressed in the chapter: Which key DNN features should you take advantage of, and why are these features important? What restrictions or other factors need to be taken into account?

❑ **Design:** After the problem is defined adequately, this section describes what features are needed to solve the problem. This will give you a broad idea of how the solution will work, or how the solution to the problem will be accomplished.

❑ **Solution:** After preparing what is going to be accomplished and why (and how it solves the problem defined earlier), we will produce and discuss the code, page, and module configurations, and so on, and any other material that will realize the design and solve the problem laid out at the beginning of the chapter. Just as the coverage of this book as a whole is weighted toward solution, so is each chapter. This is where you will get hands-on practice and create the code.

This book is intended to be read from cover to cover, so that you start from scratch and finish with a complete website solution. However, the book follows a modular structure, so every chapter is quite self-contained and implements DNN features that, if necessary, can be "turned on or off" at any time.

Whom This Book Is For

This book is *not* for advanced programmers who use DNN at the core level to create modules or extend the project. This book *is* intended for beginning-to-intermediate users, as well as some advanced users, who want to learn:

❑ How to create a great-looking DNN website and how to customize it with CSS.

❑ How to use DNN's built-in functions and modules to implement a complete professional, content-driven business website solution while providing the necessary core skills that will help you become proficient in your day-to-day usage of the framework.

While the book does not explain every last detail of the DNN technology, it does concentrate on functionality that is found "under the surface" while walking you through many processes and details that will allow you to take advantage of the DNN framework.

What You Need To Use This Book

To follow the book and build the project locally on your own computer, or to apply the downloadable and ready-to-use project files, you'll need the following:

❑ Installed DNN instance and database — at least version 4.7 recommended (Chapter 2 outlines complete prerequisites and installation details).

❑ Adobe Photoshop (version 7 or higher recommended) or other image editing software of your choice (all examples throughout the book use Photoshop 7).

❑ The HTML/CSS editor of your choice (all examples throughout the book use Dreamweaver).

Conventions

To help you get the most from the text and keep track of what's happening, I've used a number of conventions throughout the book.

Source

This section includes the source code.

```
Source code
Source code

Source code
```

Output

This section lists the output.

```
Example output
Example output

Example output
```

> Boxes like this one hold important, not-to-be forgotten information that is directly relevant to the surrounding text.

Tips, hints, tricks, and asides to the current discussion are offset and placed in italics like this.

As for styles in the text:

❑ We *highlight* new terms and important words when we introduce them.

❑ We show keyboard strokes like this: Ctrl+A.

❑ We show filenames, URLs, and code within the text like so: `persistence.properties`.

❑ We present code in two different ways:

```
In code examples we highlight new and important code with a gray background.
The gray highlighting is not used for code that's less important in the present
context, or has been shown before.
```

Source Code

As you work through the examples in this book, you may choose either to type in all the code manually or to use the source code files that accompany the book. All of the source code used in this book is available for download at www.wrox.com. Once at the site, simply locate the book's title (either by using the Search box or by using one of the title lists) and click the Download Code link on the book's detail page to obtain all the source code for the book.

> *Because many books have similar titles, you may find it easiest to search by ISBN; this book's ISBN is 978-0-470-19064-7.*

Once you download the code, just decompress it with your favorite compression tool. Alternately, you can go to the main Wrox code download page at www.wrox.com/dynamic/books/download.aspx to see the code available for this book and all other Wrox books.

Errata

We make every effort to ensure that there are no errors in the text or in the code. However, no one is perfect, and mistakes do occur. If you find an error in one of our books, such as a spelling mistake or faulty piece of code, we would be very grateful for your feedback. By sending in errata you may save another reader hours of frustration, and at the same time you will be helping us provide even higher quality information.

To find the errata page for this book, go to www.wrox.com and locate the title using the Search box or one of the title lists. Then, on the book details page, click the Book Errata link. On this page you can view all errata that has been submitted for this book and posted by Wrox editors. A complete book list including links to each book's errata is also available at www.wrox.com/misc-pages/booklist.shtml.

If you don't spot "your" error on the Book Errata page, go to www.wrox.com/contact/techsupport .shtml and complete the form there to send us the error you have found. We'll check the information and, if appropriate, post a message to the book's errata page and fix the problem in subsequent editions of the book.

p2p.wrox.com

For author and peer discussion, join the P2P forums at p2p.wrox.com. The forums are a Web-based system for you to post messages relating to Wrox books and related technologies and interact with other readers and technology users. The forums offer a subscription feature to e-mail you topics of interest of your choosing when new posts are made to the forums. Wrox authors, editors, other industry experts, and your fellow readers are present on these forums.

At http://p2p.wrox.com, you will find a number of different forums that will help you, not only as you read this book, but also as you develop your own applications. To join the forums, just follow these steps:

1. Go to p2p.wrox.com and click the Register link.

2. Read the terms of use and click Agree.

3. Complete the required information to join as well as any optional information you wish to provide and click Submit.

4. You will receive an e-mail with information describing how to verify your account and complete the joining process.

You can read messages in the forums without joining P2P but in order to post your own messages, you must join.

Once you join, you can post new messages and respond to messages other users post. You can read messages at any time on the Web. If you would like to have new messages from a particular forum e-mailed to you, click the Subscribe to this Forum icon by the forum name in the forum listing.

For more information about how to use the Wrox P2P, be sure to read the P2P FAQs for answers to questions about how the forum software works as well as many common questions specific to P2P and Wrox books. To read the FAQs, click the FAQ link on any P2P page.

1

Introducing the Project — mbrdesigncorp.com at a Glance

This chapter introduces the project that is going to be developed throughout the book. The concept behind `mbrdesigncorp.com` (a fictitious name) and this entire book is to provide a well-rounded education of DotNetNuke (DNN) and teach you how to use DNN thoroughly for your own website development. It provides you with the tools to make your everyday use of DNN much more efficient and successful. While following along, keep in mind that this website, like any other DNN website, can easily be modified to meet the needs of your own real-world requirements. As the focus of this book is directed at showing you how to leverage the power of DNN's extensive feature set, the book goes into great detail showing how to take advantage of DNN's functionality, thereby giving you a strong foundation for using it to develop your own feature-rich, professional website solutions.

This book follows a "Problem-Design-Solution" approach in each chapter: The Problem section explains the business requirements for the information designed in that specific chapter, the Design section is used to develop our roadmap for meeting those requirements, and the Solution section is where we write our code to implement the design. This is unlike traditional computer books because the focus is not on teaching basic concepts, but rather showing you how to apply your knowledge to solve real-world business requirements. If you are new to DNN, then this book will give you a good jumpstart to get immediate results. If you are a beginner-to-intermediate user and generally familiar with the basic concepts of web development with DNN, and you want to learn more about the DNN framework, then let's move forward!

Problem

Everywhere you turn on the Internet there is a proliferation of web design companies offering a multitude of similar products and services. It seems there are new companies cropping up every day that offer web design in some shape or form. Whether good or bad, it goes without saying that competition is constantly increasing. And while many web design sites are nothing more than brochure-ware displaying portfolios of work, companies must do more to distinguish themselves from others and give themselves an edge to be taken seriously as a professional organization worthy of being contacted and secured for business. While it is important for a web design company to have a nice-looking website with an impressive portfolio, successful websites also build and foster virtual relationships. They do this by providing visitors with up-to-date, fresh information about their company or the products and services they offer. DNN makes it possible in many ways to communicate with site visitors and/or registered users and deliver new content (such as information about new projects, news articles, and updates regarding new product releases) quickly and efficiently, using a myriad of built-in functional choices that set it apart from other content management systems.

Design

The Design section of each chapter is devoted to discussing the problem and designing a solution. This typically means gathering a list of business requirements and desired features to implement, as well as ideas for the overall look and feel of the site and content structure. At the beginning of the project we start by thinking about the needs of our website, and how we might use DNN to facilitate those needs. I expand on those needs using DNN's built-in functionality. As I have already discussed, our sample website solution in this scenario is mbrdesigncorp.com, the website that's going to be built as I demonstrate many key features of DNN that you should find very valuable as you work with the application on a day-to-day basis. I'll begin by compiling a list of features below that our modern, dynamic, content-based website should have, and touch upon how the use of several everyday, real-world techniques can help you to create your own DNN projects much more efficiently and successfully.

❑　A successful content-based site needs a great-looking, intuitive user interface. Appearance is important, especially for a web design company. It's the first thing users notice — well before the site's functionality or the products and services being offered. In short, if our website doesn't look appealing, visitors aren't going to take it seriously enough to even consider your products and services as a design firm. Therefore, information on the site must be well-organized and easily navigable. The ability to change a site's look and feel, independent of its content, also helps to keep the site fresh and alive in the eyes of users. The ability to create great designs and convert them into complete DNN skin packages puts this power squarely in your hands.

❑　A successful, content-based site needs to have a fresh supply of content to make users want to come back often, especially if new products are constantly being offered. As is the case with all websites, if the content becomes stale, visitors lose interest and stop visiting. This means less revenue as reduced traffic means less interest in the products and services being offered through the website. To facilitate a constant stream of new, dynamic content, the site needs a mechanism that enables the site administrator(s) to easily update it. Furthermore, if you have content editors that are not technical, the site administration must be straightforward for non-technical users. As an added bonus, the ability for site administrators to assign start and expiration dates provides added flexibility when applying content that is tied to a specific promotion or timeframe. As you learn some of the techniques for customizing certain aspects of pages and modules, I'm confident you'll find that the new skills you acquire as a result, will make day-to-day content implementation/ updates much more straightforward.

❑　A successful content-based site doesn't stop with the ability to add different types of content and manage that content easily. A successful content-based website also allows administrators to easily change design attributes based on, for example, user feedback, without having to go back to the original designer and ask for code changes. Furthermore, after your site has been built, you've added content, and you're ready for a successful launch, you may want to apply some tweaks in the form of textual color changes, font size, or even the width of your site as it is displayed in a browser. DNN sites that have properly taken advantage of CSS can make all of these examples extremely trivial.

❑ A successful content-based site that sells web design products and services owes its success to its users and customers. To build a community of active members and returning customers, users have to have a unique identity that distinguishes them from other members/customers. For this reason, the site needs a registration feature as part of a larger user authentication/ authorization infrastructure. This will also be used to define roles and grant and/or restrict access to certain content/areas of the site. When you learn about Security Roles, understand the process of securing content/pages based on permission levels, and implement the techniques contained in this book for locking down content, you greatly increase your site's level of interactivity by a huge degree.

To recap everything briefly, mbrdesigncorp.com will be created using some key core feature sets that you will most likely adopt as a regular part of creating your own DNN website solutions. First, you implement a professional, easily changeable design layer that is separate from content and function. Next, you learn all about content administration and new techniques that will allow you to take advantage of some of DNN's key feature sets, while becoming more familiar with implementing various types of content. You also learn how to customize your content and define beginning and expiration dates. Finally, you learn about roles-based security, which allows you to define and implement all types of security for users or groups of users within a DNN website.

Although the sample project is built around a fictitious website, within the list of requirements you'll recognize some of the common functionality typically expected from websites you'll find today — sites you'll develop as a result of this book, or sites you are already developing.

Solution

The Solution section of each chapter will contain the instructions and actual code for implementing all of the features and requirements outlined and designed in the previous sections. For the first chapter, however, I provide a more detailed description of exactly what the following chapters will entail, so you can get a good idea of what the final result will be like.

In Chapter 2, you learn how to install the DNN framework in various scenarios. Depending on your environment, you'll choose the scenario that is right for you. In some cases, you may want to learn how to install the DNN framework in a live server environment or on your local computer, so you can develop without the speed constraints of your Internet connection and/or server.

Chapter 3 focuses on overall design for the DNN website. The objective of this chapter is to get readers thinking out-of-the-box and dispel the myths that a DNN website has to have a certain look and feel. This chapter examines the limitations and best-practice guidelines when creating or converting website designs for DNN. By the end of this chapter, you'll have a good understanding of what is possible with design as it relates to DNN websites.

In Chapter 4, you build the site's design, including the graphics, HTML, XML, and CSS files. You begin by examining a Photoshop (PSD) file that includes the design for skins and containers. (It is assumed that you have some basic working knowledge of Photoshop.) You learn how to organize a PSD file using layers and layer sets, create slices, and save images to be used in HTML skin and container files. Then, you learn the concept of Tokens — placeholders for dynamic content — and focus on building the HTML, CSS, and XML components/attributes of HTML-based skins and containers. By the end of this chapter, you'll be able to build all of the necessary components required for an HTML-based DNN skin package.

In Chapter 5, you learn how to package the completed skins and containers into a single skin package that can be installed on your DNN website. You learn the differences when uploading skin packages at the Admin level and at the Host level, and which option is appropriate for different situations, how to preview skins and containers, how to delete skin packages, and how to apply skins and containers to our website. When you have finished this chapter, you'll be able to comfortably package, upload, and apply skins and containers to a DNN website.

In Chapter 6, you start building your website pages in preparation for content. You learn how to add top-level and sub-level pages, create hidden pages, preview pages, move pages around the site, copy pages, delete pages, define page properties, apply/change skins, and define start and expire dates for displaying pages. By the end of this chapter, you'll know just about everything there is to know about configuring pages within your DNN website.

After you have created the site structure, and you have learned how to work with pages, you are introduced to the concept of modules in Chapter 7. This chapter provides an overview of modules and explores some of DNN's regularly used, key built-in modules in detail. You learn how to install modules, add new modules to a page, add existing modules to a page, move modules to different locations on a single page, move modules to other pages, delete modules, apply containers to modules and customize module settings and properties. In this chapter, you learn how to implement, in detail, the Text/HTML, Media, Announcements, Links, Survey, and FAQ modules. At the end of this chapter, you'll be able to get a great deal more use out of a few key core modules that will become part of your normal arsenal of the modules you use for all of your DNN website implementations.

In Chapter 8, you learn about DNN's CSS hierarchy and how DNN uses CSS to control page components and attributes of dynamic items. You learn about the default CSS styles used by DNN for display and how to eliminate unnecessary CSS code. Moreover, you learn how to change website attributes by customizing the default CSS styles using skin.css, which should be used as the overriding style sheet for the site. You also learn how to create your own custom skin and container CSS styles and apply them to elements within your DNN website.

In Chapter 9, you learn all about Security Roles. You learn about DNN's membership provider and methods for creating and deleting users, verifying login credentials, changing passwords, and more. This chapter provides in-depth information about defining the type of registration for your site, specifying fields for registration, creating and editing user accounts, creating Security Roles and Role Groups, applying Security Roles to user accounts, and adding define permissions at the page and module level. By the end of this chapter, you'll be able to create secure content that is locked down and available only to users with the appropriate permissions you specify.

Finally, Chapter 10 includes a summary of the additional techniques and resources that will help to make your DNN website implementations successful. And last, but certainly not least, you learn about what you should expect to see from DNN in the near future.

Summary

This chapter provided an overview of an aggressive plan to develop a highly functional content-based website that will show you how to use a great deal of DNN's built-in functionality. I painted a broad picture about what will be discussed, designed, and implemented throughout the remainder of the book. In each chapter, you'll learn something new about DNN, and at the end of the book you will have acquired the necessary skills to create a professional, real-world website solution and take advantage of several DNN features in ways you didn't even think of. Furthermore, the site you'll develop throughout this book will most likely provide a great deal more functionality than any site you've designed in the past. And I am certain you'll learn how to do more than you ever thought was possible with the DNN framework, and probably in a smaller amount of time, too.

2

Installing DotNetNuke 4.8.2

DotNetNuke is different from the traditional website. Understanding these differences is key to understanding what DotNetNuke is, how and why it should be used for professional business website solutions, and if it is right for a given set of specific business needs. This book walks you through the steps of developing a professional website in order to demonstrate these differences. This chapter demonstrates many of the varied installation options available on local computers and web servers, thus allowing you to follow along with the examples provided in this book. After successfully completing the examples in this chapter, you will be able to install DotNetNuke to your local computer or a web server.

DotNetNuke Framework vs. HTML

Prior to installing DotNetNuke, it is advantageous to have a basic understanding of the framework and how the application is different than a traditional website. Keep in mind the following:

❑ DotNetNuke is a web application.

❑ DotNetNuke is a Content Management System.

❑ DotNetNuke is a framework.

❑ DotNetNuke is open source software.

These statements get attention and raise eyebrows, but most often generate questions. As a web application, DNN is a fully functional program running on a web server delivering dynamic data to web browsers, and can be used as-is. As a Content Management System, DNN allows easy maintenance of content by technical and non-technical people. As a framework, it is highly extensible and flexible. It uses software providers, factories, and private assemblies to allow significant extensions and changes to functionality without changing the core software. As open source software, the code is available for validation and modification.

I do not recommend that you change the core software. Core Team actively seeks requests for enhancements. If core functionality changes must be made, it is recommended that you use the built-in extensibility via the software providers and factories.

Additionally, as open source software, DNN may be downloaded and installed by anyone free of charge. With a little knowledge of the installation processes and the installation options that are available, you can have DotNetNuke running in a matter of minutes.

Problem

In order to develop the `mbrdesigncorp.com` website, DotNetNuke must first be installed on the computer that will host the website.

If this is your first DotNetNuke website, or you are simply installing DotNetNuke to follow along with the examples, I highly recommend that you install DotNetNuke on your local computer.

Most users think of a website in the traditional sense — as having several independent static web pages stored as HTML or HTM files. Later versions of web servers allowed people to use file extensions such as ASP, CFM, or PSP to add dynamic content to each of these pages, each using different scripting technologies. The dynamic parts of these pages were often stored in a database. Using ASP.NET, DotNetNuke takes this one step further. This is a little bit of an over simplification, but think of it this way: DotNetNuke has one web page where all content is loaded from the database. The "page" is assembled on-the-fly with the content being determined by the request from the browser. Not only is the content stored in a database, but so is the menu structure and page layout for every page on the site. This is what gives DotNetNuke the ability to add a new page on-the-fly. There are no pages to upload, and therefore no additional work is required to make a page look like the rest of the site. The DotNetNuke application framework handles all of this and more.

With this information it is easy to see that installing DotNetNuke is more than just uploading pages and graphics. In fact, it is more like installing a series of Windows applications that is accessed via a web browser. As with all great leaps in technology, this brings about its own set of requirements and prerequisites.

Prerequisites

As with all applications there are prerequisites. The following list introduces the major pieces of software and options required to get DotNetNuke up and running.

❑ **Web server:** In order to run the DotNetNuke application you must have a computer that will run Microsoft Internet Information Services (IIS) 5.0 or greater. IIS comes with Windows XP Professional, Windows Vista, Windows Server 2000, and Windows Server 2003, but may not be installed by default. There is one currently supported alternative to IIS. This is the file system–based web server that comes with the current versions of Microsoft web development tools, including the free express versions.

❑ **Microsoft .NET runtime:** You must have ASP.NET runtime version 2.0 or later installed. You can download this free of charge from Microsoft at www.microsoft.com/downloads.

❑ **Database:** DotNetNuke data access is provider-based. This simply means that a piece of code (called a provider) is used to talk to a specific brand database. For instance, DotNetNuke comes with a Microsoft SQL provider and thus will work with Microsoft SQL Server 2000 or any later version. Data providers are available for several different database products, and more data providers are becoming available frequently. If you are currently using a database other than Microsoft SQL Server, check www.DotNetNuke.com to see if a data provider is available for your database. For all the examples in this book, we will be using versions of Microsoft SQL Server, including the Microsoft SQL Server 2005 Express edition, which can be downloaded free of charge from Microsoft at http://msdn.microsoft.com/vstudio/express/sql.

❑ **DotNetNuke application:** In addition to the preceding requirements, you must download the DotNetNuke software. DotNetNuke comes in multiple packages for several different purposes:

   ❑ **Source Package:** Contains everything, including full application source code.

   ❑ **Starter Kit Package:** Contains only the files needed to configure a development environment in Visual Web Developer Express or Visual Studio 2005.

   ❑ **Install Package:** Contains only the files needed for a runtime deployment to a web server.

   ❑ **Upgrade Package:** Contains only the files needed for an upgrade of an existing installation (does not include module packages).

   ❑ **Documentation Package:** Contains only developer documentation.

❑ **Install Wizard:** DotNetNuke comes with an install wizard. This wizard will help you configure your DotNetNuke website. I will use all three install options of the wizard in my examples.

Installing DotNetNuke is not like installing a simple Windows program where you run one install and you are done. With all the different options for the prerequisites, not to mention the different reasons for wanting to install DotNetNuke, there is no single correct way to complete the install.

When installing this software, then, you face the following challenges:

❑ Multiple reasons for installing DotNetNuke

❑ Multiple operating systems with slightly different setup requirements

❑ Multiple compatible database programs with different setup requirements

❑ Multiple installation options in the DotNetNuke install wizard

The combination of all these options means that there is no single best way to install DotNetNuke.

Design

This chapter covers two scenarios in four examples. These four examples are designed to provide the information in a way that the options provided in this section can be mixed and matched to your installation requirements.

Scenarios

1. Installing DotNetNuke on a local computer in order to evaluate, develop, or practice using the web application. You can also use this type of setup to "build" the website and then export the content to a template to be used on your production web server. This is the scenario for the first three examples.

2. Installing DotNetNuke on a hosted web server or your company's production web server. This would be the server where people will go to view your website.

The obvious split in these two scenarios is whether the application will be available for public consumption (via the Internet or an intranet) or for use on a single computer. With two scenarios split over four examples with each using a different operating system, you can see a broad range of installation options.

Do not limit yourself to looking at only the example for your target operating system. Each example offers information and ideas that can be used in other operating systems. For instance, the first example uses Visual Web Developer and the Starter Kit, which would also work in other operating systems.

Solution

These four examples use many of the installation options available for DotNetNuke. I recommend that you read through all the examples. You may mix and match the pieces, but you must make sure that you have all the prerequisites, as listed previously, for any given installation.

❑ **Fast and easy:** Windows XP Home, Visual Web Developer, SQL Server 2005 Express, DNN Starter Kit Package, DNN install wizard Auto install option.

❑ **Most common:** Windows XP Professional, IIS, SQL Server 2005 Express, DNN Install Package, DNN install wizard Auto install option.

❑ **Newest OS:** Windows Vista, IIS, SQL Server 2005 Express, DNN Install Package, DNN install wizard Typical install option.

❑ **Production web server:** Windows 2003, IIS, SQL Server 2000, DNN Install package, DNN install wizard Custom install option.

The combination of these examples should give you the information you need to successfully install DotNetNuke.

FAST and EASY on Windows XP Home

This example is unique in that it will be the only example not using IIS. IIS is not available in Windows XP Home Edition. Using the Home Edition of Windows requires the installation of one of the Microsoft development tools that include web server software. When Installing Visual Web Developer or Visual Studio, a file-based web server is installed. This web server is available only while the development software is running. For this example, you will use Visual Web Developer.

There are several advantages of using the Starter Kit:

❑ It is the easiest, fastest, and least technical way to get a DotNetNuke application running.

❑ It will work with all the commonly used Microsoft PC operating systems.

❑ It installs everything necessary to build your own custom modules.

You should never install development software such as Visual Web Developer or Visual Studio on a production web server.

This example takes you through the following steps:

1. Download and install Microsoft Visual Web Developer (VWD).

During the installation of VWD both ASP.NET version 2 and SQL Server 2005 Express will be installed. In other examples, each of these must be done as separate steps.

2. Download and install the DotNetNuke Starter Kit.

3. Create a website with the Starter Kit.

4. Run the DotNetNuke install wizard.

This example will also work on Windows XP Professional and Windows Vista. It includes everything necessary to start developing modules as well.

Step 1: Download and Install Microsoft Visual Web Developer

Visual Web Developer 2008 Express Edition (VWD) (also known as one of the Visual Studio Express Editions) is a free development tool from Microsoft. It can be downloaded at http://msdn.microsoft.com/express/download.

If Visual Studio 2008 is already installed, there is no need to download VWD. However, you do need to make sure that all Service Packs and patches are installed, including ASP.NET version 2 and SQL Server 2005 express.

VWD can be downloaded and installed with either a web install or an ISO image. You can use either, but for this example we recommend the web install as it is much smaller.

Once the VWD install file has been downloaded, navigate to the directory where you saved the file and double-click it. Once the install program loads, the screen shown in Figure 2-1 appears. Click Next on this screen.

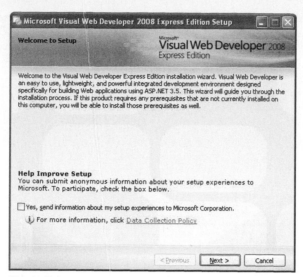

Figure 2-1

Accept the License Agreement by selecting the checkbox and click Next. Because this example uses the SQL Server 2005 Express Edition, be sure that the checkbox to install that option is selected, as in Figure 2-2. You should also select the Silverlight runtime option. After these are selected, click Next again.

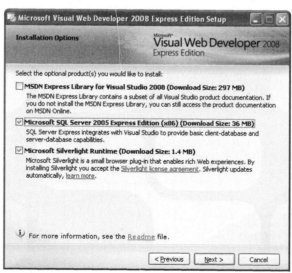

Figure 2-2

Please notice in Figure 2-3 that the install program has determined several things that this computer needs. These technologies can be manually downloaded and installed. However, it is nice to have this all done in a controlled manner and only if necessary. Click the Install button to accept the default installation folder and begin the install.

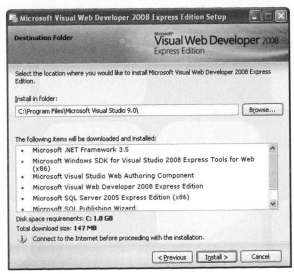

Figure 2-3

This brings up the status screen, as shown in Figure 2-4.

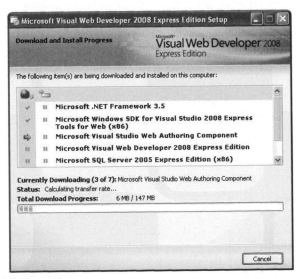

Figure 2-4

When the VWD Installation Wizard finishes, you may be asked to reboot your computer.

If you already have a version of Microsoft SQL Server installed, you can use your existing SQL Server. The Production Web Server example shows you how to use a version of SQL other than Express.

Once all three technologies have been installed, the Setup Complete screen appears, as shown in Figure 2-5.

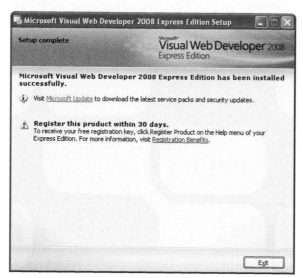

Figure 2-5

The Setup Complete screen gives you a warning that you must register the software within 30 days. Even though the software is free, it still requires registration. It is also important to note that I recommend that Windows Update be run to make sure the latest security patches have been applied. Once you have finished with any links on this screen that you wish to follow, click Exit.

After installing any software, it is a good idea to reboot to ensure that the installation is complete. The first time you open the VWD it will do a self-configuration. This needs to be done before the next step. Once the self-configuration is complete, close VWD.

Step 2: Download and Install the DotNetNuke Starter Kit

The DotNetNuke application is a free download available at www.DotNetNuke.com. Registration is required before access is granted to the download page. However, registration is free. For this example, be sure to download the Starter Kit Package.

Using Windows Explorer, navigate to the directory where the files were downloaded and double-click the DotNetNuke.vsi file. This starts the install of the Starter Kit to your VWD. The Select Content to Install screen will be displayed as in Figure 2-6. Clear the DotNetNuke Compiled Module (VB) checkbox.

This example uses Visual Web Developer Express. If you are using the full Visual Studio version, you do not need to clear the DotNetNuke Compiled Module (VB) option.

Once the correct options are selected, click Next.

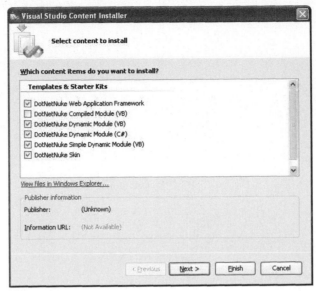

Figure 2-6

The screen in Figure 2-6 is displayed giving you the option to change your install settings or finish the install. If all of the options are correct and signify Ready to install this item, click Finish.

Once the installation is complete, click Close (see Figure 2-7). The environment is now set up to install the website.

Figure 2-7

Step 3: Create a Website with the Starter Kit

From your Start menu, run the Microsoft Visual Web Developer 2005 Express Edition. This will display the screen as shown in Figure 2-8.

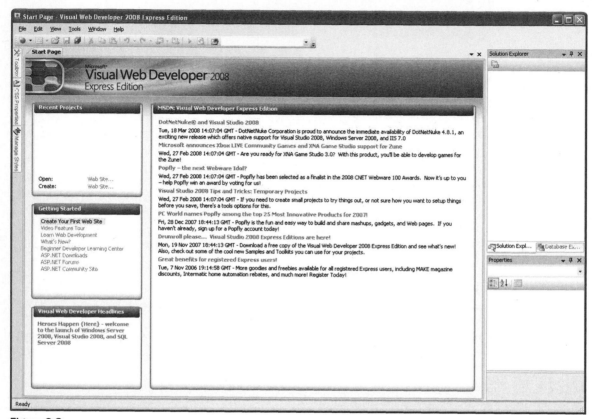

Figure 2-8

Once you click Create: Web Site, the New Web Site screen appears, as shown in Figure 2-9.

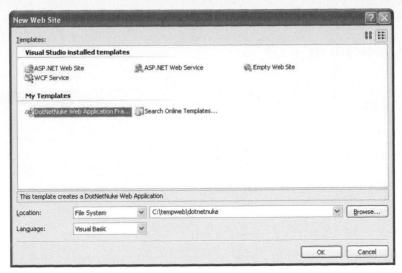

Figure 2-9

Highlight "DotNetNuke Web Application Fra. . ." as shown in Figure 2-9. Please notice the three combo boxes near the bottom of the window. You need to leave the two on the left as they are (File system and Visual Basic).

> *If IIS was being used, the HTTP option in the Location combo box could be selected. Because this example uses Windows XP Home, IIS is not installed and requires the use of the File System option.*

The combo box on the right tells the wizard where the website should be located on the hard disk drive. For this example, use C:\tempweb\dotnetnuke as in Figure 2-9.

> *If the directory does not exist, it will be created.*

Click OK. After a few minutes, a screen such as the one shown in Figure 2-10 appears.

You should read through this entire document. In keeping with the "Fast and Easy" theme of this example, I will note only two things at this time. Both are critical, and are marked in bold on the screen. The first is that you need to start the DotNetNuke Application Installation Wizard by pressing Ctrl+F5. The second is that you *must* use the Auto Installation Mode. Both of these will be covered in the next step.

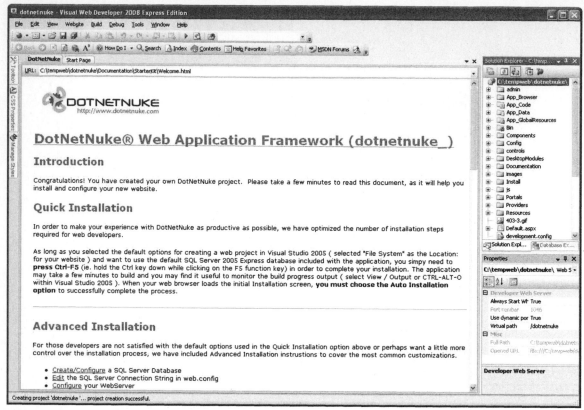

Figure 2-10

Step 4: Run the DotNetNuke Installation Wizard

Having duly noted the comments at the end of the last step, run the install wizard by pressing Ctrl+F5. (First, press and hold down the Ctrl key. While holding the Ctrl key down, press and release the F5 key. Now release the Ctrl key.) This may take several minutes, but eventually the screen shown in Figure 2-11 appears.

This is the starting page of the install wizard. The Auto radio button *must* be selected for this installation to work properly. The other install options will be covered in the following examples.

Don't worry if the graphics on this page don't show up. After the Auto radio button has been selected, click Next. The install process will start and show status updates as it proceeds. After a few minutes, a message appears stating that the wizard has finished (see Figure 2-12).

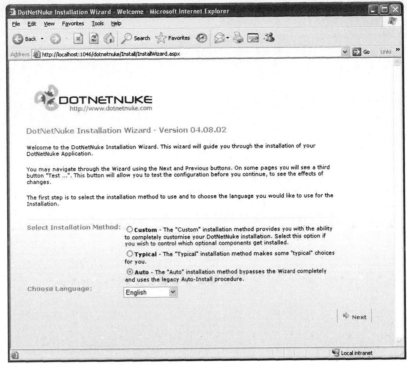

Figure 2-11

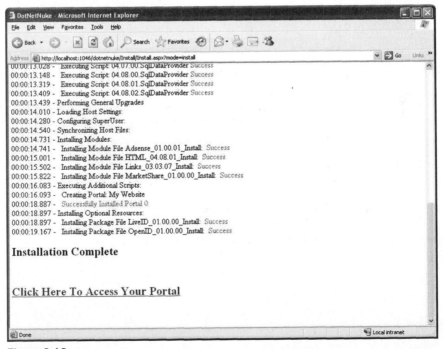

Figure 2-12

Click the link at the bottom to navigate to the home page of your new DotNetNuke website. (See Figure 2-13.) You may have to scroll down to see the link.

You may get an error about being unable to load a module; this is a known problem and will not affect your website. Simply refresh your browser by clicking the browser refresh button or press F5.

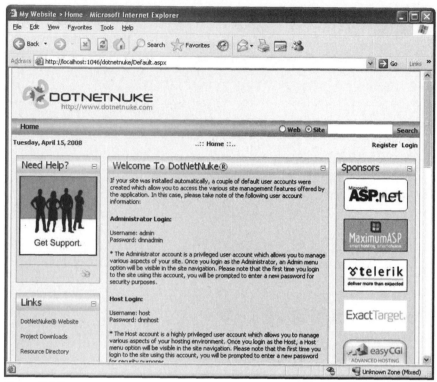

Figure 2-13

This example is the quickest and least technical approach possible to getting a DotNetNuke website up and running on a local computer. By setting up Visual Web Developer (VWD) and letting VWD install the minimally required components, many of the prerequisites for DotNetNuke are dealt with automatically. Once this environment is set up, you use the DotNetNuke Starter Kit to place all the files and scripts in their proper places. Last, you use the "Auto" option of the DotNetNuke install wizard to configure the database and website.

Most Common on Windows XP Professional

This example looks at one of the most common installations of DotNetNuke. It also serves as a good background to all the pieces that make the DotNetNuke application work. The following steps are covered:

1. Validate that IIS is installed and running.

2. Validate that ASP.NET version 2 or later is installed.

3. Validate that Microsoft SQL 2005 Express is installed and running.

4. Download and unzip DotNetNuke.

5. Configure IIS.

6. Set Directory Permissions.

7. Validate Database.

8. Run the DotNetNuke install wizard.

This may seem like a long list, but it is really very simple.

You must be running XP Professional. XP Home Edition does not include the required IIS software included in this example. You will need administrator rights for some of the system changes in this example.

Step 1: Validate That IIS Is Installed and Running

The easiest way to validate that IIS is installed and running, is to open an Internet Explorer (IE) window, and type **localhost** in the address bar. If IIS is installed and running, two browser windows open; one of them looks something like Figure 2-14.

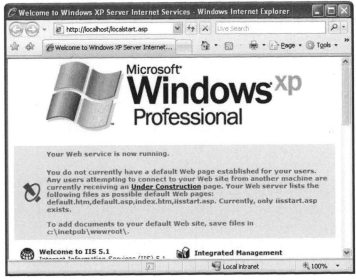

Figure 2-14

If you see this, IIS is installed and running! Go to Step 2. If IIS is not installed, you will either see an error page or be redirected to your search default search engine. In this case, IIS needs to be installed. Go to the Control Panel and click Add or Remove Programs. This opens a window that looks like Figure 2-15.

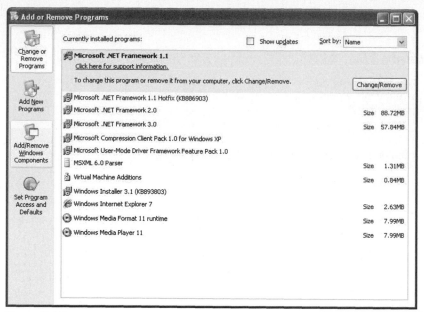

Figure 2-15

Click the Add/Remove Windows Components option, as shown on the left side of this window. This opens a window like you see in Figure 2-16.

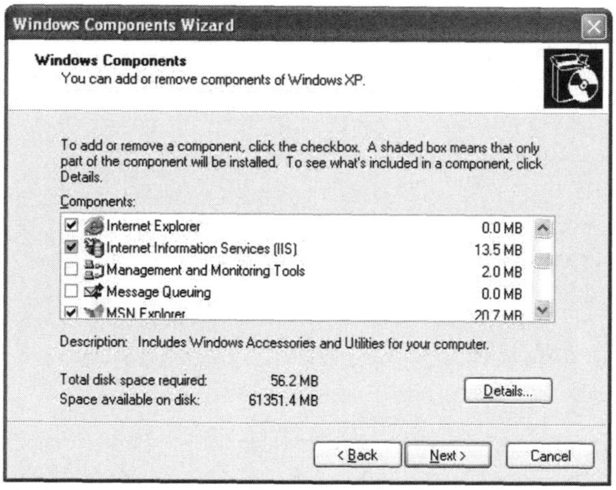

Figure 2-16

"Internet Information Services (IIS)" is in the list, as shown in Figure 2-16. If it is not selected, select it. Click Next and follow the wizard to install IIS.

Depending on how your operating system (OS) was installed, you may need your original installation disc.

Once this is complete, opening IE and typing **localhost** in the address bar brings up a window, as in Figure 2-14.

Step 2: Validate That ASP.NET Version 2 or Later Is Installed

To validate that ASP.NET version 2 is installed, go to your Control Panel and click Add/Remove Programs. Once the list is populated, scroll down and look for "Microsoft .NET Framework 2.0," as shown in Figure 2-17.

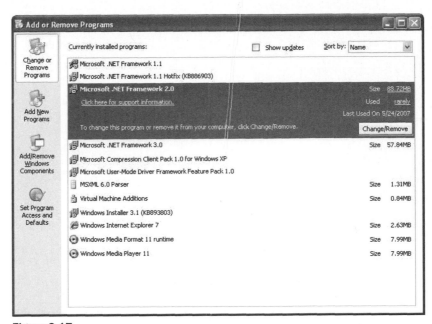

Figure 2-17

If "Microsoft .NET Framework 2.0" is in the list, it is installed and you are ready to go. If it is not in the list, then you need to download and install it. This is a free download that can be found at www.asp .net/downloads. Once the downloaded file has been saved to your disk, simply run the install package and you are done.

Step 3: Validate That Microsoft SQL 2005 Express Is Installed and Running

To validate that Microsoft SQL 2005 Express Edition is installed, check and see if the service is running. To do this, open the Control Panel and choose Administrative Tools.

If you are using the Category view in the Control Panel, you will first need to select Performance and Maintenance.

The Administrative Tools section will look like Figure 2-18.

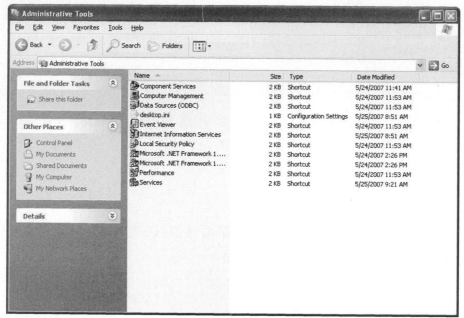

Figure 2-18

Double-click the Services shortcut to display a screen similar to Figure 2-19, with the listing dependent upon what is installed on your computer.

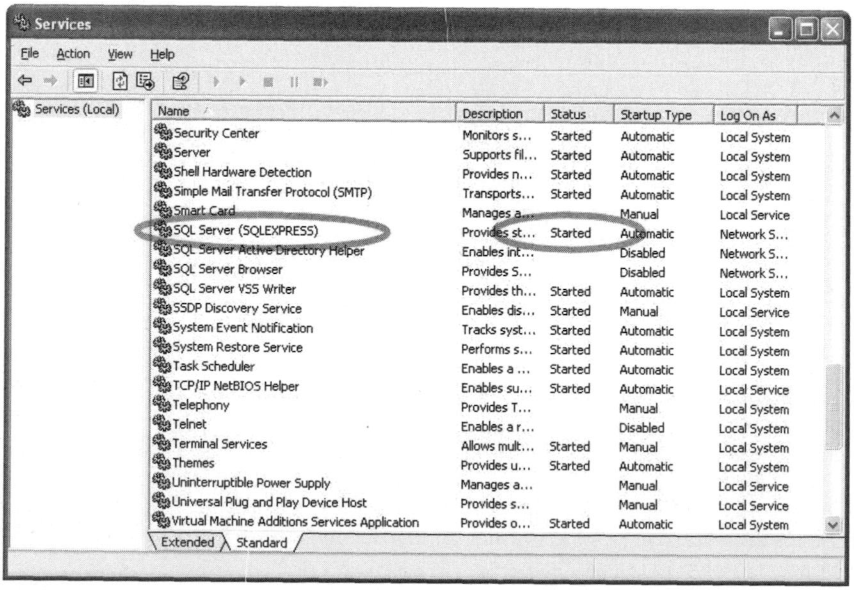

Figure 2-19

Scroll down and look for SQL Server (SQLEXPRESS) in the list. In the Status column to the right of the name, it should say Started, as in Figure 2-19. If SQL Server (SQLEXPRESS) is not in the list, it will need to be downloaded and installed.

You may have a different version of SQL server installed. Any version of MS SQL Server version 2000 and later is acceptable.

SQL 2005 express is a free download from Microsoft available at `http://msdn.microsoft.com/ vstudio/express/sql/register/default.aspx`. Currently, two different packages are available:

❑   SQL Server 2005 Express Edition SP2

❑   SQL Server 2005 Express Edition with Advanced Services SP2

Both of these packages have associated downloads. For this example, all that is needed is the SQL Server 2005 Express Edition SP2, as shown in Figure 2-20.

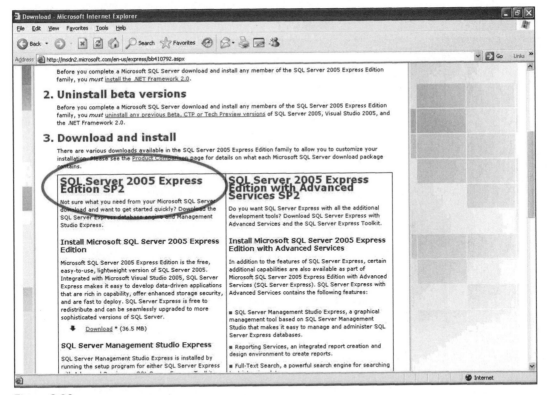

Figure 2-20

To install SQL Server 2005 Express Edition SP2, download the install package and run it. Accept all defaults in the install wizard. Once the wizard is finished, recheck the Services again. You should now see the information shown in Figure 2-19.

Step 4: Download and Unzip DotNetNuke

The DotNetNuke application is a free download available at www.DotNetNuke.com. You must register on the website to be granted access to the download. This registration is free. For this example, be sure to download the Install Package. Once the file is downloaded, unzip the files. For this example, unzip the files to the C:\Inetpub\wwwroot\dotnetnuke directory.

Step 5: Configure IIS

In this step, the website will be configured using the IIS management console. You can access this by first opening the computer Control Panel from the Start menu. In the Control Panel, select the Administration Tools link. On the Administration Tools page, select Internet Information Services to open a window like the one shown in Figure 2-21. You see a tree view on the left with information on the right about the selected nodes.

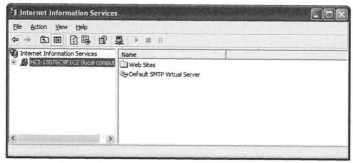

Figure 2-21

Expand the local computer node and then expand the Web Sites node by pressing the + (plus) sign to the left of the node. Under the Web Site node is a node called Default Web Site. Expand this node and locate the DotNetNuke directory where the unzipped files were saved. Click once on this node to highlight it. With the DotNetNuke Site node highlighted, right-click this same node to access the context menu, as shown in Figure 2-22.

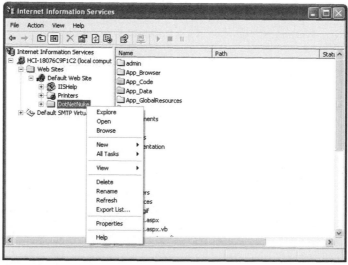

Figure 2-22

Select the Properties item in the context menu shown in Figure 2-22. This opens the Property page, as shown in Figure 2-23.

Figure 2-23

This Property page is used to tell the computer that the directory where you unzipped the DotNetNuke files should be treated as a website. There are two things on the directory tab of this Property sheet that need to be done. First, change the execute permissions to Scripts and Executables, as shown in Figure 2-23. Be sure that all the other options are as shown in Figure 2-23 as well. Second, click the Create button. The Directory tab will look like the one shown in Figure 2-24.

Figure 2-24

Now change to the Documents tab, as shown in Figure 2-25.

Figure 2-25

Depending on your setup, a new Default document, default.aspx, will need to be added if it is not in the list. To do this, click the Add button and type in **default.aspx**, as shown in Figure 2-26.

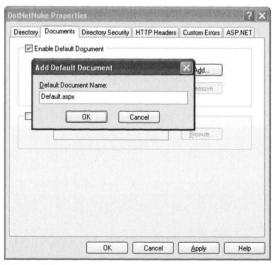

Figure 2-26

Click OK. This adds default.aspx to the bottom of the Default Document list. It can be moved to the top of the list by highlighting default.aspx and clicking the up arrow button several times. This results in a screen that looks like Figure 2-27.

Figure 2-27

Finally, on the ASP.NET tab, select the ASP.NET tab and ensure that the ASP.NET version is version 2, as shown in Figure 2-28.

Figure 2-28

If the ASP.NET version drop-down box is empty or has a version less than 2.0, change it, and then click OK. Close the Internet Information Services management window. You have now successfully configured IIS.

Step 6: Set Directory Permissions

Because the DotNetNuke application writes to the disk, the operating system must be configured to allow this. Open Windows Explorer and navigate to the directory where the extracted DotNetNuke files are located. If you have been following this example, this will be C:\Inetpub\wwwroot\DotNetNuke (see Figure 2-29).

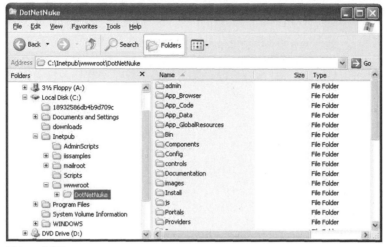

Figure 2-29

Right-click this directory and choose Properties on the context menu. Go to the Security tab. This opens a Properties page, as shown in Figure 2-30.

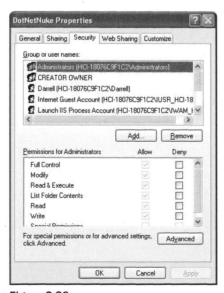

Figure 2-30

If you cannot see the Security tab as shown in Figure 2-30, you must disable Simple File Sharing. You accomplish this by doing the following:

Select Start ⇨ My Computer ⇨ Tools ⇨ Folder Options ⇨ View. Scroll to the bottom, clear the Use Simple File Sharing checkbox, and click OK.

Look in the Group or usernames list for "ASP.NET Machine Account," as shown in Figure 2-31. (The part in parentheses will be different as it will have your computer name instead of HCI.)

Figure 2-31

If it is in the list, be sure Full Control is selected and click Apply. If it is not there, it must be added so that you may assign it the permissions to write to the hard disk. In order to do so, click the Add button. This opens the Select Users or Groups dialog box, as shown in Figure 2-32.

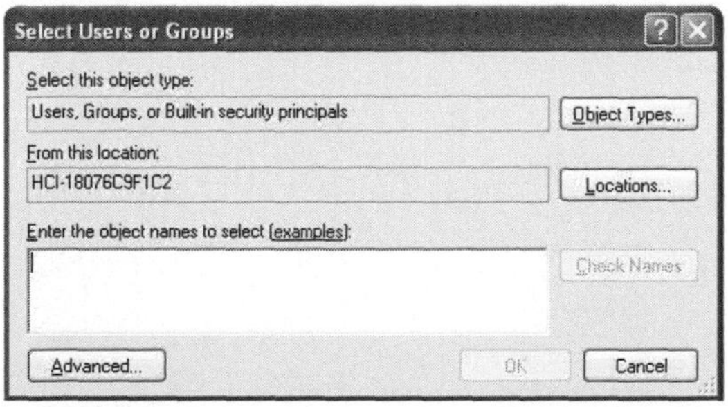

Figure 2-32

Click Advanced to display the advanced screen, as shown in Figure 2-33.

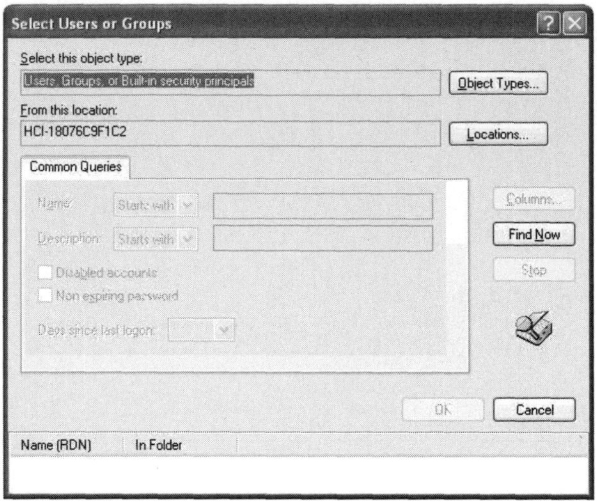

Figure 2-33

Click Find Now. This brings up a list of security objects, as shown in Figure 2-34.

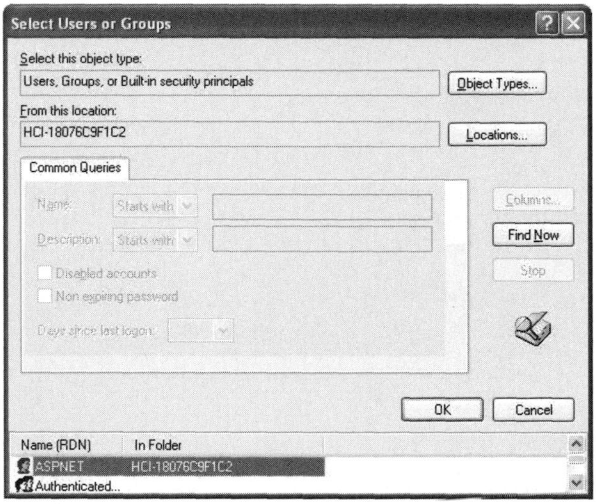

Figure 2-34

Highlight ASPNET in the list as shown in Figure 2-34 and click OK. The window appears as shown in Figure 2-35.

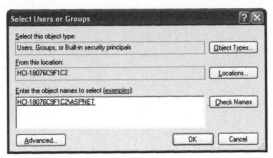

Figure 2-35

Click OK to add the ASPNET security object (see Figure 2-36).

Figure 2-36

With the ASP.NET Machine Account highlighted, select the Full Control - Allow checkbox, as in Figure 2-36. Click OK. The ASP.NET user account on your computer now has the proper permissions to run your DotNetNuke application.

Step 7: Validate Database

In earlier versions, you had to create a database to use DotNetNuke. However, with the current versions an empty SQL 2005 Express database file is provided with the install. Because this is what you are using for this example, you simply need to validate that the file is where it should be. To do this, open Windows Explorer and navigate to the App_Data directory of your website and make sure there is a file there called Database.mdf. If you are following along with this example, the path would be C:\\Inetpub\wwwroot\DotNetNuke\App_Data\Database.mdf (see Figure 2-37).

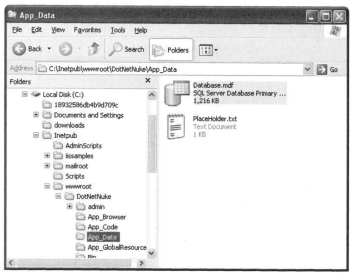

Figure 2-37

Step 8: Run the DotNetNuke Install Wizard

If you have completed the steps in this example, running the install wizard is a snap. Open an IE window and navigate to `http://localhost/dotnetnuke`. The website will begin the installation process and offer you a choice of three installation methods (see Figure 2-38).

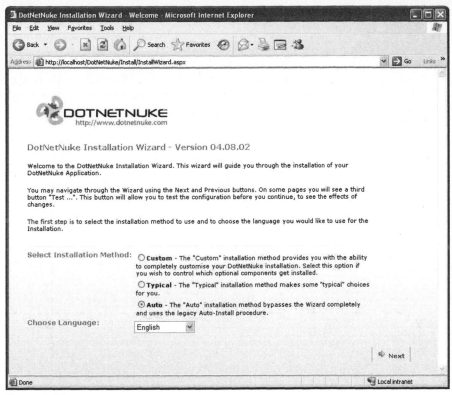

Figure 2-38

For this example choose the Auto radio button, and click Next to start the installation process and update the browser as it progresses. When the process completes, a link is provided at the bottom of the page to open the new website (see Figure 2-39).

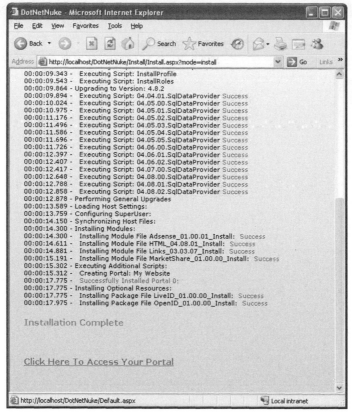

Figure 2-39

Click the link at the bottom of the page (shown in Figure 2-39). You may need to scroll down to get to this link.

In past versions, people have been known to get an error when clicking the link shown in Figure 2-39. This is not a problem. If it happens to you, just refresh your browser by either clicking the Refresh button or pressing F5.

You now have a DotNetNuke website running on your local computer (see Figure 2-40)!

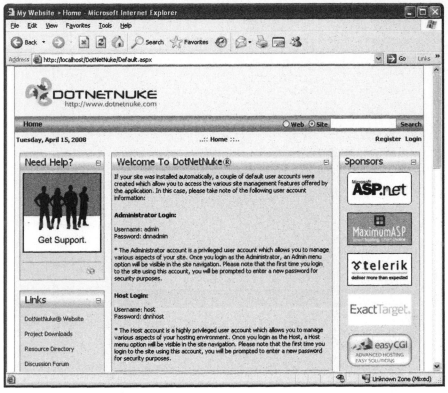

Figure 2-40

Newest OS on Windows Vista

This example uses the newest operating system from Microsoft, Vista. This example is similar to the second "Most Common" example. The same feature set applies, but there are a few subtle differences. For instance, with XP Pro, the .NET Framework had to be downloaded and installed. On Vista, the Framework is installed but by default is not available to IIS. Additionally, Vista comes with an upgraded IIS (version 7). With all the upgrades and the new user interface, it seems prudent for Vista to have its own example.

You will need to have administrator rights for some of the system changes in this example. Vista Home Basic and Starter editions do not include all the necessary IIS features for this example. You must be using Vista Home Premium, or a higher version.

Step 1: Validate That IIS Is Installed and Running

With the secure-by-default paradigm, Vista is installed with IIS turned off. This example is going to assume that IIS is not installed and will just go through the process. This tutorial will validate that IIS is set up in a manner that is compatible with DotNetNuke. From the Start menu, go to the Control Panel, as shown in Figure 2-41.

Figure 2-41

Click Programs to display a screen, as shown in Figure 2-42.

Figure 2-42

On the programs page, Click Turn Windows features on or off. If your user account is not classified as an administrator, you may not be able to complete this step. A UAC window (see Figure 2-43) will pop up and ask for the password for the administrator login or another user that has administrator privileges. At a minimum, you will need administrator rights to complete the steps in this example.

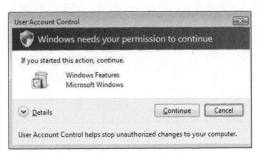

Figure 2-43

The screen shown in Figure 2-43 is a User Account Control (UAC) Message. You will see this UAC message any time software attempts to make a change to the core system. Click Continue.

In the Windows Features window, locate the Internet Information Services. If the checkbox is clear, as in Figure 2-44, click it and it will turn blue.

Figure 2-44

These checkboxes have three states. Clear means off. Blue means some of the functions are on and some are off. Checked means all functions are on.

Expand the Internet Information Services node, as shown in Figure 2-45, and make sure all the proper options are checked.

Figure 2-45

By selecting the ASP.NET checkbox, you make sure that .NET Framework 2 is installed and available for use by IIS.

Now scroll down a little more and make sure the Security section is set up like Figure 2-46.

Figure 2-46

Click OK. IIS is now running.

Step 2: Install Microsoft SQL 2005 Express Edition

If Microsoft SQL 2005 Express Edition is not installed on your system, download the install file from http://msdn.microsoft.com/vstudio/express/sql/register/default.aspx. Once you have successfully downloaded the install file, run it. The UAC will ask your permission to run the program as it will change the basic setup of the computer. Once the install starts, you are asked to accept the licensing terms and conditions, as shown in Figure 2-47.

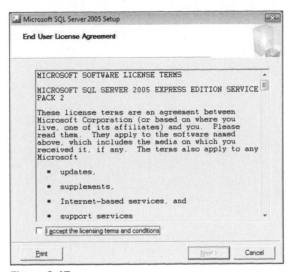

Figure 2-47

Check this box to accept the licensing terms and conditions, and then click Next. Continue with the SQL install wizard, choosing the default options. This will make sure all the necessary SQL functionality is available.

Step 3: Download and Unzip DotNetNuke

The DotNetNuke application is a free download located at www.DotNetNuke.com. You must register on the website before you are granted access to the download. Registration is free. For this example, be sure to download the Install Package. Once the file is downloaded and saved, unzip the files. For this example, unzip the files to the C:\TempDNN directory.

Step 4: Configure IIS

In Step 1, IIS was installed. Now IIS must be told to treat the files just unzipped in the C:\TempDNN directory as a website. Open the Control Panel, as shown in Figure 2-48, and click System and Maintenance.

Figure 2-48

Scroll to the bottom and select Administrative Tools (see Figure 2-49).

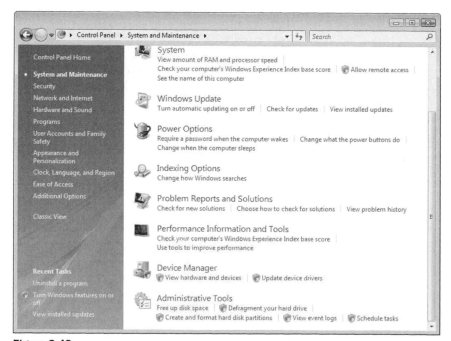

Figure 2-49

The Administrative Tools window displays. Find and double-click Internet Information Services (IIS) Manager, as shown in Figure 2-50.

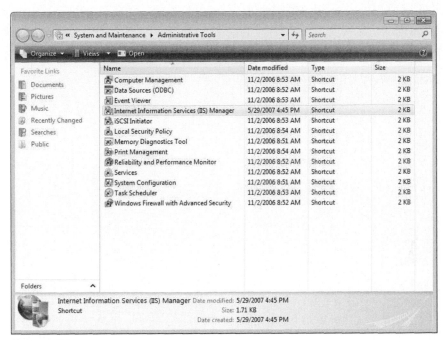

Figure 2-50

If a User Account Control message pops up, click Continue.

Expand the nodes in the Connections area and highlight Default Web Site, as shown in Figure 2-51.

Figure 2-51

Right-click Default Web Site. Click Add Application from the context menu. Type **DotNetNuke** in the Alias field. Change the Application pool to be Classic .NET AppPool. Change the Physical path text box to C:\TempDNN.

This location is where the unzipped DotNetNuke files were placed. If you placed them in a different directory, you should put that directory here.

When finished with the Add Application screen, the popup window should look like Figure 2-52.

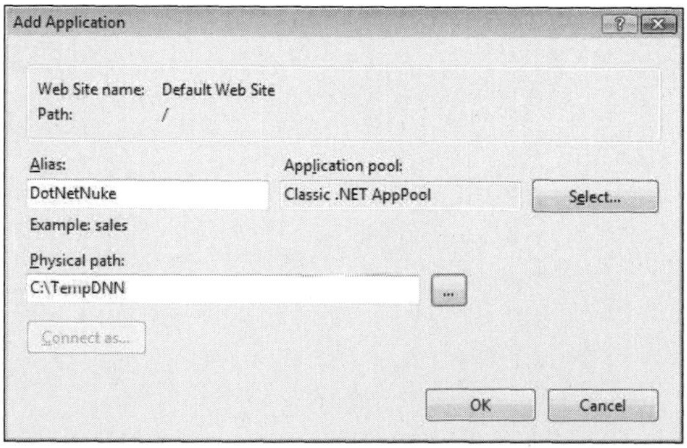

Figure 2-52

Click OK. In the Connections pane (see Figure 2-53) on the left side, click DotNetNuke to highlight it. Double-click Default Document in the lower center of the screen.

Figure 2-53

Make sure that default.aspx is in the Default Document list. If it is not, add it, and click Apply in the Actions pane on the right (see Figure 2-54).

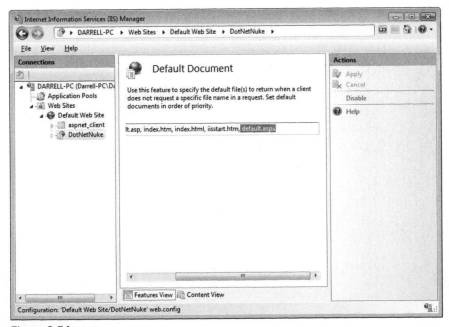

Figure 2-54

One more thing that needs to be done from the IIS Manager is to set the permissions. The permissions for ASP.NET must be set so that ASP.NET (and thus DotNetNuke) will be able to write to the hard disk drive. In other operating systems, this would be accomplished by giving ASP.NET the permissions to write to a specific directory structure. In Vista, this can be accomplished by setting the Trust Level of the ASP.NET program.

In the Connections pane on the left, double-click DotNetNuke (see Figure 2-55).

Figure 2-55

Double-click .NET Trust Levels (see Figure 2-55).

For this example, we will give ASP.NET Full trust. If it is not already selected, select "Full (internal)" in the drop-down menu, as shown in Figure 2-56, and click Apply.

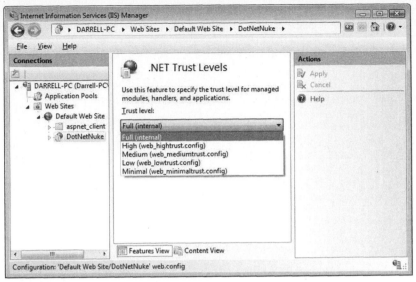

Figure 2-56

IIS is now configured for your website.

Step 5: Validate Database

This example uses the default SQL Express DB. Because you previously installed Microsoft SQL Server 2005 Express Edition in this example, all that is needed is to validate that the database file is where it should be.

From the Start menu, click Computer. Drill down to the directory where you stored the DotNetNuke files. If you are following along with this example, the files are in C:\TempDNN. The directory App_Data should contain a file called Database.mdf, as shown in Figure 2-57.

The Database.mdf file is an empty database file that is included in the install Zip file from DotNetNuke.com. If for some reason it is not in this directory, you should unzip the files again.

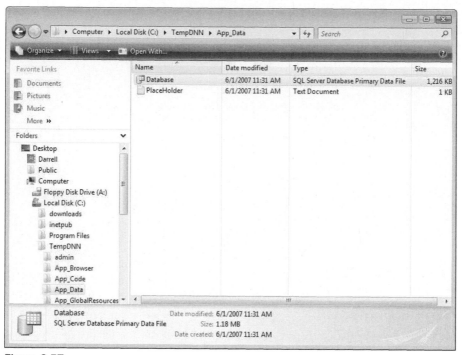

Figure 2-57

Step 6: Run the DotNetNuke Install Wizard

Now it is time to run the DotNetNuke install wizard. This wizard will set up the database, install key components and modules for the application to run, and establish two user accounts.

Open an Internet Explorer window, type **http://localhost/dotnetnuke** in the address bar, and press the Enter key. After a few moments, you are shown the first page of the wizard (see Figure 2-58).

Figure 2-58

In the previous examples, we used the Auto installation option. In this example, we use the Typical installation option. Choose the Typical radio button and click Next. In page two of the wizard, you have the option to test permissions of your setup. It is always advisable to do this (see Figure 2-59).

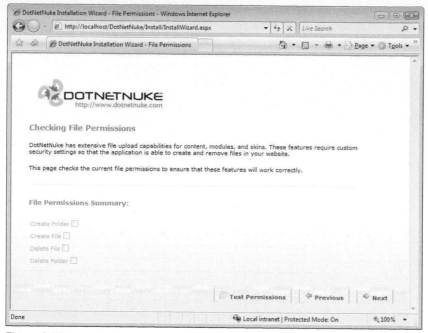

Figure 2-59

Click Test Permissions. If you have set the permissions correctly, you will see checks in all four of the checkboxes and a notice that your site has passed the permissions check, as shown in Figure 2-60.

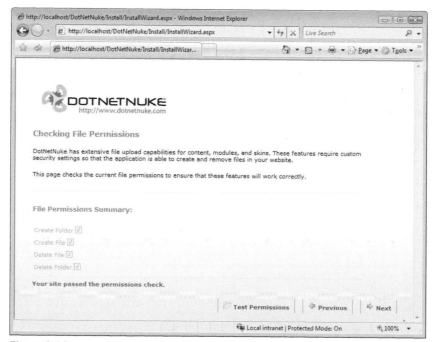

Figure 2-60

Click Next. Page three of the wizard allows you to specify and test your database connections. It is always advisable to take advantage of these opportunities to validate your setup (see Figure 2-61).

Figure 2-61

Click Test Database Connection. The success or failure of the test is displayed in the bottom left of the screen. Figure 2-62 shows a notice of a successful test. If it had not been successful, there would have been a red failure notice.

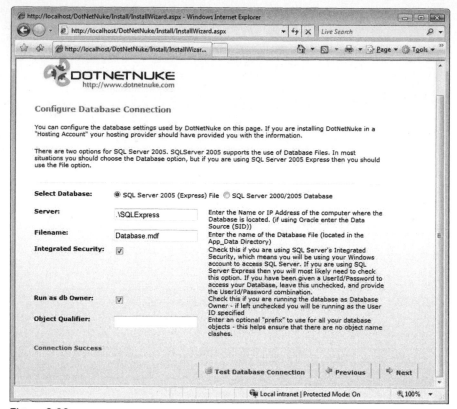

Figure 2-62

Click Next to run the Database Installation Scripts. Status updates will be displayed as the scripts progress (see Figure 2-63). Once the "Installation of Database Complete" message appears (see Figure 2-63) click Next.

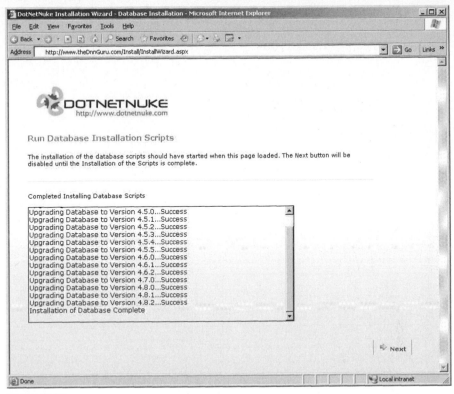

Figure 2-63

This displays the next page of the install wizard, which requires the information shown in Figure 2-64 to set up a SuperUser account. Changing the First, Last, and User names is optional. For this example, they will be left as they are. Adding a password and a vaild e-mail address is required.

It is very important that you remember your username and password.

The default password for this account has historically been dnnhost. Obviously, it would not be a good idea to use this in a live environment. In addition, when the site is started, it will warn you that the password is very unsecure. In order to see these warnings, and to ensure that you remember the password for this example, you will use the default password.

You should never use the default password on a live site.

In the Password and Confirm Password fields, type **dnnhost**. In the Email Address field, type your e-mail address (for example, yourname@yourdomain.com) and click Next.

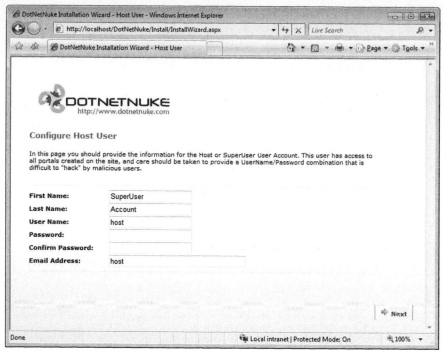

Figure 2-64

The next page of the wizard (see Figure 2-65) allows you to set up basic portal information, and the administrator information for this site.

It is very important that you remember your username and password.

The default password for this account has historically been dnnadmin. Obviously, using this in a live environment would not be a good idea. In addition when the site is started, it will warn you that the password is very unsecure. In order to see these warnings, and to ensure that you remember the password for this example, you will use the default password.

You should never use the default password on a live site.

In the Password and Confirm Password fields, type **dnnadmin**. In the Email Address field, type your e-mail address (for example, yourname@yourdomain.com). For this example, leave the rest of the fields as they are. The Portal Title can be changed later and there is only one template in the default configuration. Click Next.

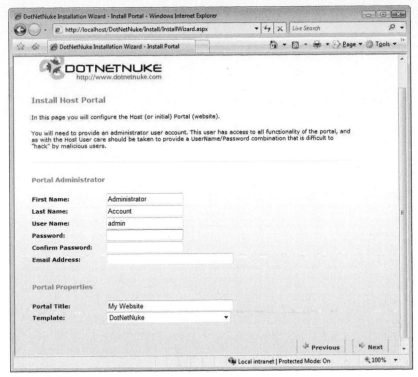

Figure 2-65

Click Finished (Goto Site), as shown in Figure 2-66, to go through the initial startup of your new DotNetNuke site.

Figure 2-66

This will take a few minutes to complete. You will eventually see the screen shown in Figure 2-67.

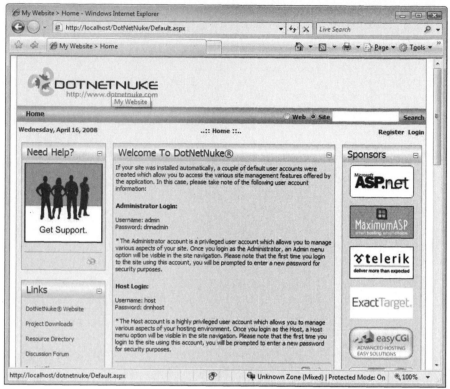

Figure 2-67

You are up and running!

Production Web Server on Windows 2003

Choosing a hosting company for your website is a very important decision. You need to consider questions such as the following:

❑ What will happen to my business if the site is offline for an extended time period?

❑ What kind of support will I get? How is personal data protected?

❑ What kinds of backups are made?

Are there other ways in which this hosting company will affect your business?

Then, all this needs to be balanced against the question, How much am I willing to pay?

The good thing is that you can find hosting from very inexpensive (a few dollars per month), to very expensive (thousands of dollars per month), depending on your business requirements. The key here is "your business requirements." Once you have defined these, additional functional requirements are imposed by the DotNetNuke application.

For this example, I assume that you have established your business requirements and that you will only be dealing with the requirements imposed by DotNetNuke.

Additionally, DotNetNuke is supported by hosting companies in two very distinct ways. In the first, you have your very own instance of DotNetNuke. No one else is using other portals on this instance or in your database. In this case, you will be able to install your own modules, make changes at the host level, and choose configuration options.

In the second, you and many other companies share the same instance of DotNetNuke and the same database. In this case, you will not be allowed access to the Host menu options. You may not be allowed to upload your own modules or, at the very least, you will have to have all code vetted by the hosting company. Many configuration options you will have no control over (such as how long a password must be).

The second option is going to be the least expensive. If you have a small budget, and just need to have a web presence, this could be the best choice for you.

Many companies advertise that they support DotNetNuke. If you choose one of these companies, it may even do the basic install for you. If this is the case, you need to ask:

- ❑ What version is the company using?
- ❑ Will you have your own instance, or will you be on a shared portal?
- ❑ How will version upgrades be handled?

Once you are satisfied with these answers, you can proceed with that company. However, for this example, let's assume that the company is not specifically supporting DotNetNuke, and that you will have to do the install yourself.

Step 1: Validate That the Hosting Environment Meets Requirements

Several specific requirements *must* be met for the DotNetNuke application to run on a hosted web server:

- ❑ The server *must* be running a Windows operating system (Windows Server 2000 or later).
- ❑ The server *must* be running Internet Information Services (IIS).
- ❑ The server *must* have ASP.NET version 2 or later installed.
- ❑ The Windows user associated with the ASP.NET service must have Full access to the root of your web directory. (This user is "Network Services" by default on Windows Servers.)
- ❑ You must have a connection to, and authorization to use, a compatible database. (This example will use Microsoft SQL 2000 Server.)
- ❑ You must set the default document to default.aspx.

Step 2: Get Database Connection Information

Your hosting company will need to give you the following information:

❑ The address or means of access to your database server. This could be an IP address (for example, 123.123.123.1) or a domain name (for example, sql1.hostingcompany.com); or the hosting company may just tell you it is on the same server where your website is located.

❑ Your specific database name or catalog.

❑ The username to log on to the database.

❑ The password to log on to the database.

You will not use this information until you start configuring the application, but getting this information ahead of time often solves a lot of problems. In Step 1, you must have a database. Not all hosting companies offer databases. Those that do offer databases may charge extra for the use of a database. When you get the information in the preceding list, you are assuring yourself that you have this requirement covered.

Step 3: Get FTP Information

You will place the application on the hosted web server with FTP (File Transfer Protocol). This has been the main method of transferring files to web servers since the days of static web pages. As this is not new, I will not go into great detail on how to FTP files to your server. You will need to obtain the following FTP information from your hosting company:

❑ FTP address

❑ FTP username

❑ FTP password

Step 4: Download the DotNetNuke Install Package

The DotNetNuke application is a free download located at www.DotNetNuke.com. You must register on the website in order to access the download. Registration is free. For this example, be sure to download the Install Package. Once the file is downloaded, unzip the files to a temporary location. You can use any directory you want — just be sure to remember where you put the files. For this example, unzip the files to the C:\DotNetNuke directory.

Step 5: Modify the web.config File

In previous versions of DotNetNuke, the web.config file had to be modified before running the Installation Wizard. Now all these changes can be done by the wizard. It is very educational to make a copy of the web.config file before and after the wizard has run so that you can see the changes. After the wizard has run, you may want to check the web.config file to make sure that the `compilation debug` attribute is set to false (unless you are wanting to debug) and that the `minRequiredPasswordLength` setting meets your company standards (default is seven characters). You can find these settings by doing a simple search. However, you may find that examining the code of the web.config file will show you many of the ways you can customize how DotNetNuke can be configured. It is really amazing what you can discover in these files!

Step 6: FTP Files to Hosting Environment

Using the FTP program of your choice and the FTP connection information provided by your hosting company, copy all the folders and files from the temporary folder where the DotNetNuke files were unzipped to the root of your website.

Step 7: Run DotNetNuke Install Wizard

Now it is time to run the DotNetNuke install wizard. Open a browser and type the web address to your site in the address bar. It is best if you use your domain name. For our example, let's use theDnnGuru.com. This will start the install wizard and show the screen in Figure 2-68.

If you do not have a domain name established, use the connection address as supplied by the hosting company.

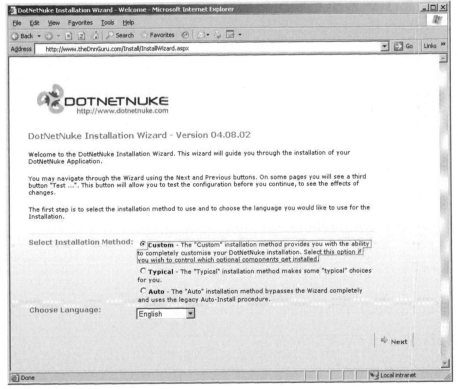

Figure 2-68

On this installation, choose the Custom installation radio button, as shown in Figure 2-68. Click the Next button in the lower-right corner. The Checking File Permissions page of the wizard allows validation that the permissions have been set properly for the DotNetNuke application to install and run (see Figure 2-69). Click Test Permissions.

Figure 2-69

After the test, the page will refresh and all four of the test checkboxes should be selected. There should also be a green message that indicates the permissions test has been passed. If the test was unsuccessful there will be a red failure notice. Failure indicates that the permissions have not been assigned properly as stated in Step 1. Once you have passed all the permissions tests, click Next.

For this example, an SQL Server 2005 database is being used. Therefore, the Sql Server 2000/2005 Database radio button needs to be selected. In the Server text box, place the address to the SQL server. If your hosting company gave you a domain name or an IP address, place that in this box. If they told you that the SQL server had been installed on your hosting box, you can just use (local), as in Figure 2-70. In the database text box, put the name of the database (sometimes called a catalog) provided by the hosting company. The hosting company should have provided the user ID and password (as described in Step 2).

For this example, the database is on the hosted computer; therefore, the Server text box will be left, as shown in Figure 2-70.

Fill in the rest of the fields with the data provided by the hosting company.

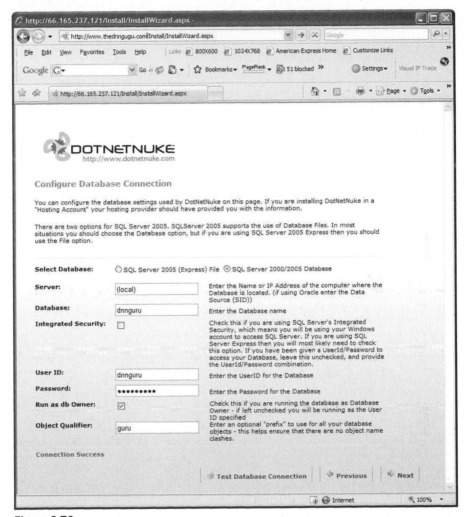

Figure 2-70

It is highly recommended that you place something in the Object Qualifier field. In this example, the word "guru" has been chosen as the Object Qualifier. Although this is not required, something should always be placed in this field. This will help make sure that the database objects created by, and under the control of, the DotNetNuke application are unique.

Click Test Database Connection.

If the wizard can find and log in to the database with the information provided, it will display a Connection Success message, as shown in Figure 2-70. Should the connection fail, please check the information provided by the hosting company.

All this information could have been placed in the web.config file prior to uploading the files to the server. Had this been done, the fields on the Configure Database Connection page would have been populated by what had been placed in the file. Anything placed on this screen is saved to the web.config file when the wizard does its magic. If you are unfamiliar with the connection string syntax, this is a much simpler way to get the correct information into the web.config file. Also, because you have the Test Database Connection link, you have instant feedback that you have it correct.

Once you get the Connection Success message, click Next.

This will open the Run Database Installation Scripts screen. As the scripts create the objects in the database, the page will update you on the status (see Figure 2-71).

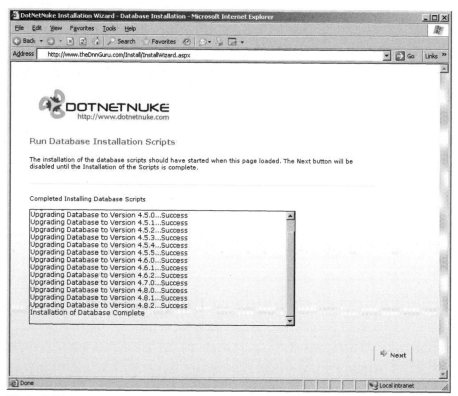

Figure 2-71

Once you get the Installation of Database Complete message, click Next.

The Configure Host User page (see Figure 2-72) is very critical. Here, the information for the default SuperUser is established. It is very important not to forget the username and password! The First, Last, and User name fields may be modified. For this example, however, they will be left as is.

Type a password and confirm it by typing it a second time.

The default password length in the web.config file is seven characters. Therefore your password *must* be at least seven characters.

Type a valid e-mail address in the Email Address field. Click Next.

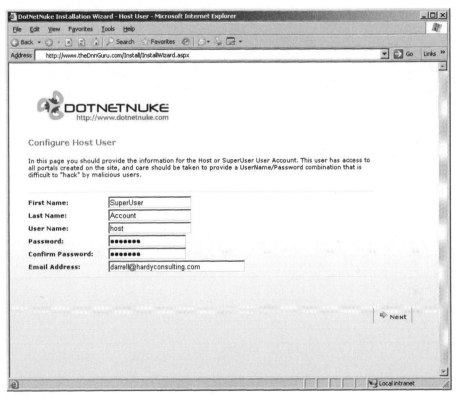

Figure 2-72

The Install Optional Modules screen (see Figure 2-73) allows the installation of the functional modules that come with the DotNetNuke application. These can installed at a later date from the Host menu. It is a good practice to not install things that are not being used. You will notice that some modules are checked for installation, and cannot be unchecked. This is because they are the most commonly used modules and are used with the default data that is installed with the site. For this example, leave this page as it is.

Click Next.

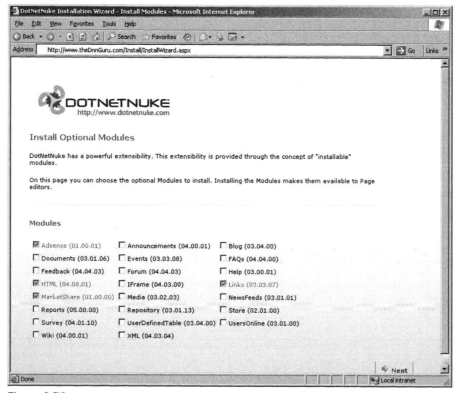

Figure 2-73

The Install Authentication Services screen allows you to install the providers for the method of authentication you will need. Once again, it is advisable not to install methods that you don't need. For this example, just leave the screen as it is (see Figure 2-74) and click Next.

There are no Skins or Containers to be automatically installed. Therefore, the screen shown in Figure 2-75 just states that there is nothing to do here and all is proceeding according to plan.

Click Next.

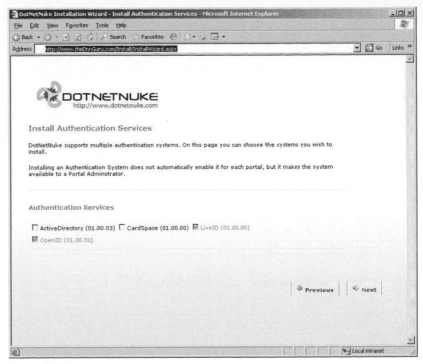

Figure 2-74

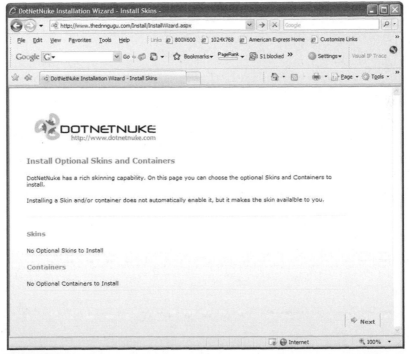

Figure 2-75

There were also no additional language packs to be automatically installed. All three of these items —
Skins, Containers, and Languages — can be installed later. Again, with nothing to do, the screen
displayed in Figure 2-76 simply states that this task has been successfully completed.

Click Next.

Figure 2-76

The Install Host Portal page (see Figure 2-77) allows the setup of an administrator for the root portal/
website. This user is one step below the SuperUser previously created. Again, the First, Last, and User
names may be modified. Be sure to remember the username and password placed on this form.

In the portal Title field, place a title for the website. Click Next.

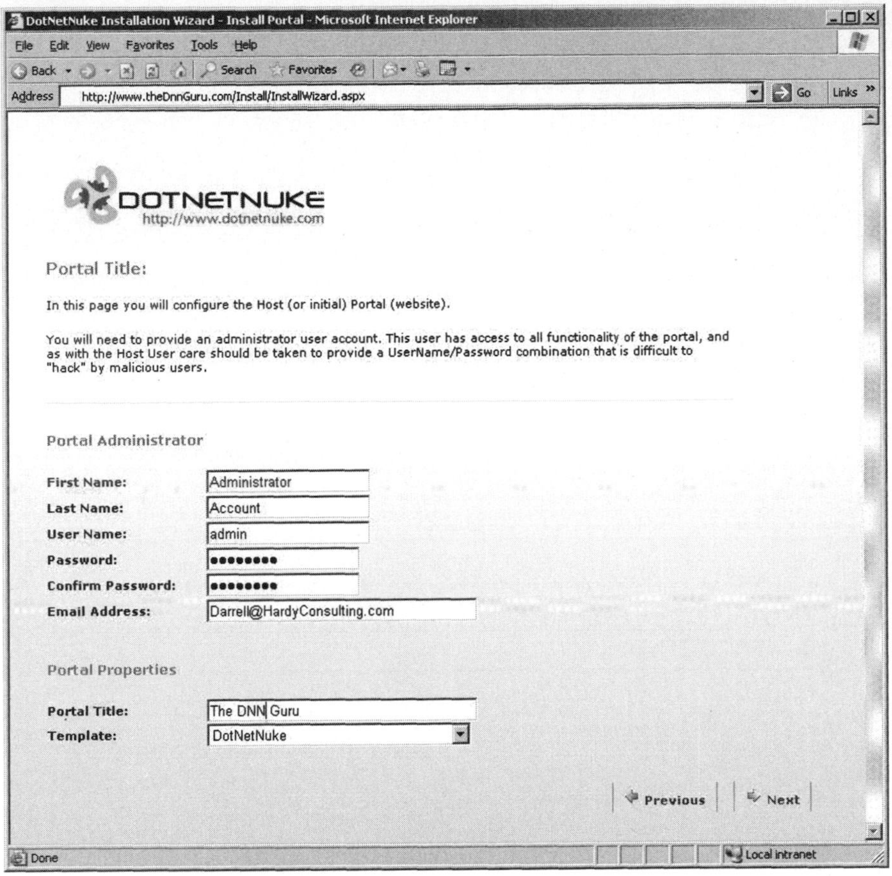

Figure 2-77

Congratulations! You have successfully installed DotNetNuke on a hosted server (see Figure 2-78). Click Finished (Goto Site).

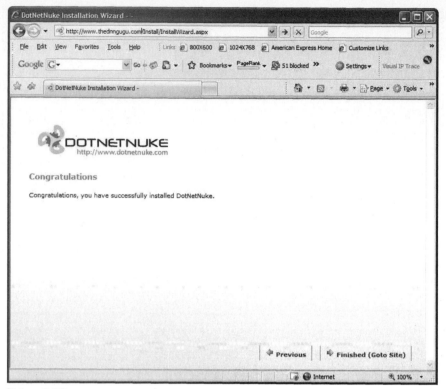

Figure 2-78

This will display the website, as shown in Figure 2-79.

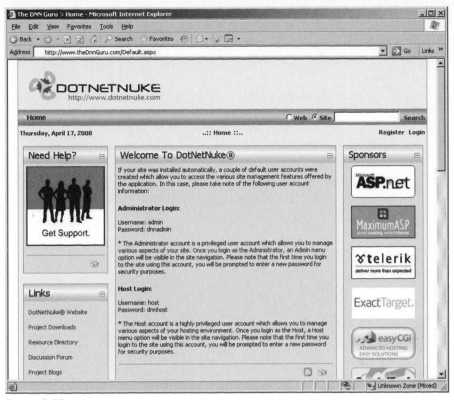

Figure 2-79

Summary

This chapter covered a great deal of information regarding several installation options for DotNetNuke. You learned how to prepare multiple environments for installation, as well as several different installation options within DotNetNuke. You may be restricted by things, such as using your existing operating system (version of Windows). Therefore, mixing the components of the examples to match your purpose, operating system, available database, and DotNetNuke installation mode will give you the tools necessary for a successful installation.

One thing that is not a restriction to installing DotNetNuke, and in fact encourages many people to evaluate it for their use, is that the DotNetNuke application may be downloaded free of charge and with no licensing or usage fee.

And finally, you learned that anyone can get started in the DotNetNuke world.

3

Designing for DotNetNuke — Skins and Skin Components

The first step in creating a new DNN website is to develop the overall look and feel, or specifically, the *skin*. The skin typically consists of the site's overall layout, use of graphics, and cascading style sheets (CSS) to define the global styles throughout. This visual architecture defines how the site is presented from the user's perspective. First, you establish the user experience you want visitors to have, and then you use the DNN framework to facilitate that user experience. The basic considerations that affect the user's experience are the menu/navigation, use of images, and page structure in terms of content. The menu must be intuitive and should be augmented by navigation hints such as a site map or *breadcrumbs* on the interior pages that remind users where they are at any given time, relative to the site as a whole. Breadcrumbs refer to a set of small links on the page whose location is defined at the skin level. These links form a trail that enables users to navigate to pages by clicking the link for a page displayed by the breadcrumb.

The good news is that DNN skins can be built using simple HTML and CSS that most developers are familiar with. However, before you write any code, you should consider all the options made possible by DNN's skinning engine, so you can understand and take advantage of the many attributes that can be implemented as part of a skin. This chapter examines the overall visual layout of a website and explains, in detail, how you can take advantage of arguably the best skinning engine available on any platform. When creating DNN skins, you will find very few limitations because the code is based on HTML and CSS. In fact, with a little out-of-the-box thinking, you'll see that you can customize almost every aspect of your DNN skin. This chapter lays down the ground rules of designing for DNN, which will be used as the basis to create the look and feel for the sample MBR Design website referenced throughout the book.

Problem

From its early days as IBuy Spy Portal, there has been a misconception that a DNN website has to have a certain look and feel. This was due in large part to the fact that developers were concentrating on writing source code without paying much attention to design, which was totally logical. As a result, early DNN skins had a "cookie-cutter" look and feel. After all, the initial focus of what is now called DNN was on function, not on design.

In the past year, things have changed quite a bit. As the DNN framework has become solidified and vilified, and now that more and more people have discovered it, the issue of design has become increasingly important, just like any other website. As a result, many so-called *skinners* — designers that create and offer DNN skins commercially — have come out of the woodwork. However, very few skinners take an out-of-the-box approach to creating DNN skins and so offer cookie-cutter designs that are similar in look and feel. This is typically what happens when designs are created simply to work on top of the DNN framework instead of creating a good design, and then tweaking it to work for DNN. The main point here is that the primary goal of the site should always be considered first: to provide a professional, intuitive, and highly functional graphical interface for users to interact with. Remember one simple fact: Appearance is important! Appearance is important! Appearance is important! You get the idea. The look and feel is the first thing presented to the end user. If your site is less than desirable, visitors will be left with a bad impression of the site. Therefore, they may not take it seriously, and they may not come back. Obviously, this is the last thing you want.

How do you go about deciding the type of design that is right for your website? That really depends on the type of content you want to deliver. For example, for the MBR Design website, we want to deliver information in a clean and concise way that is easily navigable. This will allow us to easily place appropriate emphasis on the elements that are most important — such as portfolio examples. It seems like a no-brainer, but the bottom line is to keep things simple from the outset.

Designing the user interface (UI) for your DNN website is fairly straightforward because you simply follow certain guidelines defined by the framework itself. When considering the dynamic navigation component, you decide if you want horizontal navigation or vertical navigation, and where you want the menu component to reside on your pages. For page layout, you simply decide the location of other dynamic DNN components, such as the Login, Breadcrumb, or Copyright controls. Similarly, you define the content structure of your pages — the areas for dynamic, administrable content — by defining the location of content panes within your skin(s). All of the components of the UI are defined at the skin level and can easily be changed by modifying the skin(s). So, it is quite easy to apply fundamental changes at any time during the site development phase.

Design

This section focuses on overall design for DNN websites. The objective of this chapter is to get you thinking outside-the-box and to dispel the myth that a DNN website has to look a certain way. In this chapter you learn:

❑ The definition of a skin and information about the individual components that make up a complete HTML-based skin package

❑ A comparison of HTML-based skins vs. ASCX-based skins

❑   Skin content structure and the placement of dynamic controls

❑   Limitations and best-practice guidelines when creating or converting website designs for DNN

As you learn about skin components, I'll provide samples of early and current skin designs to demonstrate how skins have evolved over the past few years, so you have a good understanding about what is possible. After you've completed this chapter, you'll put all of the knowledge you've learned to use in Chapter 4 by designing and creating an entire skin package from scratch. But before you get into the actual implementation, I'll present a thorough overview of the skinning process, and what is involved.

An Introduction to Skinning

The term "skinning" has many different interpretations depending on the audience. At the most basic level, skinning provides you with a static layout but allows you to change colors and styles and possibly override images with your own custom graphics. The term "skinning," as it relates to DNN, refers to the ability to customize every aspect of the user interface without changing the actual content. The advantages of DNN skinning are that web page layout and application logic are separated and can be designed and modified independently of each other. This abstraction of "form" and "function" is sometimes referred to as a two-tiered presentation model. This two-tiered approach affords both developers and designers a high degree of independence when it comes to updating and/or maintaining a website, and can substantially reduce the time and effort required in the post-release phases of a professional website solution.

Skin Objects

Within the HTML skin files, skin objects are used as placeholders to represent some type of dynamic functionality, such as a menu, login link, or copyright notice. These placeholders are inserted into the actual HTML at locations you define as [TOKEN] text. When a skin package is uploaded and processed, the HTML files are parsed, along with other files required within a skin package, and the [TOKENS] are replaced by the appropriate application logic, resulting in the skin objects being replaced with specific dynamic content associated with them.

Skin objects contain a feature known as attributes that allows you to customize the appearance of skin objects within your skin. When creating HTML skins, attributes are specified in a separate skin.xml file — this preserves the presentation of the HTML skin file for the designer (see the section "XML Files" later in this chapter).

> *There are many skin objects that can be used within your DNN skins such as* [LOGIN], *which is used to display a Login link, or* [CURRENTDATE], *which is used to display the current date.*

When creating ASCX-based skins, it is necessary to register a Skin Object (control) once like so:

```
<%@ Register TagPrefix="dnn" TagName="LOGIN1" Src="~/Admin/Skins/Login.ascx" %>)
```

However, after a control is registered, you can have multiple instances of it within a skin, as long as each instance of the control has a unique ID. Therefore, the actual user control tag is placed in the skin file, where it is meant to be displayed like so:

```
ie. <dnn:LOGIN1 runat="server" id="Instance1" />
ie. <dnn:LOGIN1 runat="server" id="Instance2" />
```

Content Panes

Content Panes are used to organize the structure of content within a DNN website. Simply put, a Content Pane is just a place where content can be displayed. Similar to Skin Objects, the location of Content Panes is also defined within the HTML. This free-form approach offers the ultimate in design flexibility but also imposes some complications in terms of seamless plug-and-play skinning. For true plug-and-play skins, the layout, name, and quantity of content panes has to be consistent from skin to skin. This will ensure that your content flows the same when you apply a different skin with the same content structure.

Within the DotNetNuke skinning solution, each skin can have different content pane names (IDs), layouts, and an unlimited quantity of content panes per skin. However, each content pane within the same skin must have a unique ID, and at least one content pane must have an ID of "ContentPane." This is how DNN knows that an HTML file that has been created and uploaded is a skin file. If one of the content panes in a skin file does not include an ID of ContentPane, DNN will generate an error that says a skin file does not exist.

Content panes are quite flexible because you can choose to have them collapse and become invisible when they contain no content. Having content panes collapse when no content has been applied to them is a way to achieve layout flexibility without the need to create an additional skin. For example, if you have a skin with a header pane at the top, you can insert a nice branded image into the header pane to make an attractive looking homepage. But you can also use the same skin on the interior pages without inserting an image into the header pane, causing it to collapse, thus creating more real estate for interior-page content, which is typically more copy-heavy.

Content panes are specified at the skin level and the structure cannot be modified within the DNN interface. Changing the content structure can be accomplished only at the skin level (when creating/modifying your skins.

Design Process

Now that you have a brief understanding of skinning and some of the terminology, let's move on to the actual design process and the components involved. Although this process may be slightly different than how a web page designer is accustomed to building HTML pages, the concept is very similar except that the content is no longer static (stored in the HTML page itself), but added dynamically via the DNN portal interface (actually done on the web site and stored in the database).

To make the process of creating skins as simple and as flexible as possible, HTML is used as the basis of the skin definition. This is a huge advantage, as you don't have to learn a new technology to create a skin for DNN. You can use the HTML design tools you are most comfortable with to create and maintain your own skins. The examples in this book use Dreamweaver for HTML design and CSS.

Designing for Web Accessibility

An important part of the design process is to understand Web accessibility and the importance of accommodating users with disabilities. Web accessibility means that people with disabilities can use the Web. More specifically, Web accessibility means that people with disabilities can perceive, understand, navigate, and interact with the Web, and that they can contribute to the Web.

Web accessibility also benefits people without disabilities. For example, a key principle of Web accessibility is designing Web sites and software that are flexible to meet different user needs, preferences, and situations. This flexibility also benefits people without disabilities in certain situations, such as people using a slow Internet connection; people with "temporary disabilities", such as a broken arm; and people with changing abilities due to aging.

Another important design consideration is that Web accessibility is required by laws and policies in some cases. Therefore, when creating a skin design it is becoming increasingly important to think about the intended audience.

But before you start creating your skin, it is important to have a good understanding of the components used in the skinning process.

Skin Components and Proper Naming Conventions

Skins are installed as single-packaged Zip files. Each skin package, at a bare minimum, consists of a single folder that contains at least one HTML file, a CSS file, an XML file, and any graphics/images, if any, related to the skin package. It is a good practice to name your skin folder something specific to your skin, so it is distinctive, and you can easily identify it from a list of skin names. In most cases, we tend to use the name of the site in an abbreviated format with no spaces. For example, the sample website project being built throughout this book is for a fictitious company called MBRDesignCorp. Therefore, we'll use MBR as a basis for naming all folders and files.

Skin definitions can be created using two different methods, HTML or ASCX (user controls). If you are a web designer with limited or no exposure to ASP.NET, then the HTML option is best. On the other hand, if you are proficient in ASP.NET and plan on creating your skin in a tool, such as VS.NET, then ASCX is best. Basically, the only difference between the two methods is the file extension of the skin definition file and the use of tokens versus actual user control tags. This book takes an in-depth approach to skinning using the HTML method.

HTML Files

Skins and containers are typically built using tables-based HTML with extensive CSS, or tableless DIV-based HTML with extensive CSS — the design and main website audience usually dictate which process to be used (tables-based or tableless). Our sample MBR project portal will include three separate tables-based HTML skin designs (some skin packages have more depending on the specific requirements of a project — remember, you can have an unlimited number of skins in a given skin package). Our three skin types for MBR will be separated into three distinct views needed for almost any portal site that is created. Let's assume that for our MBR skin package there is one of each skin type in the following bulleted list:

- ❑ **MBRhome.html:** This is the skin that will be seen on the home page and any other launch page within the website.

- ❑ **MBRinterior.html:** This is the skin that will be applied to all interior pages throughout the site.

- ❑ **MBRadmin.html:** This will be a full screen view (single content pane because it usually needs more flexible widths) seen by admins, or logged-in users in some cases.

- ❑ **MBRsplash.html:** This is the splash or intro page of the website.

The number of HTML files that can be contained in one skin package is unlimited. However, the need to have more than the skin versions in the preceding list should make you rethink your structural layout, because the design of the skin itself has nothing to do with content. What you may consider a different skin layout can often be handled within the content structure itself when using collapsible content panes.

CSS Files

One thing that designers often have a difficult time grasping is how CSS is applied to DNN skins. Therefore, it is important to understand how DNN websites utilize CSS.

Every installation of DNN includes a default.css file. This CSS file includes all of the default CSS styles used by DNN and exists to fill in the gaps that a designer may overlook during the skinning process. The default.css file also handles classes, which may be used by the content of some third-party modules that the designer cannot plan for.

Each DNN portal also has a portal.css, which simply has a number of empty default classes that are available to the designer.

All other CSS files associated with a skin package are created by the designer. These CSS files must follow the exact naming convention as the HTML file they correspond to (htmlname.css), or be named skin.css. The skin.css file is special because it is the common CSS file that should be shared by all HTML files in your skin package. The only time you should use a separate htmlname.css file is when you have CSS classes unique to a particular skin file, or when you need to override specific classes in the skin.css for a particular skin type. In most cases, you will need only a single skin.css file, which is shared by all of the HTML skin files within a skin package.

There are two other ways DNN utilizes CSS: with container files, which is discussed later on, and from within actual modules being used in a DNN website. As a designer, you have no control over the module.css files and also have no idea if and when they are going to be used. Luckily, the majority of the time, module.css classes don't affect design and are rarely used.

The following shows the order in which all of the CSS files are loaded, and where they actually reside within the folder hierarchy of a DNN website:

- ❑ **Default.css:** Located in an area accessible to the designer only via File Transfer Protocol (FTP)

- ❑ **Skin.css:** Located in the skin package folder (Portals/PortalID/Skins/MBR/skin.css)

- ❑ **Portal.css:** Located in the root folder of the portal install (Portals/PortalID/portal.css)

- ❑ **Htmlname.css:** Located in the same directory as skin.css

- ❑ **Container.css:** Located in the Portal container directory (Portals/PortalID/Containers/ Containername/Container.css)

- ❑ **Module.css:** Located in the home directory of the module and accessible only via FTP

The bottom line is that, despite the amount of CSS files that are present within a single DNN portal, it is a good practice to use the skin.css file only for storing and applying any and all CSS classes for a skin package.

XML Files

XML files are the final piece to the skinning puzzle. And the good news is that there is nothing mysterious about what is included in these files or how to use them. Simply put, a single XML file is used to define the global attributes and allows you to customize the appearance of skin objects by overriding default values set by the DNN portal framework. These attributes apply to all skins with a single package. When your skin package is uploaded and parsed for use in a portal, DNN looks to this XML file to add custom settings to the generated ASCX file(s) the portal will display to end users. In simple terms, this XML file allows you to define skin object attributes such as CSS class names.

Parsing is the process upon installation, which converts your HTML skin files to make them usable by the portal.

The following is an example of an XML document with settings for one token. Each tag instance is called a node.

```
<Objects> 1 per file
<Object> multiple per Objects node
  <Token>[LOGIN]</Token> Token used in html file - 1 per Object node
  <Settings> Node used for logical grouping - 1 per Object
<Setting> Beginning of a setting - multiple per Settings node
  <Name>TEXT</Name> Name of setting for token - 1 per setting node
  <Value>LOG IN</Value> Value of setting for token - 1 per setting node
</Setting> End of a setting - multiple per Settings node
      <Setting>
  <Name>CssClass</Name>
  <Value>Login</Value>
</Setting>
    </Settings>
</Object>
</Objects>
```

If you are not familiar with using XML, don't worry. It's just a human readable language displayed in a hierarchical format. XML code is very similar to HTML tables code — for each opening tag there must be one closing tag. For a detailed list of attributes that can be applied to tokens, please see the DotNetNuke Skinning.pdf included in the DotNetNuke file downloads at www.dotnetnuke.com. It explains the attributes that can be applied to the available tokens and defines the default value if no value is present.

ASCX-Based Skins

As previously discussed, when uploading HTML-based skins, DNN parses the HTML skin files and generates ASCX files on-the-fly to display the appropriate dynamic functionality defined by our tokens. This is one way to build skins. The other option, which is better suited for developer types, is to create ASCX-based skins that DNN does not have to parse to display dynamic controls. Unlike HTML-based skins, which include placeholder tokens, when creating ASCX-based skins, dynamic user controls must first be registered at the top of the ASCX skin file like the following menu, login, and user controls:

```
<%@ Register TagPrefix="dnn" TagName="SOLPARTMENU1" Src="~/Admin/Skins/
SolPartMenu.ascx" %>
<%@ Register TagPrefix="dnn" TagName="LOGIN"
Src="~/Admin/Skins/Login.ascx" %>
<%@ Register TagPrefix="dnn" TagName="USER"
Src="~/Admin/Skins/User.ascx" %>
```

After your user controls have been registered, the code for each user control must be placed directly in the HTML code of your skin file, where you want the user control to be displayed on your live page like the following menu control:

```
<dnn:SOLPARTMENU1 runat="server" id="dnnSOLPARTMENU1"
display="horizontal" userootbreadcrumbarrow="false" usesubmenubreadcrumbarrow="false"
rootmenuitemselectedcssclass="MenuItem_MouseOver"
rootmenuitemactivecssclass="MenuItem_Selected"
rootmenuitemcssclass="MenuItem" menubreakcssclass="MenuBreak" cssseparator="separator"
submenucssclass="SubMenu" submenuitemselectedcssclass="SubMenu_MouseOver"
usearrows="false" rightseparator="<img src=&quot;images/separator.jpg&quot;>"
menualignment="justify"/>
```

Note the piece of code `runat="server"`. This tells DNN that a dynamic user control is being loaded. This snippet must be present to inject a user control on a live page.

Unlike HTML-based skins, where you define user control attributes with a separate XML file, you can see that all of the user control attributes are defined and placed directly in the ASCX file, along with the user control, in this case for the dynamic menu.

Which Method Is Right for You?

There are advantages to building ASCX-based skins. ASCX-based skins don't have to be packaged into a single file, uploaded and parsed by DNN. You can simply upload ASCX-based files via File Transfer Protocol (FTP), refresh your page, and updates are applied. There are some caveats to creating ASCX-based skins, however. As I said earlier, ASCX skins are more for developer types because there is more code to be concerned with. And, if you are not careful or comfortable coding ASCX files, it is easy to change something that causes your code to "break," causing DNN to display an error when trying to load your page.

HTML-based skins are built with the least common denominator in mind — designer types that are more familiar with creating HTML web layouts using Dreamweaver or other WSIWYG editors and less familiar with in-depth ASCX code. XML knowledge is a requirement for defining user control attributes within HTML-based skins. However, XML code is quite easy for designers to understand and implement within their DNN skins.

Solution

Now that you have a good overview of the individual components that bring a skin package to life, let's deconstruct a few skins in an effort to understand how the concept of design applies to them.

Let's start with a skin design example that is indicative of early DNN skin designs. In Figure 3-1, notice the simple skin design, which has a very boxy look and feel. This is how typical early DNN skins were created as more emphasis was placed on development rather than design.

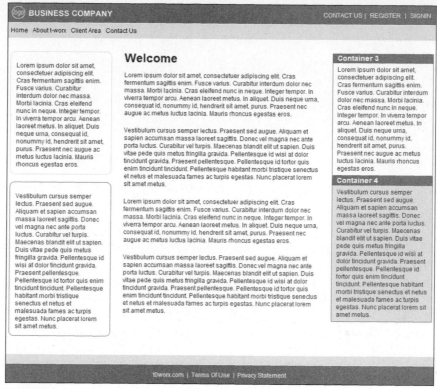

Figure 3-1

Notice the seemingly three-column format of the content. Then, notice the tokens (user controls) used in this design: the logo in the upper-left corner, the register and signin links in the upper-right corner, the horizontal menu, and the copyright, terms, and privacy tokens in the footer.

Now let's look at the underlying structure of our simple skin example to understand what is happening with the display of the skin.

Let's analyze the content pane structure in Figure 3-2 first. As you can see, the content structure has been defined with the following content panes:

- ❑ LinkPane

- ❑ TopPane

- ❑ LeftPane

- ❑ ContentPane (Remember, at least one of the panes within a skin must have an ID of "ContentPane.")

- ❑ RightPane

- ❑ BottomPane

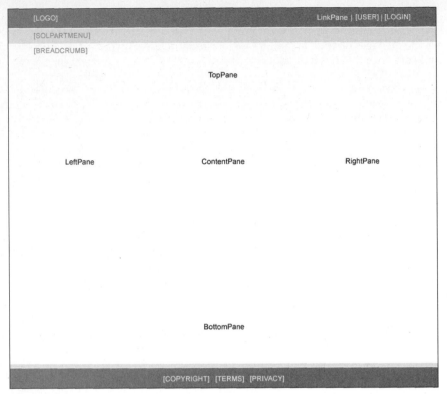

Figure 3-2

These denote the individual panes, defined only at the skin level, that content can be added to. Notice how the content pane structure actually looks different than the design in Figure 3-1. That is because all of the content panes are not being utilized in our skin. The TopPane and BottomPane content panes in our skin have been coded with the `visible="false"` attribute, which makes them collapse because no content has been applied to them. And because the TopPane and BottomPane content panes are collapsed, the other content panes within our skin expand to take up the additional space no longer being used by our TopPane and BottomPane collapsed panes. This is a great way to build additional layout flexibility into your skins without creating additional skin versions.

Also notice how the skin utilizes another content pane called LinkPane to insert the CONTACT US link next to the REGISTER link. It's advantageous to use multiple content panes within your skins to give administrators the ability to apply changes to your website easily, such as changing a key phone number or address, or in this case, simply adding a link.

Next, let's use Figure 3-2 and focus on the tokens being used in our skin design. First, notice that we have used the [LOGO] token to display the logo. Using the [LOGO] token allows you to display a common logo on all pages of your site via Admin ⇨ Site Settings ⇨ Appearance ⇨ Logo. See Figure 3-3 for an example of a logo that has been applied via the [LOGO] token.

Next, notice the [USER] and [LOGIN] tokens (refer back to Figure 3-2). The [USER] token displays the account name of a person when logged in and any words you define in the XML when not logged in. The [LOGIN] token simply provides a link that allows a person to click and log in to the website. Using the XML file within an HTML-based skin package, the text that is displayed by the [USER] and [LOGIN] tokens can be displayed textually however you want. For example, the [USER] token can be defined to display the words "Click Here to Register," or simply "REGISTER," as in the Figure 3-2 example. The [LOGIN] token can be defined to display the words "Log in Now to Receive a Special Offer" or simply "LOGIN," as in the Figure 3-2 example.

Figure 3-2 also displays the additional tokens used in the sample skin. They are:

❑ [SOLPARTMENU]: This token displays our dynamic menu. With the XML file within an HTML-based skin package, many attributes can be defined to control the look and feel of the dynamic menu, including whether the menu is displayed vertically or horizontally, as in our skin example. There are also several attributes that control the display of the menu within the skin.css file used within the HTML-based skin package.

❑ [COPYRIGHT]: This token displays the copyright information on a DNN website. The words displayed by the [COPYRIGHT] token can be defined via Admin ⇨ Site Settings ⇨ Copyright.

❑ [TERMS]: This token links to the default Terms of Use page within a DNN website, which can easily be customized via Admin ⇨ Language ⇨ Language Editor ⇨ Resource Name: MESSAGE_PORTAL_TERMS.Text.

❑ [PRIVACY]: This token links to the default Privacy Statement page within a DNN website, which can easily be customized via Admin ⇨ Language ⇨ Language Editor ⇨ Resource Name: MESSAGE_PORTAL_PRIVACY.Text.

The sample skin we have just examined includes most of the "default" tokens that are used with most DNN skins. However, many other tokens can be used within a DNN skin to display different types of dynamic content. The next skin design, displayed in Figure 3-3, includes additional tokens typically used by many DNN sites and is more indicative of some of the modern DNN skins being created today.

Figure 3-3

Notice how the design has a less standard (boxy) DNN look and feel, which is a complaint heard often by clients looking for cutting-edge DNN designs.

In Figure 3-5 below, notice the number of content panes within the second design example. Creating skins with several content panes is a good way to provide flexibility in terms of layout options when applying content to a DNN website. The number of content panes that can be added to a skin, and the way they react to live content, is limited only by your imagination.

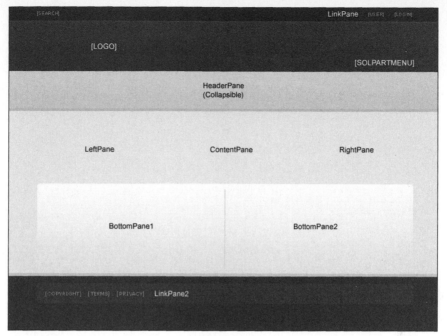

Figure 3-4

Also in Figure 3-5, notice the HeaderPane being utilized in this sample skin design. Using a HeaderPane within a skin is a good way to use the same skin for the home page and interior pages of a DNN website, while making the same skin appear different to the end user. For example, in Figure 3-4, a large image is used in the HeaderPane to display the main branding image on the home page of a DNN website. Figure 3-6 below shows the same skin applied to an interior page with a smaller image used in the HeaderPane, thereby providing more real estate for interior-page content. You can also use the `visible="false"` attribute to collapse the HeaderPane by leaving it empty, which would provide even more real estate for interior-page content.

Figure 3-5

The sample skin design shown in Figure 3-5 uses many of the same tokens as our first design example, plus a few other tokens. Let's review the different tokens being used by our second skin sample which are as follows:

❑ [SOLPARTMENU]: Notice how the menu has been stylized to appear as tabs. This token displays a third-party menu component being used by this skin. Several third-party menu components are available for DNN, with their own set of attributes that can be applied to control the look and feel of the menu. One source for good (and not-so-good) third-party menu components, modules, and skins for DNN is www.snowcovered.com, which is the best-known marketplace for DNN commercial products. Another quality source for certified DNN components, modules, and skins is the DotNetNuke Marketplace (www.marketplace.dnn.com). What makes this site a quality source is the fact that many modules and skins sold here go through a review process by the DNN core team. Only if they pass the core team's rigorous review process are they listed for sale in the DNN Marketplace. Because of this certification process, you can be assured you are purchasing components, modules, and skins of the highest quality available for DNN. Yet another great source for DNN (and ASP.Net) components is Telerik (www.telerik.com). Telerik offers truly best-of-breed products, including several components that add professional-level functionality and display to your DNN website.

❑ [CURRENTDATE]: This token displays the date on a DNN website. The XML file within an HTML-based skin package can be used to define the format of the date being displayed.

❑ [BREADCRUMB]: This token displays a link trail that indicates your location within your DNN website at any given time. The links displayed by this token enable users to easily navigate to hierarchical pages within their DNN website. The XML file within an HTML-based skin package can be used to define the level at which your breadcrumbs start to display.

❑ [SEARCH]: This control displays a site search or web search function on a DNN website. The XML file within an HTML-based skin package can be used to specify one or both of these search methods.

Now let's take a look at the skin design, shown in Figure 3-6, that will be used for the sample MBR Design website that you are going to build on throughout this book.

Figure 3-6

As you can see in Figure 3-6, the MBR Design is simple, clean, and easy to navigate, with the use of just a few containers and a nice header image that really pops. Let's deconstruct the MBR Design skins in Figure 3-7.

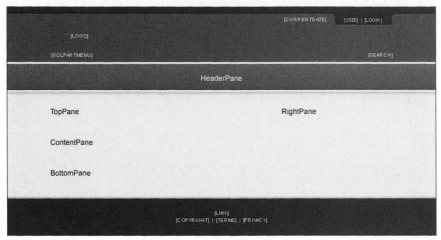

Figure 3-7

As you can see, the MBR Design skins also utilize many of the same standards tokens used by other DNN skins. It also includes a HeaderPane that can be used for key branding imagery, or left empty to create more content real estate for interior pages.

Limitations and Best Practice Guidelines

Many DNN websites start with an original, custom skin design. However, many DNN sites also start from existing templates or designs that are converted into DNN skins. Now that you have a good understanding of how skins are constructed using tokens and content panes, it will be helpful to follow a few guidelines that will make your skin design projects a success, whether you are creating a design from scratch or using an existing design.

A Few Tweaks Can Go a Long Way

Just about any design can be converted into a DNN skin with a little creativity. Many people like to use Template Monster templates (www.templatemonster.com) or other existing templates as a starting point for a website design. In some cases however, aspects of certain templates need to be tweaked to be more DNN-friendly — mainly to accommodate a DNN menu correctly. Figure 3-8 displays a Template Monster template that needs to be converted into a DNN skin.

Figure 3-8

However, a few tweaks are required to make this design play nicely within the DNN environment. Figure 3-9 shows the template with a couple of necessary tweaks to convert the template into a functional DNN skin.

Figure 3-9

As you can see in Figure 3-9, the menu has been changed to accommodate a DNN menu component (displayed as buttons in this example) while maintaining the overall integrity of the original template design.

Next, the [REGISTER] and [LOGIN] tokens have replaced the Shopping Cart link in the top-right. Virtually, everything else in the design can be built to appear exactly as it is displayed in the original template using tokens, content panes, and containers. Of course, I recommend using content panes when possible so you have total control of any content at the Admin level, such as the links at the bottom and the Paypal/credit card buttons shown in Figure 3-9.

Design Skins with Minimum Widths

Because of the dynamic nature of a DNN website, it is important to realize that DNN skin designs must react to content that is always changing. Early DNN skinners found this out the hard way as they created fixed-width skins that were not built with the flexibility to expand or contract with content. This becomes obvious as content is applied to a DNN site that is wider than the fixed width of the skins. Figure 3-10 shows an example of the top portion of skin that was not designed to accommodate content that was wider than the original fixed-width design.

Figure 3-10

As you can see, while we are not logged in, the top of this skin looks just fine. However, take a look at Figure 3-11, and see what happens when an Admin logs in.

Figure 3-11

As you can see in Figure 3-11, the image area under the logo appears to be "broken" with gaps in the image. This is because the skins were developed like a typical, static website with no consideration for dynamic content. And as you have also seen, this is not obvious until content is applied that causes this behavior (such as when logging in). For this reason, it is recommended that you always create skins with a minimum width opposed to a fixed width. It takes only a little extra time in most cases to code skins properly to make sure this never happens. It will be worth the frustration of having to fix the skins later when you are trying to meet website production deadlines. And trust me, the last thing you want is a client calling you with the news that the skins they paid for are "broken."

DNN Menus

There are actually very few restrictions when it comes to creating DNN skins. The DNN menu is one component whose display is restricted to either a vertical or horizontal format on a straight line. And, because DNN is totally dynamic, it is impossible to create a DNN menu that is displayed on a curve.

However, the benefits of the dynamic state of the DNN menu far outweigh these so-called limitations. For example, as you have seen in the design samples, you have a great deal of control over the look and feel of a DNN menu. There are many different menu components that give you a great deal of freedom to apply unique styling to the different unselected, active, and hover states of your DNN menu. Moreover, you can easily change the names, locations, and order of menu items within a DNN website very easily while maintaining any styling you have applied as part of the design.

The Location of User Controls

Another minor restriction is deciding where to place the dynamic controls, which can only be defined and changed at the skin level. You cannot move these dynamic controls within the DNN interface itself, but you can apply several attributes that define the look and feel of DNN controls to match a site design. Another important note about user controls is that they cannot exist inside content panes. Therefore, skins have to be coded for user controls to coexist with content panes within the HTML structure of DNN skins.

Content

You cannot apply modules horizontally within a single content pane. Modules can exist only within a vertical relationship to one another inside a content pane. However, a little creativity when designing skins and content can go a long way to mitigate this so-called restriction. It is quite easy to make your DNN content appear just about any way you can think of depending on your content pane structure.

With these restrictions aside, you really have a great deal of flexibility when creating DNN skins and displaying content with DNN websites. All that is required is some experience with applying content to DNN websites and a little creative thinking outside-the-DNN-box.

Summary

In this chapter, you learned the definition of a skin, how DNN skin designs have changed over the past few years, and the importance of design when creating skins for DNN. You've also learned about many of the necessary components used in building DNN skins, the differences in applying DNN components within HTML and ASCX-based skins, how skins are constructed with tokens and content panes, and how to achieve successful results using a few best practice design guidelines.

In most cases, you can use many of the principles you have learned for traditional, static website designs. Add to these principles the basic concepts of using DNN components with static HTML, and it's just a matter of time before you can turn your static website designs into DNN skins.

Now that you have a good understanding of what is possible when creating skins for DNN, let's put that knowledge to use by building an entire DNN skin package in Chapter 4.

4

Preparing the Design and Creating an HTML-Based Skin Package

As you learned in the previous chapter, creating a website design for DNN is very similar to creating a traditional website design, while adding some special components that turn a static, lifeless web page into an intuitive, dynamic environment. Indeed, a feature-rich, dynamic environment takes the ability to edit and maintain a website to a whole new level. This type of web environment is becoming the standard type of website experience expected by many website owners today. While the final destination is entirely different, the path to prepare a finished website design for DNN remains the same. You start with an image editor, such as Photoshop, to develop a design/proof of concept. Then, you slice up the design to create the necessary individual images for use in HTML files and export them for coding in an HTML editor. Finally, you use an HTML editor, such as Dreamweaver, to create HTML-based code that represents the necessary files in a given skin package. This process requires various skills, but it is a process that can be learned efficiently with a little knowledge of Photoshop and Dreamweaver.

Problem

Let's face it — most designers use Photoshop as a basis for website design. However, because of the pressures of deadlines, many designers simply don't take the time to properly organize their files with layers and layer sets. This creates several headaches when preparing designs for HTML or having to change aspects of the layered Photoshop file itself:

❑   When using Photoshop files that are not organized appropriately, it is not clear which design components are defined by the different layers that may exist. This is apparent, for example, when using certain pre-built templates as a basis for website design that may have hundreds of layers that have not been named according to the design elements contained on them. This is also apparent when designers use the default names

(Layer 1, Layer 2, and so on) given by Photoshop when creating new layers. It can be quite frustrating to show and hide layer after layer just to find the correct layer that contains an element you want to change.

❑ In many cases, certain components within a design may have several layers. For example, the navigation component may have background images, text, on and off states, and separator images. When these types of components are not part of the same layer set, it becomes very difficult to make changes that may affect the component as a whole, such as moving the navigation to a different location within the design. Doing this layer by layer is time-consuming and inefficient.

❑ Designs created in Photoshop typically contain several different images. It is difficult to revise and save versions of these individual images when "slices" have not been utilized. When applying "slices," you define the name and specific heights and widths of individual images or areas within a design that get saved with the Photoshop file. When "slices" are applied, it is easy, for example, to create a new design color scheme by re-coloring a Photoshop file and simply changing the names of "slices" and saving them. When "slices" are not utilized, it is difficult to make design changes down the road because image areas have not been defined and saved with the original Photoshop file.

The idea that time is saved by not going the extra mile to properly organize layered Photoshop files is a myth. Organizing designs with layers and layer sets takes very little time on the front end and offers many advantages. To make the process of changing or updating a design as painless as possible, it is highly recommended that designers take the time to organize their Photoshop files appropriately.

While organizing source files is important, so too is the way you choose to build your HTML. There is a misconception about using Photoshop or other image editing software to create HTML because many designers still think of design in terms of static web pages. In the static web design world it is acceptable to create fixed-width designs because when a static web page is loaded in a browser, it does not change. Therefore, many designers of static web pages simply apply slices to their design files and let their image editing software create fixed HTML for them. However, in the dynamic web design world, it is important to prepare designs that will accommodate changing content. For example, creating the MBR Design header that expands seamlessly, regardless of the width of content that is applied, is a great way to facilitate the requirements of dynamic content. If HTML is not properly coded for dynamic content, a design can easily appear "broken" if it does not expand seamlessly.

Design

This section focuses on using Photoshop 7+ to prepare the MBR Design look and feel for conversion into a DNN skin package and create the actual graphics required for the design. This section also focuses on using Dreamweaver 8+ to create the actual HTML, CSS, and XML files that are required for the MBR Design skin package. The objective of this chapter is to show you, at a low level, how to create a skin package from start to finish. Therefore, it is assumed that you have some working knowledge of Photoshop and Dreamweaver. In this chapter you learn:

❑ How to use Photoshop to prepare and organize MBR Design skin design using layers and layer sets

❑ How to use Photoshop to create slices and save all of the necessary images used in the MBR Design skins

❑   How to use Dreamweaver to create all of the necessary HTML, CSS, and XML component files required for the MBR Design skin package

As I just mentioned, you will learn the basic skinning process from start to finish while building all of the necessary components required for an HTML-based DNN skin package. After you complete this chapter, you will package and install the skin package on the MBR Design website. But before you can install the skin package, you need to build it. So let's get a move on!

Solution

Like any other website project, creating a DNN skin typically starts with Photoshop or other image editing software to create a mock-up of what the final site may look like prior to any coding in HTML. After a mock-up has been created, it is submitted to the decision maker(s) for approval before you proceed with the coding. After the final mock-up is approved, it can be sliced into small pieces and exported for use in HTML. During the process of creating a mock-up, which typically includes several different individual layers, it is essential to keep the file organized with intuitively named layers and layer sets. This makes the process of editing a mock-up easy and efficient. The sample MBR Design project follows these same guidelines. Let's open the initial MBR design in Photoshop and analyze how the file has been organized.

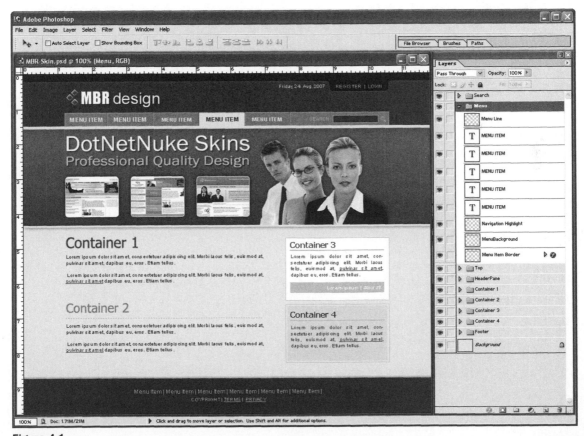

Figure 4-1

As you can see in Figure 4-1, our initial MBR design is a good representation of how the final website is going to appear. You can also see, by looking at the Layers palette, the different layer sets that have been created for the various graphical components on the page. Within each layer set, several individual layers that are required for each individual graphical component have been grouped together and clearly named according to their functional representation within the design. For example, the menu layer set has been expanded to show all of the individual menu component layers. Using layer sets like this keeps your file nicely organized for editing and makes it easy to edit or move entire components with minimal effort.

To give you a better idea of how the MBR design is broken down in terms of separate components, Figures 4-2 through 4-10 show the components contained within each individual layer set.

Figure 4-2

The Search Layer Set in Figure 4-2 includes the elements that represent the [SEARCH] token attributes.

The Menu Layer Set in Figure 4-3 includes the elements that represent the dynamic menu attributes — in this case, for the SolpartMenu. This can represent any DNN menu component.

Figure 4-3

The Top Layer Set (see Figure 4-4) includes the [CURRENTDATE], [USER], [LOGIN], and [LOGO] token attributes, as well as the top ribbon background that gets repeated horizontally in a browser.

Figure 4-4

The HeaderPane Layer Set (see Figure 4-5) includes the repeating HeaderPane background graphics, including a slice for the HeaderPane image(s).

Figure 4-5

The Container1 Layer Set includes the attributes that represent Container 1 (see Figure 4-6).

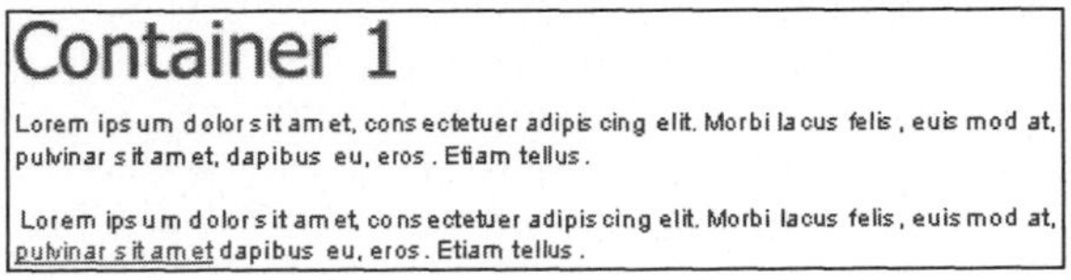

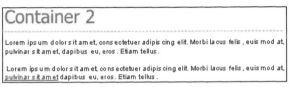

Figure 4-6

The Container2 Layer Set includes the attributes that represent Container 2 (see Figure 4-7).

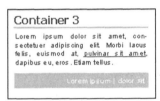

Figure 4-7

The Container3 Layer Set includes the attributes that represent Container 3 (see Figure 4-8).

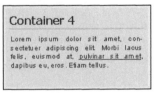

Figure 4-8

The Container4 Layer Set includes the attributes that represent Container 4 (see Figure 4-9).

Figure 4-9

The Footer Layer Set includes the [LINK], [COPYRIGHT], [TERMS], and [PRIVACY] token attributes as well as the background for the footer area that repeats horizontally in a browser (see Figure 4-10).

Figure 4-10

Poor Organization Can Lead to Wasted Time and Increased Costs

This chapter illustrates how good organization of your Photoshop files can make the editing process simple and efficient. It is also important to be aware of how poor organization can potentially affect a project's timeline and costs. Figure 4-11 displays a Photoshop file that has not been organized appropriately for editing purposes.

Figure 4-11

As you can see by looking at the Layers palette, the layers have not been named. They simply contain the default names created by Photoshop when the layers were either created or duplicated. Therefore, there is no way to know which layer corresponds to each design element unless you start turning layers on and off to see which layers are affected. This is typically what happens when designers are in too much of a hurry to name their layers based on the elements included on them. Also notice that no layer sets have been utilized. For these reasons, it would be very difficult to edit designs such as this with hundreds of independent layers, without spending hours deciphering which individual graphical component coincides with each individual layer. This is not recommended!

When using Template Monster templates (www.templatemonster.com), allow for 2–4 hours of extra time to properly organize the included Photoshop files as they typically contain hundreds of unnamed layers, like the example shown previously in Figure 4-11.

The benefits of saving layers and layer sets when creating website designs (or any type of designs for that matter) are obvious. Layers and layer sets give you total freedom to change your design colors, backgrounds, or any other attribute quite easily. If a client called with scope changes midway though a project that included an entire color palette change to a design, it would be very difficult if all of the graphics were composed into a single JPEG. But knowing you have saved an appropriately organized layered Photoshop file gives you the comfort that you can make any necessary revisions to a design quickly and efficiently.

Creating Slices with Photoshop

Now that you know the importance of preparing clean, organized, layered Photoshop files, let's use Photoshop to slice and dice all of the images required for your skin, so you can build your HTML-based skin package.

Photoshop has many great features. One of the best for creating website designs is the use of "slices." Slices allow you to define individual image areas that get saved along with the Photoshop file, making it easy to change or rename images later. You can even export HTML along with your slices. However, when creating HTML for dynamic content environments such as DNN, it is necessary to create many styles and customize the HTML markup. Therefore, it is typically better to export individual images, or smaller "chunks" of HTML that can be applied to HTML skin files.

There are two ways to create slices in Photoshop. The first option requires the following four steps:

1. Select the Slice Tool (see Figure 4-12).

Figure 4-12

2. Drag an area to define as a slice (see Figure 4-13).

Figure 4-13

3. Select the Slice Select Tool (see Figure 4-14).

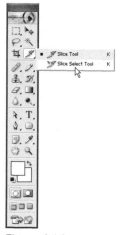

Figure 4-14

4. Double-click on the slice to open the Slice Options window and name the slice (see Figure 4-15).

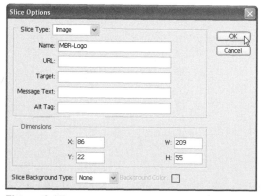

Figure 4-15

The second option requires the following three steps but lets you create a slice directly from a layer:

1. Select a layer you want to create a slice from by selecting it in the Layers palette (see Figure 4-16). Then, select New Layer Based Slice from the Layer menu. This creates a slice with the same dimensions as the item on your selected layer.

Figure 4-16

2. Select the Slice Select Tool (see Figure 4-17).

Figure 4-17

3. Double-click on the slice to open the Slice Options window and name the slice (see Figure 4-18).

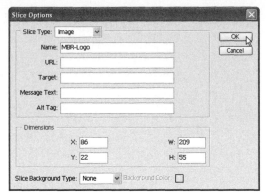

Figure 4-18

Saving Slices as Images for HTML

Now that you have effectively learned how to create slices in Photoshop, let's create all the slices and save the images required to build the MBR Design skin HTML files.

Figure 4-19 highlights the necessary slices for creating the MBR Design HTML-based skins. They are as follows:

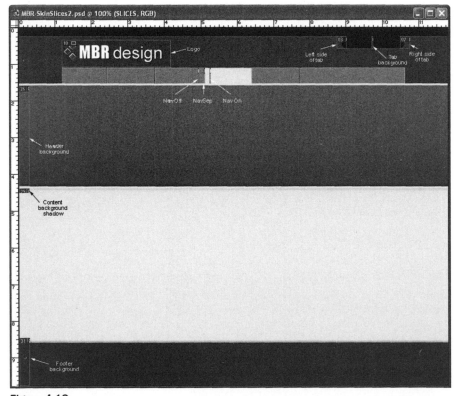

Figure 4-19

- ❑ **Logo:** This image will be saved in a separate folder you'll name Content and applied globally to the website via Admin ⇨ Site Settings. It will not be used in the actual skin files.

- ❑ **Left side of tab:** The left corner of the User/Login tab.

- ❑ **Tab background:** The background that will be used to make your login tab expand horizontally.

- ❑ **Right side of tab:** The right corner of the User/Login tab.

- ❑ **NavOff:** The unselected state of the top-level menu items.

- ❑ **NavSep:** The separator between the top-level menu items.

- ❑ **NavOn:** The hover and selected state of the top-level menu items.

- ❑ **Header background:** The background that will be used to make your header expand horizontally.

- ❑ **Content background shadow:** This image will be used to duplicate the shadow horizontally at the top of the content area.

- ❑ **Footer:** The background that will be used to make your footer expand horizontally.

Save for Web

After the slices are created for your design, four steps are required to save the images in preparation to create the HTML skins:

1. Selecting Save for Web from the File menu (shown in Figure 4-20).

Figure 4-20

2. In the Save For Web dialog box, select slices by shift-clicking on each slice (you can select the magnifying glass icon from the tool palette on the left and zoom in if necessary); select the file format settings on the right and click the Save button (shown in Figure 4-21).

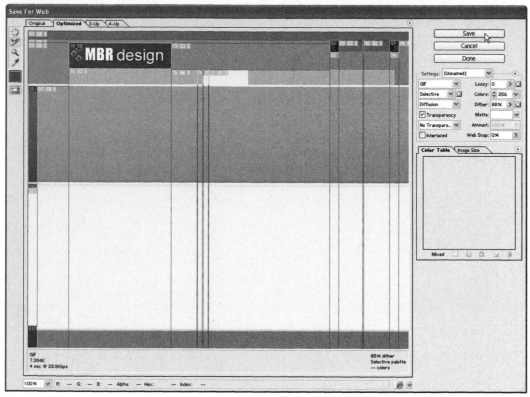

Figure 4-21

3. Because you want to save only the individual images defined by your slices with no HTML, select Images Only in the drop-down menu next to Save as Type. Then, select Other in the drop-down menu next to Settings (shown in Figure 4-22).

Figure 4-22

4. Under Optimize Files, clear the Put Images in Folder checkbox and click OK. This saves the images in a specified folder without creating an additional subfolder (shown in Figure 4-23).

Figure 4-23

5. Finally, select Selected Slices in the drop-down menu next to Slices and click the Save button to save only the slices that are selected (see Figure 4-24).

Figure 4-24

This saves all of the slices that have been selected to a specified folder, in this case to a folder called "images," to be used for creating the HTML-based skins (shown in Figure 4-25).

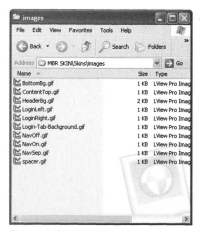

Figure 4-25

You can use these same methods for creating slices to use for containers as well as skins, although containers typically include fewer images because of the small amount of HTML required for them.

The benefits of using Photoshop and saving slices when preparing website designs is also obvious. Slices provide the ability to make design customizations easily because the areas that define all of the images are saved with the image names you assign. For example, if the entire color scheme of a design changes midway through a project, you could easily change all of your layered elements to achieve the desired colors, and simply save your slices again and replace the original images created from them because they are always the same image names unless you change the slice names. You don't have to worry that the images are the correct size or even the correct images if you don't alter the slices. If, by a series of unfortunate events, your slices happen to change or be deleted, that is another story. The bottom line is, if you want to painlessly edit or customize existing designs you create, be sure to save slices so you can do so any time you desire.

Creating DNN Skins — A Few Guidelines

Now that you have properly organized your source file and used slices to create all the required images for your skins, let's jump right in and build the DNN skin package! But before you get started with the actual code, it's a good idea to lay down some guidelines.

First, all skin files will be placed in a single folder named Skins. When creating skins it is important to name them intuitively so users can easily differentiate between different skin versions within a single skin package when accessing them via a drop-down menu within the DNN interface.

The Skins folder will include:

- One HTML file and one JPEG (preview) file per skin version with consistent filenames:
    - skinname.html
    - skinname.jpg
- One common skin.xml file: There is an exception to this rule. If there are one or more skin versions with specific, unique XML attributes required, it is necessary to create a "skinname.xml" file that is consistent with the unique skin filename that includes the unique XML attributes for that skin.
- One common skin.css file: There is an exception to this rule. If one or more skin versions with specific, unique CSS attributes are required, it is necessary to create a skinname.css file that is consistent with the unique skin filename and includes the unique CSS attributes for that skin.
- An "images" folder containing all skin-related graphics.

Figure 4-26 shows a preview of what your completed MBR Design skin folder will contain.

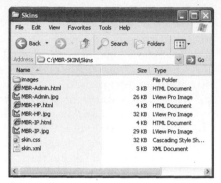

Figure 4-26

As you can see in Figure 4-26, in accordance with our initial guidelines, there are three skin HTML files, a single common XML file, a single common skin.css file, and one images folder that contains all of the skin-related images that have been saved via Photoshop using slices.

Skins will be built using tables-based HTML with extensive CSS.

Skin HTML will be built with a minimum width that expands horizontally and seamlessly for wider content. To make sure skins stretch properly without "breaking," you should use an underlying table that defines the width of the site in pixels via CSS, so that the site width can easily be changed in the CSS without your having to change the skin HTML. The underlying table will contain nested tables with widths of 100% defined in the CSS.

Unique IDs must be used for each defined content pane as well as the `runat="server"` reference (`ID="UniquePaneName" runat="server"`). One and only one content pane must have a specific ID of ContentPane in order for DNN to properly parse the skin package upon installation. If two or more content panes are defined with the same ID, DNN displays a "pane already exists" error message upon installation and will not install.

When creating HTML-based skins, it is important to make sure all content panes are entirely empty. Placing HTML characters in content panes displays them until they are removed at the skin level. Placing images in content panes causes errors and your DNN pages will not load.

The HTML-based MBR Design skins will be built with the following tokens:

- ❑ [LOGO]
- ❑ [CURRENTDATE]
- ❑ [USER]
- ❑ [LOGIN]
- ❑ [SOLPARTMENU]
- ❑ [SEARCH]
- ❑ [BREADCRUMB]

❑   [COPYRIGHT]

❑   [TERMS]

❑   [PRIVACY]

The guidelines outlined serve as a good basis for DNN skin production in general, and some are even necessary to ensure your skins actually work. Of course, if you prefer tableless HTML, or if tableless skins are a requirement for a project, you can certainly code your HTML-based DNN skins with divs, although you will find the DNN skinning process much more difficult using divs. So be prepared to spend some extra time if that is the route you choose, or are required, to take.

Remember that several components are required when building HTML-based skins. I'll focus on the HTML and CSS skin files first because it necessary to create several CSS styles as you build the HTML code.

Coding the Interior-Page Skin

Three skins are required for the MBR Design skin package: a home page skin, an interior-page skin with breadcrumb, and a matching admin skin so administrators can edit in a consistent skinned environment. First, you create the interior-page skin version because it has more required components than the home page or admin skin versions. After you complete the interior-page skin, you will duplicate it and easily create the home page skin by modifying the code and some of its components. Then, you'll use the home page skin as a basis to create an admin skin.

When creating HTML-based skins, it is necessary to start with a blank HTML document that does not include <Head> or <Body> tags. When a DNN skin package ultimately gets uploaded, DNN parses the files contained in an HTML-based skin package, generates ASCX files on-the-fly, and inserts the necessary chunks of HTML it requires. Therefore, the following simple code serves as the starting point for the interior-page MBR Design skin:

```
<table ID="BGTable" class="BGTable" width="100%" height="100%"
cellpadding="0" cellspacing="0" border="0">
  <tr>
    <td height="100%" valign="top"><!--BeginBGStructureTable--><!--
EndBGStructureTable--></</td>
  </tr>
</table>
```

Notice the only item in the code is one table (BGTable) with the BGTable CSS class applied, which defines the height, width, and background color attributes below:

```
/* Skin BG Color and Content Alignment */
.BGTable { /* Alignment MUST be defined in the HTML skin file for cross-
browser compatibility */
  width: 100%;
  height: 100%;
  padding:0px 0px 0px 0px;
  background-color: #efece3;
}
```

Also, notice that height and width attributes have been added directly to the HTML code of the BGTable and to the BGTable CSS style. This is to ensure cross-browser compatibility with height and width attributes.

The BGTable table serves two purposes within this specific skin. First, it serves as the background color for your website. It is important to note that applying background color or image attributes to the default "body" CSS style can make editing content difficult with many text editors. This is because the background attributes that are applied to the "body" CSS style are displayed in the background of many text editors. For example, if you have a background color attribute of black applied to the default "body" CSS style, when editing content your text editor may display the black background attribute, making it very difficult to edit text if the color of your normal text is also black or a dark color. Using this method is an effective workaround.

Second, the BGTable serves as the underlying area that the remainder of the HTML code will be added to. The comment "<!--BeginBGStructureTable--><!-- EndBGStructureTable-->" indicates the empty BGTable cell where the next table will be nested.

Defining the Structure

Now you're going to nest another table named BGStructureTable inside the BGTable, which begins to define the skin structure:

```
<table id="BGStructureTable" height="100%" width="100%" border="0"
cellspacing="0" cellpadding="0">
  <tr>
    <td width="49%" class="BreadcrumbPane"><img src="images/spacer.gif"
alt="spacer" /></td>
    <td width="2%" class="BreadcrumbPane">You are here : [BREADCRUMB]</td>
    <td width="49%" class="BreadcrumbPane"><img src="images/spacer.gif"
alt="spacer" /></td>
  </tr>
  <tr>
    <td class="TopBg BreadcrumbBorder"><img src="images/spacer.gif"
alt="spacer" /></td>
    <td class="TopBg"><!--BeginLogoTable--><!--EndLogoTable--></td>
    <td class="TopBg BreadcrumbBorder"><img src="images/spacer.gif"
alt="spacer" /></td>
  </tr>
  <tr>
    <td height="100%" class="ContentBG"><img src="images/spacer.gif"
alt="spacer" /></td>
    <td height="100%" class="ContentBG" valign="top"><!--BeginContentTable--
><!--EndContentTable--></td>
    <td class="ContentBG" height="100%"><img src="images/spacer.gif"
alt="spacer" /></td>
  </tr>
```

```
  <tr>
    <td class="BottomBg"><img src="images/spacer.gif" alt="spacer" /></td>
    <td valign="top" class="BottomBg"><!--BeginFooterTable--><!--
EndFooterTable--></td>
    <td class="BottomBg"><img src="images/spacer.gif" alt="spacer" /></td>
  </tr>
</table>
```

The BGStructureTable you have added does several things. First, it defines the way your content gets displayed in a browser, as it contains four rows and three columns with both height and widths set to 100 percent. Notice that the first rows of each of the three columns has a % width applied to them (49%, 2%, and 49%) equaling 100 percent. The outside columns set to 49 percent will keep your middle column floating in the middle of a browser at a width specified by another table that will be nested.

Second, the BGStructureTable contains your first token — the [BREADCRUMB] token — in the top-middle table cell. This displays the breadcrumb link trail within your skins.

Within the BGStructureTable you have also applied CSS styles to the table rows that define different horizontally tiling backgrounds (header, content, footer) for your skin. Notice in two of the table cells, two different classes have been used for one CSS selector (<td class="TopBg BreadcrumbBorder">). When writing CSS, it is often very useful to use multiple classes because you can start with a base CSS class to set up some default styling (in this case, the TopBg style), and then add an additional class to add more meaning (the BreadcrumbBorder style).

The following code shows the CSS styles used for elements within the BGStructureTable:

```
.BreadcrumbPane {
  font-family: Arial, Verdana, Tahoma,sans-serif;
  font-size: 10px;
  font-weight: normal;
  color: #c1c9cb;
  text-align:left;
  vertical-align:middle;
  padding:0px 5px 0px 5px;
  white-space:nowrap;
  height:17px;
  white-space:nowrap;
  background:#061532;
}
.BreadcrumbBorder {
  border-top:1px solid #47555e;
}
.TopBg{
  background:#374850;
  border-bottom:4px solid #edede5;
}
```

Figure 4-27 shows a preview of the progress you have made so far.

Figure 4-27

Adding Navigation and Other Key Components to the Top of the Skin

Now let's add another table named LogoTable within the BGStructureTable, indicated by the comment `<!--BeginLogoTable--><!-- EndLogoTable-->`, which will include several other tokens — the `[LOGO]`, `[CURRENTDATE]`, `[USER]`, and `[LOGIN]` tokens. The LogoTable includes yet another nested table named NavTable that contains the `[SOLPARTMENU]` and `[SEARCH]` tokens.

```
<table ID="LogoTable" width="100%" border="0" cellpadding="0"
cellspacing="0" class="MainTable">
  <tr>
    <td width="100%" class="LogoPane">[LOGO]</td>
    <td class="CurrentdatePane">[CURRENTDATE]</td>
    <td valign="top" width="19"><img src="images/LoginLeft.gif"
alt="LoginLeft" width="19" height="25" /></td>
    <td class="LoginPane">[USER] | [LOGIN]</td>
    <td valign="top" width="19"><img src="images/LoginRight.gif"
alt="LoginRight" width="19" height="25" /></td>
  </tr>
  <tr>
    <td colspan="5" class="NavPaneBG">
      <!--BeginNavTable--><table ID="NavTable" width="100%" height="31"
border="0" cellpadding="0" cellspacing="0">
  <tr>
```

```
        <td class="NavPane">[SOLPARTMENU]</td>
        <td class="SearchPane">Search   [SEARCH]</td>
      </tr>
          </table><!--EndNavTable--></td>
      </tr>
    </table>
```

As you can see, the LogoTable has a CSS style of MainTable applied to it with a width of 780 pixels. A width of 780 pixels was chosen for the few people that are still browsing in 800 × 600 mode, although the standard default display resolution has shifted to 1024 × 768 in the past couple of years. I also happen to think sites that are simple in presentation, with the content always floating in the middle of the browser, are easier to read. Because of the way you coded the BGStructureTable table structure, the MainTable CSS style applied to the LogoTable actually defines the minimum width of the content within the skins because as the width of this table changes, so do the other middle-column cells with the BGStructureTable. This has been done so the width of the skin can easily be modified by simply changing the width of the MainTable CSS style. The MainTable CSS style appears here with all of the other CSS styles used for elements within the LogoTable:

```css
/* Width of Skin */
.MainTable {
  width: 780px;
}
.LogoPane {
  vertical-align: top;
  text-align:left;
  font-family: Arial, Verdana, Tahoma,sans-serif;
  font-size: 11px;
  font-weight: bold;
  color: #FFFFFF;
  white-space:nowrap;
  height:60px;
  width:100%;
  border-top-width: 1px;
  border-top-style: solid;
  border-top-color: #47555e;
  padding-top: 5px;
  padding-right: 1px;
  padding-bottom: 5px;
  padding-left: 1px;
}
.CurrentdatePane {
  vertical-align: top;
  font-family: Arial, Verdana, Tahoma,sans-serif;
  font-size: 10px;
  font-weight: normal;
  color: #788C93;
  text-align:right;
  white-space:nowrap;
  padding:4px 10px 5px 10px;
  height:20px;
  text-transform:uppercase;
  border-top-width: 1px;
  border-top-style: solid;
```

(continued)

(continued)

```
      border-top-color: #47555e;
   }
   .LoginPane {
      vertical-align: top;
      font-family: Arial, Verdana, Tahoma,sans-serif;
      font-size: 10px;
      font-weight: normal;
      color: #c1c9cb;
      text-align:center;
      white-space:nowrap;
      height:20px;
      text-transform:uppercase;
      background:url(images/LoginBg.gif) top left repeat-x #374850;
      padding-top: 5px;
      padding-right: 10px;
      padding-bottom: 5px;
      padding-left: 10px;
   }
   .NavPaneBG {
      vertical-align:top;
      border-top: none;
      border-right: 1px solid #B6C3C6;
      border-bottom: none;
      border-left: 1px solid #b6c4c5;
      height:31px;
      background-color: #788c93;
      background-image: url(images/NavMiddle.gif);
      background-repeat: repeat-x;
      background-position: left top;
   }
   .NavPane {
      font-family: Arial, Verdana, Tahoma,sans-serif;
      font-size: 11px;
      font-weight: bold;
      color: #FFFFFF;
      vertical-align:top;
      white-space:nowrap;
      height:31px;
      width: 100%;
   }
   .SearchPane {
      vertical-align: middle;
      text-align:right;
      font-family: Arial, Verdana, Tahoma,sans-serif;
      font-size: 10px;
      font-weight: normal;
      color: #B6C3C6;
      white-space:nowrap;
      padding-right: 10px;
      padding-left: 10px;
      text-transform:uppercase;
   }
```

Figure 4-28 displays a preview of the top of your skin after adding the LogoTable and NavTable.

Figure 4-28

Adding Content Panes

You have added the necessary code to properly display the top portion of your skin. Now, let's add some additional code that will form the content panes within the skins. You'll start by adding another table to the cell within the BGStructureTable indicated by the comments `<!--BeginContentTable --><!-- EndContentTable -->`.

```
<table ID="ContentTable" width="100%" height="100%" border="0"
cellpadding="0" cellspacing="0" class="ContentTable">
  <tr>
    <td height="100%" class="LeftPane" id="LeftPane" runat="server"
visible="false"></td>
    <td valign="top" class="ContentPane" id="ContentPane" runat="server"
visible="false"></td>
  </tr>
</table>
```

This is a very simple table with one row and two columns that contains just two content panes: the LeftPane and the ContentPane. It is important to reiterate the snippets required by DNN that define the content panes in your skin:

```
id="LeftPane" runat="server"
id="ContentPane" runat="server"
```

Each content pane must contain a unique ID as well as the `runat="server"` reference. And remember, one of the content panes within a DNN skin must be named ContentPane (not case-sensitive), so DNN can properly parse the HTML and generate an ASCX skin file from it. If DNN cannot locate a content pane within a skin HTML file named ContentPane, it will display an error upon installation and the skin will not be installed.

Also note the visibility snippet:

```
visible="false"
```

The visibility snippet is important if you want the content panes to collapse when no content is applied to them.

The CSS styles used for the elements found in the ContentTable are as follows:

```
.ContentTable {
  height: 100%;
  width: 100%;
}
.LeftPane {
  font-family: Arial, Verdana, Tahoma,sans-serif;
  font-size: 11px;
  font-weight: bold;
  color: #034681;
  vertical-align:top;
  vertical-align:top;
  text-align:left;
  width: 240px;
  padding-top: 5px;
  padding-right: 35px;
  padding-bottom: 5px;
  padding-left: 0px;
}
.ContentPane {
  font-family: Arial, Verdana, Tahoma,sans-serif;
  font-size: 11px;
  font-weight: bold;
  color: #034681;
  vertical-align:top;
  padding-top: 5px;
  padding-right: 0px;
  padding-bottom: 5px;
  padding-left: 0px;
}
```

Notice that the ContentTable CSS style with a width of 100 percent has been applied to the ContentTable. With this attribute, any table with the ContentTable CSS style applied to it will always stretch to fill 100 percent of the width of the cell it has been placed in. This is important when the width of the skin changes to keep content in different table cells the same width.

Creating the Footer

Let's add one final table to your code that will define the footer at the bottom of your skin by inserting another table within the BGStructureTable indicated by the comments `<!--BeginFooterTable -->`<`<!-- EndFooterTable -->`.

```
<table ID="FooterTable" class="ContentTable" width="100%" border="0"
align="center" cellpadding="0" cellspacing="0">
  <tr>
    <td class="Links">[LINKS]</td>
  </tr>
  <tr>
    <td class="Copyright">[COPYRIGHT] | [PRIVACY] | [TERMS]</td>
  </tr>
</table>
```

The FooterTable also has a very simple layout with one column and two rows. This table contains the remainder of the tokens used in your skin — the [LINKS], [COPYRIGHT], [PRIVACY], and [TERMS] tokens. The CSS for the elements found in the FooterTable is as follows:

```
.ContentTable {
  height: 100%;
  width: 100%;
}
.Links {
  vertical-align: top;
  font-family:  Arial, Verdana, Tahoma,sans-serif;
  font-size: 10px;
  font-weight: normal;
  color: #c0c8ca;
  text-align:center;
  padding:2px 0px 2px 0px;
  white-space:nowrap;
}
.Copyright {
  vertical-align: top;
  font-family:  Arial, Verdana, Tahoma,sans-serif;
  font-size: 10px;
  font-weight: normal;
  color: #788c93;
  text-align:center;
  padding:2px 0px 10px 0px;
  white-space:nowrap;
}
```

Notice that the ContentTable CSS style with a width of 100 percent has also been applied to the FooterTable to ensure it, too, will stretch to the same width as other content within the skins.

Figure 4-29 previews the completed interior-page skin. I've added labels to the content panes just so you can see them in relation to the overall skin structure. But remember to make sure content panes are completely empty when saving HTML skin files.

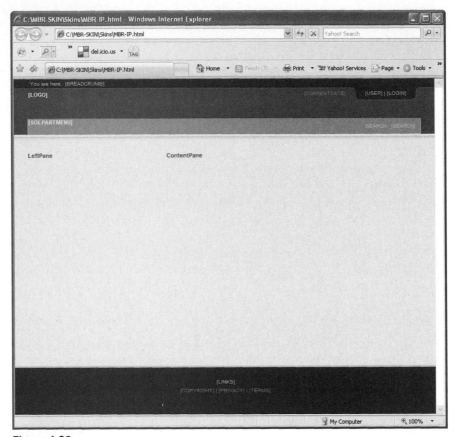

Figure 4-29

Coding the Home Page Skin

Now that you have completed the interior-page skin HTML, you need to duplicate it as the basis for the home page skin that will not contain a breadcrumb control. The home page skin will also be different because it will contain an additional content pane called HeaderPane. You will also remove the LeftPane and add a RightPane so the main content structure will be reversed. These modifications require the following steps.

1. Replace the [BREADCRUMB] token in the top of the skin with the following code:

```
<td width="2%" class="BreadcrumbPane"><img src="images/spacer.gif" width="1"
height="17" /></td>
```

Use a spacer.gif to make sure the breadcrumb pane retains the proper height of 17 pixels.

2. For the HeaderPane, simply add a new <TR> using the following code in the appropriate location within the HTML:

```
<tr id="HeaderPane">
  <td height="0" class="HeaderPane"></td>
    <td height="0" class="HeaderPane" id="HeaderPane" runat="server"
visible="false"></td>
    <td height="0" class="HeaderPane"></td>
  </tr>
The CSS for the HeaderPane is shown below:
.HeaderPane {
  font-family:  Arial, Verdana, Tahoma,sans-serif;
  font-size: 11px;
  font-weight: bold;
  color: #FFFFFF;
  vertical-align:top;
  height: 0px;
  background-color: #297EBE;
  background-image: url(images/HeaderBg.jpg);
  background-repeat: repeat-x;
  background-position: left bottom;
  text-align: center;
  /*height:234px;*/
}
```

3. Remove the LeftPane and add the RightPane by changing the ContentTable code:

```
<table class="ContentTable" width="100%" border="0" cellpadding="0" cellspacing="0">
  <tr>
    <td class="ContentPane" id="ContentPane" runat="server" visible="false"></td>
    <td height="100%" class="RightPane" id="RightPane" runat="server"
visible="false"></td>
  </tr>
</table>
```

Figure 4-30 previews the completed home page skin. Again, I've added labels to the content panes just so you can see them in relation to the overall skin structure.

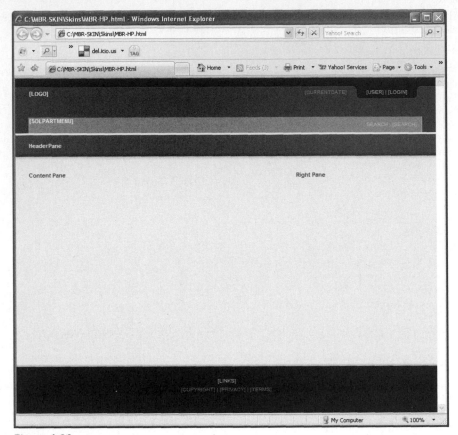

Figure 4-30

Coding the Admin Skin

Now that you have completed the two skins required for applying content within your website, you need to create a matching Admin skin with a single content pane for displaying administration functions. You'll easily do this by duplicating the home page skin and making a few simple modifications or, more accurately, a few deletions.

The first thing you'll remove, since the [SEARCH] token is not required while in admin mode, is the right column of the NavTable, as evidenced by the following code, which displays the final result after deleting the [SEARCH] token:

```
<table ID="NavTable" width="100%" height="31" border="0" cellpadding="0"
cellspacing="0">
  <tr>
  <td class="NavPane">[SOLPARTMENU]</td>
  </tr>
</table>
```

Next, remove the following code you added to the home page skin for the HeaderPane because the only content pane required for the admin skin is a single content pane:

```
<tr id="HeaderPane">
  <td height="0" class="HeaderPane"></td>
  <td height="0" class="HeaderPane" id="HeaderPane" runat="server"
visible="false"></td>
  <td height="0" class="HeaderPane"></td>
  </tr>
```

Finally, modify the ContentTable to have a single content pane:

```
<table width="100%" border="0" cellpadding="0" cellspacing="0"
class="ContentTable">
  <tr>
    <td height="100%" class="ContentPane" id="ContentPane" runat="server"
visible="false"></td>
  </tr>
</table>
```

Figure 4-31 previews the final skin as part of the MBR Design skin package — the admin skin. Again, I've added the ContentPane label, just so you can see it in relation to the overall skin structure.

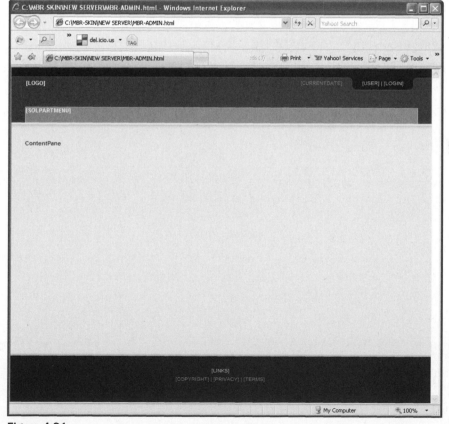

Figure 4-31

Analyzing the Menu CSS

Now that you have spent some time creating the HTML skins required for the MBR Design skin package and applied some CSS styles in the process, it is a good time to analyze the CSS styles required for the dynamic menu. The MBR Design skin uses the Solpart Menu component. Let's take a look at all of the CSS styles required for the Solpart Menu:

```
.MainMenu_SubMenu TD
{
  font-family: Arial,   Verdana, Tahoma,sans-serif;
  font-size: 9pt;
  font-weight: normal;
  padding: 2px;
}
```

```
.MainMenu_SubMenuItemSelHover TD
{
  color: #374850;
  height:31px;
  font-family:  Arial,   Verdana, Tahoma,sans-serif;
  font-size: 9pt;
  font-weight: bold;
  background: url(images/NavOn.gif) repeat-x top left #ecede5;
  padding: 0px 10px 0px 10px;
}
```

```
.MainMenu_TabRootMenuItem TD
{
  color: #eeeee6;
  height:31;
  font-family:  Arial,   Verdana, Tahoma,sans-serif;
  font-size: 9pt;
  font-weight: bold;
  background: url(images/NavOff.gif) repeat-x top left #798c93;
  padding: 0px 10px 0px 10px;
}
```

```
.MainMenu_TabRootMenuItemSel TD
{
  color: #374850;
  height:31px;
  font-family:  Arial,   Verdana, Tahoma,sans-serif;
  font-size: 9pt;
  font-weight: bold;
  background: url(images/NavOn.gif) repeat-x top left #ecede5;
  padding: 0px 10px 0px 10px;
```

```
}
```

```
.MainMenu_TabMenuItemHover TD
{
  color: #374850;
  height:30px;
  font-family:  Arial,   Verdana, Tahoma,sans-serif;
  font-size: 9pt;
  font-weight: bold;
```

```
    background: url(images/NavOn.gif) repeat-x top left #ecede5;
    padding: 0px 10px 0px 10px;
}

.MainMenu_TabMenuItemSelHover TD
{
    color: #374850;
    height:31px;
    font-family:  Arial,  Verdana, Tahoma,sans-serif;
    font-size: 9pt;
    font-weight: bold;
    background: url(images/NavOn.gif) repeat-x top left #ecede5;
    padding: 0px 10px 0px 10px;

}

.MainMenu_MenuContainer {
    border-bottom: #FFFFFF 0px solid;
    border-left: #E7EDE3 0px solid;
    border-top: #FFFFFF 0px solid;
    border-right: #404040 0px solid;
    background-color: Transparent;
    width: 1px;
    padding: 0px;
}

.MainMenu_MenuBar {
    border-bottom: #FFFFFF 0px solid;
    border-left: #E7EDE3 0px solid;
    border-top: #FFFFFF 0px solid;
    border-right: #000000 0px solid;
    cursor: pointer;
    cursor: hand;
    height:31px;
}

.MainMenu_MenuItem {
    cursor: pointer;
    cursor: hand;
    color: #374850;
    font-family:  Arial,  Verdana, Tahoma,sans-serif;
    font-size: 9pt;
    font-weight: bold;
    font-style: normal;
    border-left: #FFFFFF 0px solid;
    border-bottom: #FFFFFF 0px solid;
    border-top: #FFFFFF 0px solid;
    border-right: #FFFFFF 0px solid;

}

.MainMenu_MenuIcon {
    cursor: pointer;
    cursor: hand;
    margin: 0px 0px 0px 0px;
```

(continued)

(continued)

```
    font-family:  Arial,  Verdana, Tahoma,sans-serif;
    font-size: 9pt;
    font-weight: bold;
    font-style: normal;
    background-color: #ecede5;
    border-left: #ecede5 0px solid;
    border-right: #ecede5 0px solid;
    border-bottom: #ecede5 0px solid;
    border-top: #ecede5 0px solid;
    width: 1;
```

```
}
.MainMenu_SubMenu {
  z-index: 1000;
  cursor: pointer;
  cursor: hand;
  margin: 1px 0px 0px 0px;
  font-family:  Arial,  Verdana, Tahoma,sans-serif;
  font-size: 9pt;
  font-weight: bold;
  font-style: normal;
  color: #374850;
  background-color: #ecede5;
  border-bottom: #788c93 1px solid;
  border-left: #788c93 1px solid;
  border-top: #ecede5 1px solid;
  border-right: #788c93 1px solid;
  filter:progid:DXImageTransform.Microsoft.Shadow(color=#FFFFFF,
Direction=180, Strength=0);
  padding-top: 0px;
  padding-right: 0px;
  padding-bottom: 0px;
  padding-left: 0px;
}
.MainMenu_MenuBreak {
  width: 4px;
  border: 0;
```

```
}
```

```
.MainMenu_MenuItemSel {
  background-color: #788c93;
  cursor: pointer;
  cursor: hand;
  color: #ecede5;
  font-family:  Arial,  Verdana, Tahoma,sans-serif;
  font-size: 9pt;
  font-weight: bold;
  font-style: normal;
}
```

```
.MainMenu_MenuArrow {
  font-family: webdings;
```

```
    font-size: 10pt;
    color: Black;
    cursor: pointer;
    cursor: hand;
    border-right: #000000 0px solid;
    border-bottom: #000000 0px solid;
    border-top: #000000 0px solid;
}
```

```
.MainMenu_RootMenuArrow {
    font-family: webdings;
    font-size: 10pt;
    cursor: pointer;
    cursor: hand;
}
```

As you can see, there are several CSS styles that define the look and feel of the Solpart Menu. And getting comfortable with customizing them can take some time and patience. However, if you focus on just a few items and use them as a basis for customizations, the learning curve can be overcome quickly.

First, in the case of a navigation bar such as the MBR Design skins, note the images that represent the states of the menu — mainly NavOn.gif, NavOff.gif, and NavSep (the separator image between menu items covered in the XML discussion that follows). These images can be any type of web-safe format such as JPG or PNG. You should pay special attention to the height of these images and, how they relate to the menu design. Just changing these images and customizing the styles that contain these images can change the look and feel of the navigation considerably.

❑ The MainMenu_MenuBar is typically set to the same height as the various states of the menu items. You can also use this CSS style to apply a different background to the navigation bar independent of the menu items themselves.

❑ The MainMenu_MenuItem CSS style controls the default attributes of menu items (mainly text color).

❑ The MainMenu_MenuIcon CSS style defines the styling of the icon background and border. Typically, all borders are set to 0 (zero) and the background color is set to the same color as the MainMenu_SubMenu CSS style.

❑ The MainMenu_SubMenu CSS style controls the look and feel of the submenu items.

❑ The MainMenu_MenuItemSel CSS style controls the hover state of the submenu items.

In most cases, changing height attributes, navigation "on" and "off" images, MenuItem color, MenuIcon background color, SubMenu text color, background color and border size/color, and MenuItemSel text and background color are the only modifications required for customizing the Solpart Menu. The other CSS styles you see as part of the Solpart Menu group of styles typically do not get changed much, if at all.

This is a high-level approach at defining how the Solpart Menu styles are applied. The best way to understand the different menu attributes, and how they specifically affect the display of the menu collectively, is to install the MBR Design skin as a starting point and begin editing the CSS to see what different results are achievable. Keep in mind that the Solpart Menu is not the only menu component available for DNN. In fact, there are several menu components that can be used with DNN, which is why I have not gone into too much detail with menu customizations. Many menu components have a great deal more flexibility than Solpart. However, the Solpart Menu is a good component to start the learning process because it has been widely used with DNN from the beginning.

Skin XML

In Chapter 3, I explained that the skin.xml is used to define the global attributes that allow you to customize the appearance of skin objects. I also explained that all skins use a consistent, standard set of XML attributes referencing consistent CSS styles for each attribute. Let's take a look at some of the objects used in the skin.xml to see how the skin.xml plays a key role in the parsing of HTML-based DNN skins. Let's start with a simple object — the [COPYRIGHT] token:

```
<Object>
  <Token>[COPYRIGHT]</Token>
  <Settings>
    <Setting>
      <Name>CssClass</Name>
      <Value>Copyright</Value>
    </Setting>
  </Settings>
</Object>
```

The <Object></Object> tags simply indicate a different [TOKEN] is being used in a skin.

The <Token>[COPYRIGHT]</Token> tags define the specific [TOKEN] whose attributes are being customized.

The <Settings></Settings> tags indicate a new attribute is being defined for a [TOKEN].

Each [TOKEN] has certain, specific attributes that can be customized. Specific attributes are defined using the <Setting></Setting> tags. In the preceding [COPYRIGHT] example, the <Name> of the setting we have applied has a CssClass <Value> of Copyright, which is a CSS style defined in the skin.css included in the skin package. Sound complicated? It really isn't. All this is saying is "Use the Copyright CSS style to display the dynamic copyright control when the site loads in a browser."

Let's looks at another <Object>:

```
<Object>
  <Token>[LOGIN]</Token>
  <Settings>
    <Setting>
      <Name>TEXT</Name>
      <Value>LOG IN</Value>
    </Setting>
    <Setting>
      <Name>LogoffText</Name>
      <Value>LOG OUT</Value>
    </Setting>
    <Setting>
      <Name>CssClass</Name>
      <Value>Login</Value>
    </Setting>
  </Settings>
</Object>
```

As you can see, the [LOGIN] token has more attributes that can be defined in the XML. These attributes are also easy to decipher. This is saying, "When not logged in, display the login text as the words LOG IN," "When someone is logged in, display the logout text as the words LOG OUT," and finally, "Use the Login CSS class to display the LOG IN/LOG OUT links."

Let's take a look at one more <Object> that contains a set of attributes for the Solpart Menu:

```xml
<Object>
  <Token>[SOLPARTMENU]</Token>
  <Settings>
    <Setting>
      <Name>display</Name>
      <Value>horizontal</Value>
    </Setting>
    <Setting>
      <Name>rightseparator</Name>
      <Value><![CDATA[<img src="images/NavSep.gif" width="2"
height="31">]]></Value>
    </Setting>
    <Setting>
      <Name>rootmenuitemcssclass</Name>
      <Value>MainMenu_TabRootMenuItem</Value>
    </Setting>
    <Setting>
      <Name>rootmenuitembreadcrumbcssclass</Name>
      <Value>MainMenu_TabRootMenuItemSel</Value>
    </Setting>
    <Setting>
      <Name>rootmenuitemselectedcssclass</Name>
      <Value>MainMenu_TabMenuItemHover</Value>
    </Setting>
    <Setting>
      <Name>Rootmenuitemactivecssclass</Name>
      <Value>MainMenu_TabMenuItemSelHover</Value>
    </Setting>
    <Setting>
      <Name>submenucssclass</Name>
      <Value>MainMenu_SubMenu</Value>
    </Setting>
    <Setting>
      <Name>submenuitemselectedcssclass</Name>
      <Value>MainMenu_SubMenuItemSelHover</Value>
    </Setting>
    <Setting>
      <Name>userootbreadcrumbarrow</Name>
      <Value>false</Value>
    </Setting>
    <Setting>
      <Name>usesubmenubreadcrumbarrow</Name>
      <Value>false</Value>
    </Setting>
  <Setting>
      <Name>rootbreadcrumbarrow</Name>
      <Value>false</Value>
```

(continued)

(continued)

```
      </Setting>
      <Setting>
        <Name>submenubreadcrumbarrow</Name>
        <Value>false</Value>
      </Setting>
      <Setting>
        <Name>usearrows</Name>
        <Value>false</Value>
      </Setting>
    </Settings>
  </Object>
```

As you can see, the `[SOLPARTMENU]` object contains several attributes that can be defined. Pay particular attention to the following `<Setting>`:

```
    <Setting>
      <Name>display</Name>
        <Value>horizontal</Value>
    </Setting>
```

This controls the "horizontal" or "vertical" orientation of the menu. If you want the menu to display vertically, you simply change horizontal to vertical. Just make sure your HTML-based skin has been coded appropriately to accommodate a vertical menu.

This `<Setting>` is also important in styling your menu easily, using the menu CSS styles mentioned previously:

```
    <Setting>
      <Name>rightseparator</Name>
      <Value><![CDATA[<img src="images/NavSep.gif" width="2"
height="31">]]></Value>
    </Setting>
```

I mentioned the NavSep image earlier. This `<Setting>` is where you define the separator image name. You also define the height of the separator image within this `<Setting>`. Notice how the height of theNavSep is the same as the NavOff image in the preceding CSS. In most cases, the NavOff, NavOn, and NavSep images, or whatever you choose to name these images, are the same height. Also, be aware that you must use the `![CDATA[<img src="images/NavSep.gif" width="2" height="31">]]` path required by DNN for inserting images.

So, what have you learned from these basic XML examples? Based on the different, specific attributes that can be defined for each `[TOKEN]`, and based on CSS styles you can add to the skin.css, you can quickly customize the look and feel of the dynamic controls displayed within a DNN skin. You simply use your selected `[TOKENS]`, look up their valid attributes, and add the attribute names as `<Setting>` values.

Creating DNN Containers — A Few Guidelines

So far you've done a fair amount of coding to create three different skins — a skin that is used for the home page on the MBR Design website, an interior-page skin that includes a breadcrumb to be used for all interior pages, and a matching admin skin for use while in admin mode. You also created some CSS along the way and learned how to customize the display of dynamic components using XML.

This was a large chunk of the work necessary for building the MBR Design skin package. However, let's not forget the other essential elements that will be applied to content throughout the website — the containers.

The guidelines for creating containers are very similar to those for creating skins.

All container files will be placed in a single folder named Containers. When creating containers, it is also important to name them intuitively so users can easily differentiate between several different containers within a single skin package when accessing them via the DNN interface.

The Containers folder will include:

- ❑ One unique HTML, JPG (preview), and XML file per container version with consistent filenames:
    - ❑ containername.html
    - ❑ containername.jpg
    - ❑ containername.xml
- ❑ A common container.css file.
- ❑ An images folder containing all skin-related graphics.

Figure 4-32 shows a preview of what your completed MBR Design container folder will contain.

Figure 4-32

As you can see in Figure 4-32, in accordance with our initial container guidelines, there are three container HTML files, three corresponding JPG preview files, three corresponding XML files, a single common containers.css file and one images folder that contains all of the container-related images that have been saved via Photoshop using slices.

Containers will be built using tables-based HTML with extensive CSS.

Container HTML will be built with a 100% width so containers fill the width of contents completely.

All containers will contain one and only one content pane with the ID of contentpane as well as the `runat="server"` reference (ID="contentpane" runat="server").

When creating HTML-based containers, it is important to make sure the content pane is entirely empty. Placing HTML characters in the content pane will display them until they are removed at the skin level.

The HTML-based containers will be built with the following tokens:

❑ [SOLPARTACTIONS]

❑ [ICON]

❑ [TITLE]

❑ [VISIBILITY]

All container XML files will include a unique Title attribute to keep your container names unique when calling container CSS styles to prevent cascading when different containers are loaded on one page.

All container CSS files will include unique style names with the containername prefix — this prevents CSS cascading issues when multiple containers from the same package are applied to one page.

Creating HTML-Based Containers

Just like skins, the guidelines outlined in the "Creating HTML-Based Containers" section serve as a good basis for creating DNN containers in general, and some are even necessary to ensure your containers actually work. And although the MBR Design samples use tables-based containers, you can certainly create your containers with div-based HTML. One of the great things about DNN is that the choice is yours when it comes to creating containers (and skins)!

Let's take a look at one of the container HTML files within the MBR Design skin package:

```
<table width="100%" border="0" cellpadding="0" cellspacing="0"
class="BigBlueTitleWidth">
  <tr>
    <td class="BigBlueTitleTopMIddle"><table id="ContentTable" border="0"
cellpadding="0" cellspacing="0" class="BigBlueTitleWidth">
      <tr>
        <td width="0" class="BigBlueTitleActionscell"
visible="false">[SOLPARTACTIONS]</td>
    <td valign="middle" class="BigBlueTitleActionscell" visible="false">[ICON]</td>
        <td width="100%" class="BigBlueTitleTitle">[TITLE]</td>
        <td class="BigBlueTitleVisibilitycell" visible="false">[VISIBILITY]</td>
      </tr>
      <tr>
        <td colspan="4" class="BigBlueTitleContentpane"
id="ContentPane" runat="server"></td>
      </tr>
    </table></td>
  </tr>
</table>
```

```
<table width="100%" cellpadding="0" cellspacing="0" id="ActionTable" borer="0">
  <tr><td><img src="images/spacer.gif" / height="8" width="1"></td></tr>
  <tr>
    <td align="right"
class="BigBlueTitleBottomAction">[ACTIONBUTTON:1][ACTIONBUTTON:2][ACTIONBUTTON:3]
[ACTIONBUTTON:4][ACTIONBUTTON:5][ACTIONBUTTON:6]</td>
  </tr>
</table>
```

As you can see, creating HTML-based containers is very similar to creating HTML-based skins except that containers require a lot less HTML/CSS code. Like skins, container files cannot include <Head> or <Body> tags, as DNN parses the files contained in an HTML-based skin package, generates ASCX files on-the-fly, and inserts the necessary HTML it requires. Also note that, unlike skins, containers have only one content pane. However, they do require the same runat="server" reference, so DNN can generate the proper ASCX container files.

The BigBlueTitle container in the preceding code includes two tables. The first is primarily responsible for maintaining content and visually includes just a title and underline (via the BigBlueTitleWidth CSS class) separating the title from the content.

As I explained previously, containers have their own set of [TOKENS] that provide different functions. The [SOLPARTACTIONS] token inserts an "action" drop-down menu on each module, so module content can be administered. The [ICON] token allows you to insert an icon via the DNN interface. The [TITLE] token inserts a dynamic title that can be edited directly via the DNN interface. And the [VISIBILITY] token provides the ability to collapse or expand a module's content area.

As you can see in the preceding code, CSS is used extensively to control the layout elements within your container code and to achieve proper styling. It is best to create all styling, if possible, using CSS, so customizations can easily be applied to containers via CSS. Also notice that many of the table cells include the visible="false" snippet. This ensures that table cells collapse properly when previewing content, or when certain features are disabled on a container.

The CSS for the BigBlueTitle container is as follows:

```
.BigBlueTitleTitle {
  font-family: "Trebuchet MS";
  font-size: 25pt;
  font-weight: normal;
  color: #1a528c;
  text-align:left;
  text-decoration:none;
  padding:3px 5px 3px 2px;
}
```

```
.BigBlueTitleWidth {
  width: 100%;
  font-family: Arial, Helvetica, sans-serif;
  font-size:  8pt;
  font-weight: normal;
  color: #000000;
  border-bottom:1px dashed #cccccc;
```

(continued)

129

(continued)

```
  }
```

```
.BigBlueTitleContentpane {
  text-align: left;
  vertical-align: top;
  font-family: Arial, Helvetica, sans-serif;
  font-size:  8pt;
  font-weight: normal;
  color: #000000;
  padding-top: 5px;
  padding-right: 0px;
  padding-bottom: 5px;
  padding-left: 4px;
}
```

```
.BigBlueTitleActionscell {
  text-align: left;
  vertical-align: middle;
  font-family: Arial, Helvetica, sans-serif;
  font-size:  8pt;
  font-weight: normal;
  color: #000000;
}
```

```
.BigBlueTitleVisibilitycell {
  height: 20px;
  text-align: right;
  vertical-align: middle;
  font-family: Arial, Helvetica, sans-serif;
  font-size:  8pt;
  font-weight: normal;
  color: #000000;
  padding-right:5px;
}
```

```
.BigBlueTitleBottomAction {
  text-align: right;
  vertical-align: top;
  font-family: Arial, Helvetica, sans-serif;
  font-size:  8pt;
  font-weight: normal;
  color: #000000;
  padding:5px;
}
```

Remember that it is important to name each container CSS class with a unique name to avoid cascading issues!

Figure 4-33 previews the BigBlueTitle container.

Figure 4-33

The second table is used for ActionButtons, which are admin features that map to ModuleActionTypes within DotNetNuke.Entities.Modules.Actions. You add ActionButtons and specify their attributes using container XML files.

Container XML

Similar to skins, containers have associated XML that allows you to define attributes for container controls. Some of the typical controls that are used for containers are the [SOLPARTACTIONS] token, which controls module admin functions via a drop-down arrow; the [TITLE] token, which is used to define the unique Title CSS class; the [VISIBILITY] token, which controls the visibility icon/function; and the [ACTIONBUTTON] token, which allows you to define additional container controls.

As you can see from the following partial XML code, container XML Objects are applied the same way as skin XML Objects, although containers have a totally different set of XML Objects that can be defined using <Settings>.

```
<Objects>
  <Object>
  <Token>[SOLPARTACTIONS]</Token>
  </Object>
  <Object>
    <Token>[TITLE]</Token>
    <Settings>
       <Setting>
      <Name>CssClass</Name>
      <Value>BigBlueTitleTitle</Value>
  </Setting>
    </Settings>
  </Object>
  <Object>
    <Token>[ACTIONBUTTON:1]</Token>
    <Settings>
      <Setting>
      <Name>CommandName</Name>
      <Value>AddContent.Action</Value>
    </Setting>
```

(continued)

(continued)

```
      <Setting>
        <Name>DisplayIcon</Name>
         <Value>True</Value>
      </Setting>
      <Setting>
        <Name>DisplayLink</Name>
        <Value>True</Value>
      </Setting>
      </Settings>
    </Object>
  </Objects>
```

Summary

This chapter covered two main areas. The first was the organization and preparation of DNN skin designs. You learned the importance of organizing source files with layers and layer sets to ensure complete flexibility when editing website design components. Also, you learned about the advantages of slices: how to create them and define their attributes, and how to save images from them to be used in the coding of HTML-based skin files. You also learned about the importance of saving slices along with your layered source file so you can easily apply edits later.

This chapter also detailed all of the required components that bring an HTML-based DNN skin package to life. You learned how to create skin and container HTML by including the necessary [TOKENS] that ultimately get parsed by DNN to display the appropriate application logic in the form of specific dynamic controls. You learned how to customize the look and feel of the dynamic Solpart menu skin component. You learned how to use XML to define the global attributes of skin and container [TOKENS]. In addition, you learned how to code content panes with unique IDs and include the necessary code snippets required by DNN.

It is important to note that the techniques outlined in this chapter are not the be-all and end-all of DNN skinning. These are techniques that have worked quite well for me based on over four years of experience using DNN. But because HTML and CSS are the basis for creating DNN skins, there really is no right or wrong way as long as you understand the components, and how they work together within the DNN environment. However, the process of creating a DNN skin package requires a fair amount of planning to ensure your desired result is reached. If you follow the guidelines I have outlined, your journey to successful skinning will be a pleasant one.

Speaking of the journey, let's take the next logical step forward in the journey to building a professional DNN website solution, by building on what you have learned in Chapter 4 to package the DNN components together into a single installation file and apply the skins to a live DNN website!

5

Packaging, Installing, and Applying Skins to a Live DNN Instance

Much of the last chapter was spent in the trenches so to speak, organizing, preparing, and coding all of the necessary files required for the MBR Design skins. However, let's not get too excited — not yet anyway. There's more to do before the skins can be applied — they need to be packaged. *Packaging* is the process of grouping all HTML-based skin and container files into a single "skinname.zip" file that can easily be uploaded and installed on a DNN instance.

There are a couple of reasons for packaging HTML-based skin and container files. First, a Zip file is required by DNN for installation. As I explained in Chapter 4, when an HTML-based DNN skin package is installed, DNN parses the files and generates ASCX files on-the-fly. These ASCX files are the files DNN uses to display the front-end of a DNN website. If you are working with ASCX skin files instead of HTML files, it is possible to simply upload ASCX-based skin and container files via FTP (File Transfer Protocol) because ASCX files don't have to be parsed by DNN before they become usable. However, because you are using HTML-based skin and container files, and because it is a requirement, you need to package them.

The second reason for packaging HTML-based skin and container files is something I'll emphasize throughout this book — proper organization! In Chapter 4, I explained the importance of organizing design components in Photoshop using layers and layer sets, but why stop there? When properly packaged and installed, skin and container files are nicely grouped together when applying them to pages and containers, respectively, on a DNN website. It is possible to package individual skins/containers and install them separately as skinname.zip/containername.zip. But, as you will see, packaging all skins and containers together makes it easier for users to apply them within a DNN website. It also separates them from other skins and containers that may be installed on the same DNN website.

Problem

Many "skinners" do not package all skin and container files nicely into a single install file. They choose to package skins and containers into separate install files. Technically, this is acceptable. However, it is not unusual for a DNN website to have several different skins and/or containers applied to the same instance. For example, the MBR Design skins have several different versions that provide different content structure. This provides a lot of flexibility in terms of page/content layout within the site. Having skins and containers nicely grouped together maintains good organization. What's more, some of the skins and/or containers applied to a DNN website may not be named intuitively, which only adds to the confusion when determining which skins and containers are the correct versions that should be applied, especially when there are several skins and containers installed on the same instance. Luckily, it is easy to minimize the confusion with a little forward thinking when packaging skins and containers, as you're going to do with the MBR Design skins. However, you would be surprised how many designers still don't apply names to their files that are easy to understand. Some designers name their files skin1.html or container2.html. This type of naming convention provides absolutely no indication of what the skin or container may look like without applying them to a page. This makes editing a DNN website inefficient and annoying to say the least.

Design

This section focuses on packaging DNN skins with intuitive filenames to make site administration straightforward and efficient. This section also focuses on installing DNN skins and applying them to a live DNN instance. In this chapter you learn:

- ❑ How to create a single-packaged skin install file
- ❑ The difference between installing a skin package at the Admin level and at the Host level
- ❑ How to install a single-packaged skin install file
- ❑ How to install separate container.zip files
- ❑ How to preview installed skins
- ❑ How to apply skins and containers to a DNN website globally
- ❑ How to delete skin packages

If you ask any experienced DNN developer which key features set DNN apart from other Content Management Systems (CMS), open source or otherwise, you will find the skinning engine to be at, or near, the top of the list. In fact, you'll be hard-pressed to find another CMS framework that makes it so easy to change or apply a skin to a website. Not even Microsoft Sharepoint, DNN's closest competitor (and an expensive one at that) can offer this capability. The capability to upload a single Zip file and apply a different look to a website in seconds is very powerful indeed. But you'll be happy to know that, even though the technology is quite powerful, the actual process of packaging, installing, and applying a skin to a DNN website is not a complicated procedure, as you will now see.

Solution

After skin and container files have been created, packaging is very straightforward and requires two different groups of files — skins and containers, of course. A single-packaged skinname.zip install file contains one Zip file that includes all skin-related files and one Zip file that includes all container-related files. Again, if you prefer, you can create separate skinname.zip and containername.zip files and install them independently on a DNN website. But it's best to package skins and containers into a single skinname.zip install file to keep everything nicely organized and to make it intuitive for administrators when applying skins to pages and containers to modules.

Let's take another look at the files contained in the MBR Design skins folder in Figure 5-1.

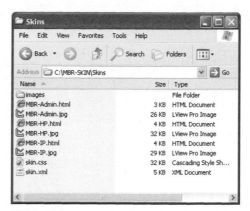

Figure 5-1

Just to recap, you can see that our MBR Design skin folder contains HTML skin files, corresponding JPEG preview files, a skin.css file, a skin.xml file, and an images folder that contains all the graphics required for our skin MBR Design skins. It is important to note again the intuitive filenames that have been applied to the HTML skin files in Figure 5-1. These are the actual skin names, minus the file extensions, that will be displayed via the DNN interface. If the skins were named skin1.html, skin2.html, and skin3.html, it would be impossible to remember which skin was the appropriate skin to apply to the homepage. I hope you can understand why it is so important to apply names to your skins that give administrators an idea of what that they look like and/or their purpose.

Likewise, in the container folder shown in Figure 5-2, you can see that our MBR Design container folder includes HTML container files, corresponding JPEG previews files, corresponding XML files, a container.css file, and an images folder that contains all the graphics required for our MBR Design containers. Also notice the container HTML filenames. It is even more important to apply intuitive filenames to containers because there are typically many more containers than skins included within a given skin package.

Figure 5-2

Creating the Zip Files

Creating the actual packaged install file requires three quick and easy steps. The first step is to zip all of the skin files together into a single Zip file named skins.zip. The second step is to zip all of the container files together into a single Zip file named containers.zip. The third and final required step is zipping the skins.zip and containers.zip into the MBR-Skin.zip file, which will be the actual skin package file that gets installed on the MBR Design DNN website. See? I said it was quick and easy.

Installing an HTML-Based Skin Package

Now that the install file has been created, it's ready for installation on a live DNN instance. The process of installing the packaged file is almost as quick and easy as creating the actual packaged file itself. However, when uploading skins, it is important to understand the difference between installing them at the Admin level and at the Host level. Depending on your situation, you can decide which scenario is best for you.

To begin the skin installation, you must first launch an instance of DNN and log in as shown in Figure 5-3 (it is assumed you have already installed DNN).

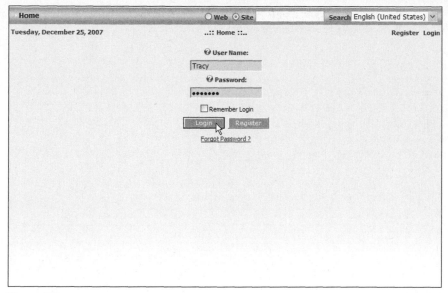

Figure 5-3

Installing Skins at the Admin Level

Installing skins at the Admin level allows skins to be accessed by the current portal only. This is typically desired when several different portals, operating as independent websites, have been created on a single DNN instance. Under this scenario, skin packages are unique to each portal and not shared.

To begin installation at the Admin level, follow these steps:

1. Navigate to the Admin ⇨ Skins menu item, as shown in Figure 5-4.

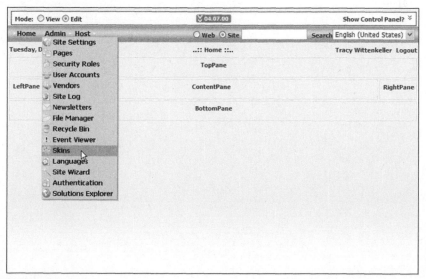

Figure 5-4

2. While on the Admin ⇨ Skins page, hover over the action arrow next to the word "Skins" and select Upload Skin, as shown in Figure 5-5.

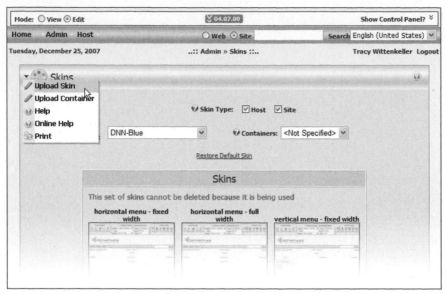

Figure 5-5

3. Click the Browse button to locate a packaged skin file on your local computer to install, as shown in Figure 5-6.

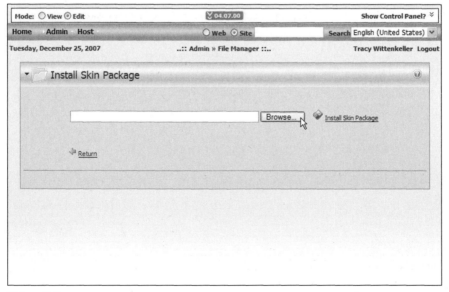

Figure 5-6

4. Select a packaged skin file on your local computer and click the Open button, as shown in Figure 5-7.

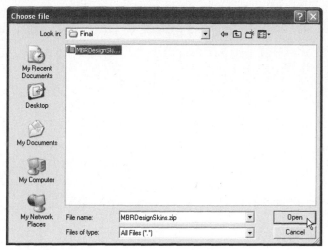

Figure 5-7

5. Click Install Skin Package, as shown in Figure 5-8.

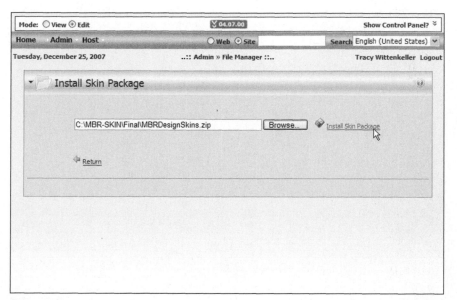

Figure 5-8

After you click Install Skin Package, DNN installs the skin package and displays all the details of the installation process via the Resource Upload Logs, as shown in Figure 5-9.

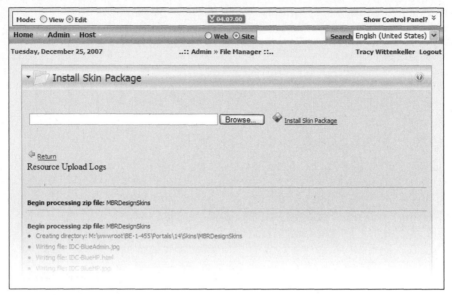

Figure 5-9

Figure 5-9 displays only the first few lines of the Resource Upload Logs. However, if you scroll through the Resource Upload Logs, you will see several lines of details regarding all of the uploaded files contained in a skin package. Figure 5-10 displays the end of the Resource Upload Logs after hundreds of lines of details.

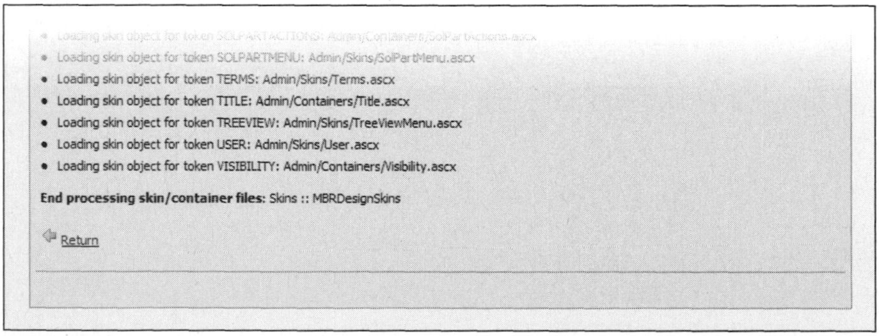

Figure 5-10

Installing Skins at the Host Level

Installing skins at the Host level is identical to installing skins at the Admin level, with the exception of the first step. In Step 1, instead of navigating to Admin ⇨ Skins, navigate to Host ⇨ Skins. Then, simply follow Steps 2 though 5 outlined previously to install a skin package.

Installing skins at the Admin level allows skins to be accessed by the current portal only. Installing skins at the Host level allows skins to be accessed by all portals on the same DNN instance. Admin-level skins are accessed by selecting the Admin radio buttons at the page or global level. Host-level skins are accessed by selecting the Host radio buttons at the page or global level. This is demonstrated in the next chapter.

Installing Separate container.zip Files

As I mentioned, you can install separate skin package (skin.zip) and container package (container.zip) files if you choose at the Admin or Host level. The process is the same for skin packages as it is when installing a packaged install file. However, to install a separate container package, you have to select Upload Container from the Skins action menu, as shown in Figure 5-11. Then just follow the same steps as outlined to select your file and install it.

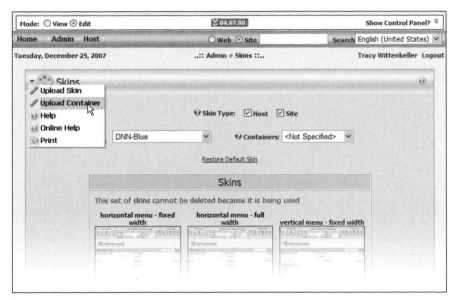

Figure 5-11

Previewing Skins and Containers

After the MBR Design skin package has been uploaded and installed successfully, you can easily preview skins and containers, if you have included JPEG previews in your skin package. If you create and include preview images within your skin package, DNN automatically generates thumbnails for display. This is especially helpful when several skins and containers have been installed on a website, and you need a reminder of what the skins and containers look like. To preview skins and containers that have been installed, follow these steps:

1. Navigate to Admin ⇨ Skins (or Host ⇨ Skins), as shown in Figure 5-12. As a default, DNN displays thumbnail previews of the skins and containers that are currently applied to the MBR Design website. (In this case, you will see previews of the default DNN-Blue skins.)

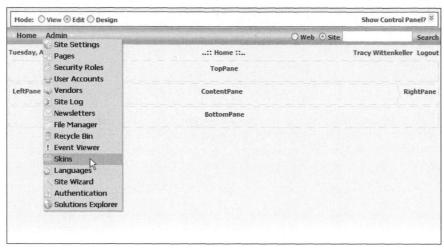

Figure 5-12

2. Because you only want to view the MBRDesign skins that have been installed at the Admin level, click the Host radio button to deselect it and display only the Admin-level skins. Then, select the MBRDesign skins from the drop-down list, as shown in Figure 5-13.

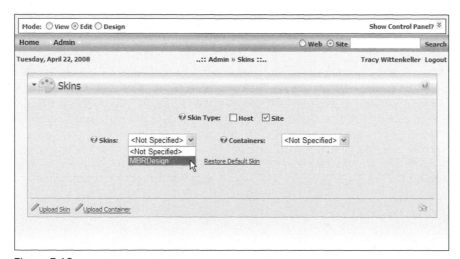

Figure 5-13

3. As you can see in Figure 5-14, only the MBRDesign skin and container previews are displayed.

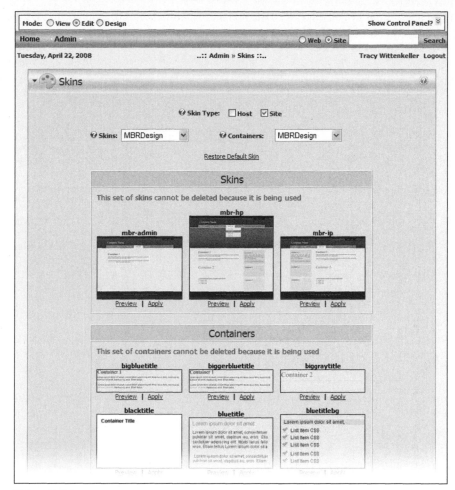

Figure 5-14

4. To view a full-size preview image of a skin or container, simply click a thumbnail image (or Preview link) to view it in a separate window. The dimensions of full-size preview images will depend on the size of the JPEG preview images you have created and included with your skin package.

I recommend that you provide good quality, detailed preview images. It's a great way to provide a roadmap of the skins and containers that are included as part of a skin package, and it makes it very easy and efficient for Administrators to select and apply the correct skins and containers appropriately.

Deleting/Uninstalling Skin Packages

After a skin package has been uploaded and installed, it is quite easy to uninstall it. Why would you want to do this? Well, maybe you decide to make extensive changes to a skin package after it has been installed. Sometimes, because of caching, instead of simply installing over a previously installed skin package (with the same exact name), it is good to delete a skin package before installing a new update, especially when several changes have been made. This ensures that you are starting with a clean slate in terms of the skin package you have updated and installed again. If you have installed a skin package over a previous version with the same name, and you don't see some of your new changes taking effect, it's a good indication that you need to delete the current version on the server and re-install an update.

It is important to note that after performing a skin package deletion, the Skinname folder is not always deleted from the server. Therefore, depending on the version of DNN you are running, you may also need to navigate to the appropriate Skinname folder via FTP and delete the empty folder that may be left behind.

Another reason for deleting a skin package is that you simply decide to use a different skin package than one that has already been installed. There is no reason to leave an unwanted skin package lingering on the server taking up space.

To delete a skin package, follow these steps:

1. Log in as Host and navigate to the Admin ⇨ Skins menu item.

   As a default, DNN displays the skins that are currently being used, as shown in Figure 5-15. Notice that the DNN-Blue skin cannot be deleted, as it is the package currently being used by the Portal.

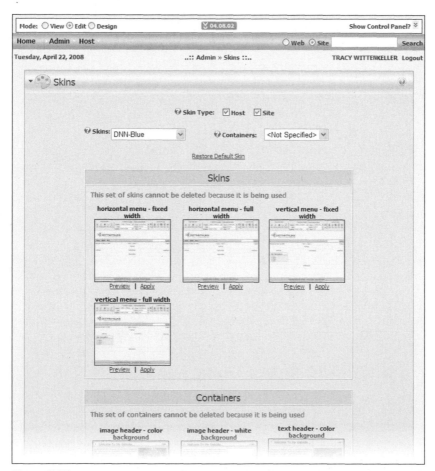

Figure 5-15

2. Because the MBRDesign skins were installed at the Admin level, clear the Site checkbox next to Skin Type: to display Host-level skins only. Then, select a skin package or skin pack from the drop-down menu to delete (in this case, the DNN-Gray skin), as shown in Figure 5-16. If you want to delete a container pack (and not a skin package or skin pack), select a set of containers from the drop-down menu on the right.

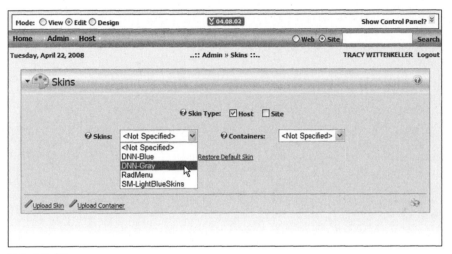

Figure 5-16

This will display the selected set of skins and containers in Preview mode, as shown in Figure 5-17.

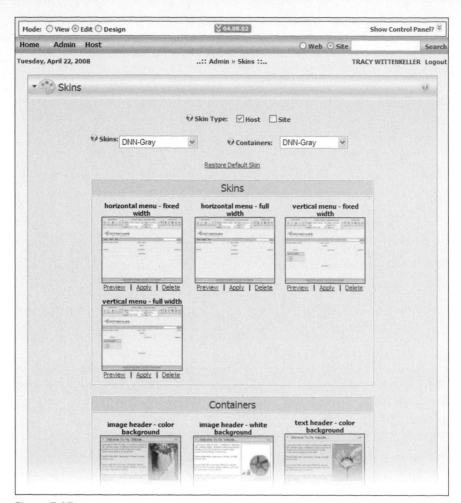

Figure 5-17

3. Scroll to the bottom of the Admin ⇨ Skins page and click Delete Skin Package, as shown in Figure 5-18.

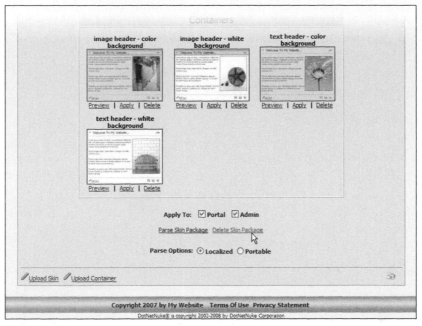

Figure 5-18

4. A dialog box is displayed asking "Are You Sure You Wish To Delete This Item?" (see Figure 5-19). Click OK to confirm the deletion of the selected skin package. Optionally, if you only want to delete individual skins or containers within a package, just click Delete under the appropriate skin or container preview image.

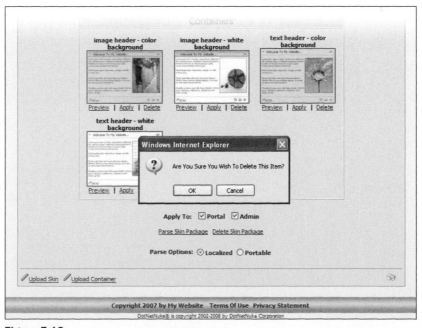

Figure 5-19

You have successfully deleted a skin package.

If the current Portal is using a skin or container within a skin package, the skin package itself cannot be deleted.

Applying Skins and Containers Globally to a Live DNN Instance

After a skin package is uploaded and installed successfully, you can finally apply skins and containers globally to your site. However, when applying skins and containers you must remember how you installed them, at the Admin level or at the Host level, so you can select and apply them appropriately via the DNN interface.

Let's apply the MBR Design skins using the following steps (you'll upload and install them at the Admin level):

1. Under the Admin menu, select Site Settings, as shown in Figure 5-20.

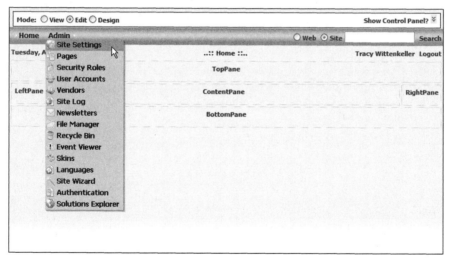

Figure 5-20

2. Click "+" next to the word Appearance to expand the Appearance Settings, as shown in Figure 5-21.

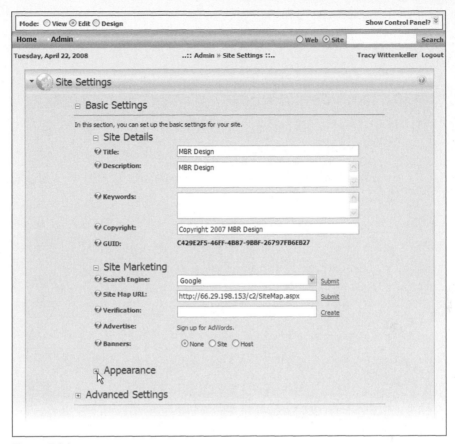

Figure 5-21

3. Scroll down to the view Skin/Container area, as shown in Figure 5-22.

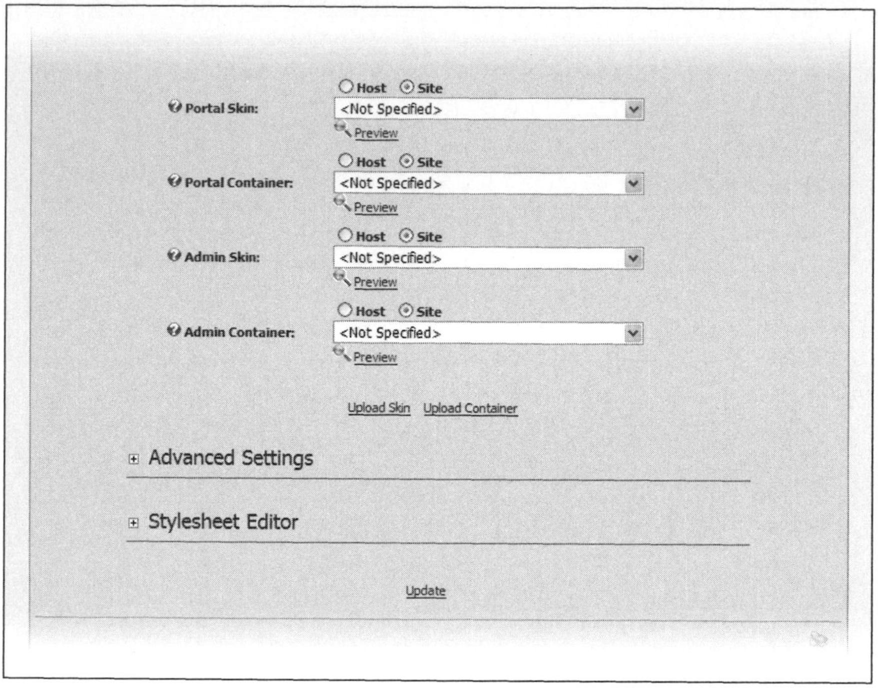

Figure 5-22

When a new DNN instance is created, Host-level skins that have been defined as the default skins within the configuration of the DNN application are automatically applied. In Figure 5-22, you can see that the Admin-level skins are being used because the radio buttons next to Admin are selected. Also note that the drop-down lists next to Portal Skin, Portal Container, Admin Skin, and Admin Container are defaulted to <Not Specified>. These are the drop-down lists that allow you to select the skins and containers you want to apply globally. When <Not Specified> is displayed in the drop-down list (again, this is the default), the default skins defined within the configuration of the DNN application are applied. In this case, the default skins are the DNN-Blue skins that were packaged with this installation of DNN.

Because you want to apply the MBR Design skins that have been installed at the Admin level, you need to be able to select them from the drop-down lists. In order to do that you must first ensure that the Site radio buttons next to Portal Skin, Portal Container, Admin Skin, and Admin Container are selected. Each time you select the Host or Site radio buttons, the drop-down lists will refresh to display the skins/containers that are available at each level. After you select the Site radio buttons, all of the skins that have been installed at the Admin level will be available to choose from. So you can then select the appropriate MBR Design skins and containers from the drop-down lists, as shown in Figure 5-23.

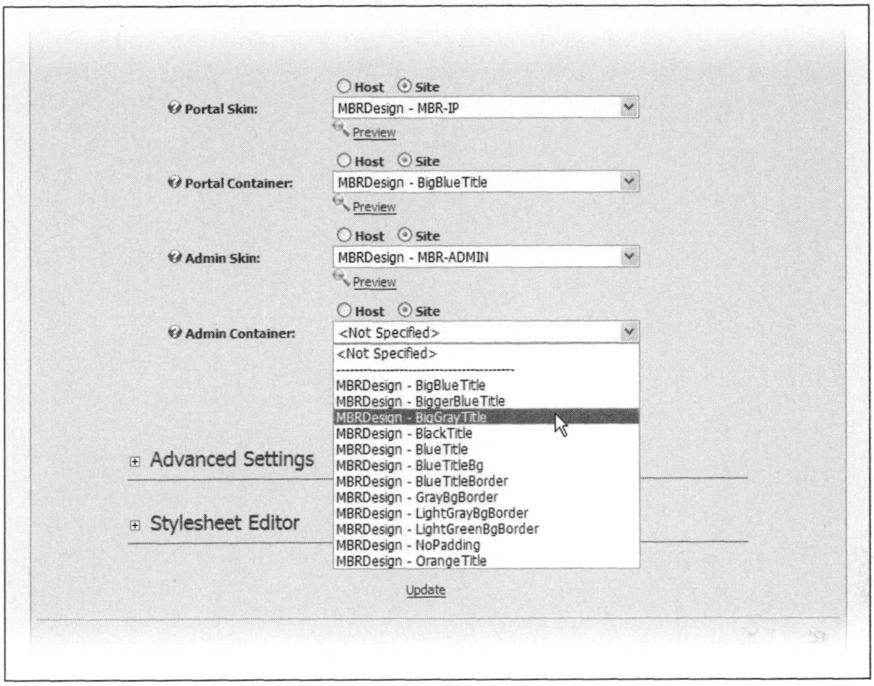

Figure 5-23

There may be times when you want to use Host-level skins as Portal or Admin skins, and Admin-level containers as Portal or Admin containers, or vice versa. Any combination of Host- or Admin-level skins and/or containers is perfectly fine. Just remember the relationship skins and containers have to a DNN instance when uploading them at the Host and at the Admin level.

Now that you have selected the appropriate skins and containers, there is just one thing left to do to apply them to the website on a global basis; you must click the Update link at the bottom of the Admin ⇨ Site Settings page. After you click the Update link, the current Admin-Site Settings page will refresh displaying the MBR-Admin skin, as shown in Figure 5-24. After the page refreshes, you will notice that the look and feel of the website has changed entirely.

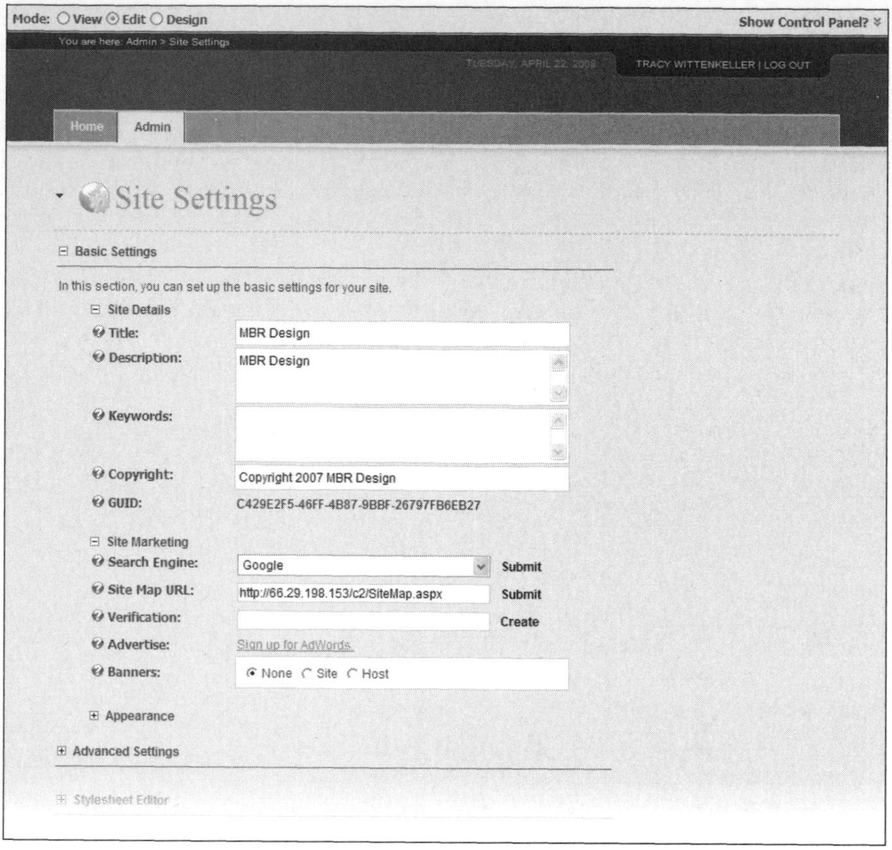

Figure 5-24

You have just learned how to apply skins and containers on a site-wide or global basis. Therefore, any skins and/or containers that have been added to the website using the defaults defined via Admin ⇨ Site Settings will change as the global defaults are changed. This also means that any new pages that are added to the website will inherit the default Portal Skin as defined via Admin ⇨ Site Settings. And any new modules that get added to the website will inherit the default Portal Container as defined via Admin ⇨ Site Settings. For example, if you add a new page to the site, the MBRDesign-MBR-IP skin will be applied to it because you have changed the default Portal Skin to MBRDesign-MBR-IP. If you add a new module to the site, the MBRDesign-BigBlueTitle containers will be applied to it because you have changed the default Portal Container to MBRDesign-BigBlueTitle.

Skins and containers can also be applied at the page level and module level, respectively, as you will see in the next two chapters. Therefore, each page on your site can have a different skin applied to it, and each module on your site can have a different container applied to it!

Summary

This chapter provided an overview of how to package, install, and apply skins to your DNN website. First, you learned the advantages of packaging skin and container files together and the importance of naming conventions. Next, you learned the difference between installing skin and container files at the Admin level versus the Host level. Then, you learned how to preview and delete skins and containers after they have been installed. Finally, you learned how to apply skins and containers to a DNN website globally.

You should be quite excited about what you have learned thus far because it means our MBR Design website is starting to take shape and take on the look and feel of the intended design. As I said at the beginning of this chapter, the ability to apply a different look and feel to a DNN website by uploading a single Zip file is very powerful and gives you a great deal of control over your site's design.

Now that you have experienced first-hand the ease at which you can install and apply different skins and containers to a DNN website, you're going to continue the development of the MBR Design website by building the website hierarchy in preparation for the site content. In the next chapter, you experience DNN's flexibility when it comes to adding, editing, moving, and deleting pages.

6

Working with Pages

Up to this point you've done a lot of the heavy lifting required to prepare your website solution for content — and now all of your hard work is about to pay off as we embark on the next stage of development — adding and editing pages required for the website.

The previous chapter discussed the power of changing the look and feel of an entire DNN website in minutes. Perhaps even more powerful is the capability to add and manipulate the page options and structure within your website easily at any time. As you will see, the capability of DNN to change a site's page structure without "breaking" references to links or content provides a compelling, intuitive, and efficient way to easily edit and maintain a website's hierarchy.

Problem

When developing static websites, pages must be created and edited offline as independent HTML files and uploaded to the server to have changes/updates take effect on a live website. Typically, a qualified webmaster who has a working knowledge of HTML, CSS, and other web technologies does this. First, the webmaster has to be contacted and briefed about the required updates. Next, the webmaster must schedule time for the required updates. And finally, when the webmaster finds time in his/her schedule, the necessary required files have to be downloaded, edited, uploaded, and then tested. This creates a highly inefficient system for making even the simplest of updates to a website.

Static websites also don't provide flexibility, efficiency, or intuitiveness in terms of making changes to a website's hierarchy. Typically, several files have to be updated in order to make a simple change, such as moving a page within the site to another location within the same site. A system such as this is not an efficient way to update a website.

It isn't just static websites that lack flexibility, adeptness, or intuitiveness — many Content Management Systems have a less-than-straightforward approach when it comes to administering pages. Some do not even allow you to edit pages directly. In many cases, you have to navigate to a separate Admin area to apply updates, and then click a Preview button, which launches a separate window, just to see what you've done. One of the really cool things about DNN is the fact that you edit content directly on live pages, so you see what your updated pages will look like as you work on them, which makes the content editing process extremely intuitive and efficient. This is how an effective Content Management System should work, as you will see as you use DNN to update the MBR Design website.

Design

Wouldn't it be nice to have the freedom to add pages to your website directly within your browser? Or rename pages in seconds? Or copy a page with all of its content? Or move pages within your site with just a couple clicks of a mouse and have the site hierarchy change and update in real time? Or add keywords? Or change page skins? Or hide pages from the main navigation? Or . . . well, the idea here is that, with DNN you have the power to control your website hierarchy with very little-to-no technical knowledge quite easily — and there are several options for doing so. This section focuses on working with pages on a DNN website. In this chapter you learn:

- ❑ How to add top-level pages
- ❑ How to add sub-level pages
- ❑ How to configure Basic Page Management settings
- ❑ How to create hidden pages
- ❑ How to preview pages
- ❑ How to move pages within the site
- ❑ How to copy pages
- ❑ How to delete pages
- ❑ How to configure Advanced settings
- ❑ How to apply/change page skins
- ❑ How to define start and end dates for displaying pages

By the end of this chapter, you will know just about everything there is to know about configuring pages within your DNN website. When you see just how flexible it is to add or update pages in DNN, I'm confident you'll never think about a Content Management System the same way again.

Solution

Adding content to a DNN website starts with adding pages. The MBR Design website is no exception. But before content can be added, the site hierarchy has to be defined. Once that is done, as you will see, you can easily add pages in accordance with your site outline.

Adding Top-Level Pages

Currently, the MBR Design website has only one page, the Home page, which was created automatically with the DNN installation. However, you need to add additional top-level pages to the website based on the site map, shown in Figure 6-1. So let's get right to it.

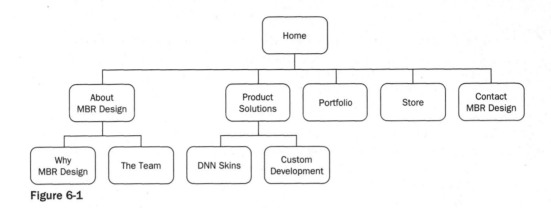

Figure 6-1

The first thing you need to do is log in to the new MBR Design portal, as shown in Figure 6-2.

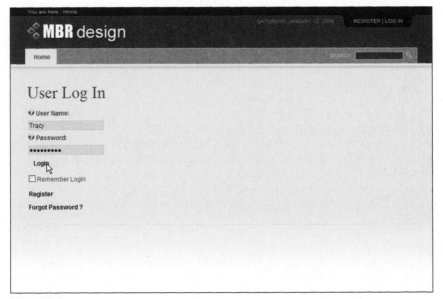

Figure 6-2

After you log in, you need to expose the Control Panel by clicking the double arrow next to Show Control Panel, as shown in Figure 6-3. If you like, you can configure the Control Panel to be maximized or minimized (opened or closed) automatically by navigating to Admin ⇨ Advanced ⇨ Usability Settings ⇨ Control Panel Visibility and selecting either the Minimized radio button or the Maximized radio button.

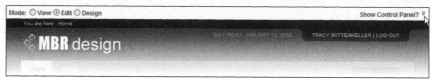

Figure 6-3

After clicking the double arrow, the complete Control Panel is exposed, as shown in Figure 6-4.

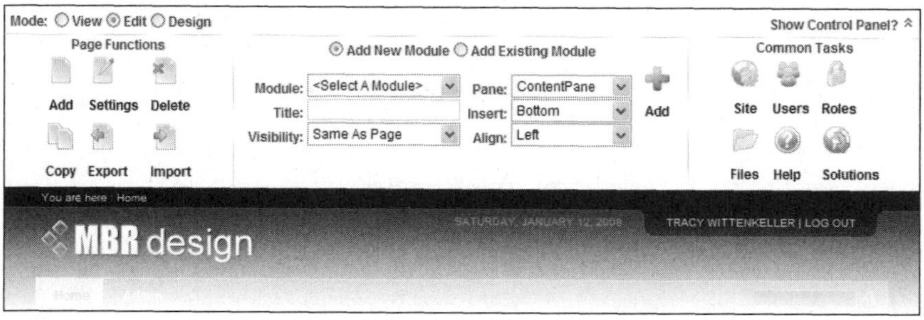

Figure 6-4

The Control Panel contains key functions for administering a DNN website. This includes the Page Functions menu on the left, which is our area of focus at the moment. The buttons in the Page Functions menu provide quick access to often-used page management functions. You'll use the Page Functions menu to add your first page.

Clicking Add under Page Functions will load the Page Management settings for your first page, as shown in Figure 6-5.

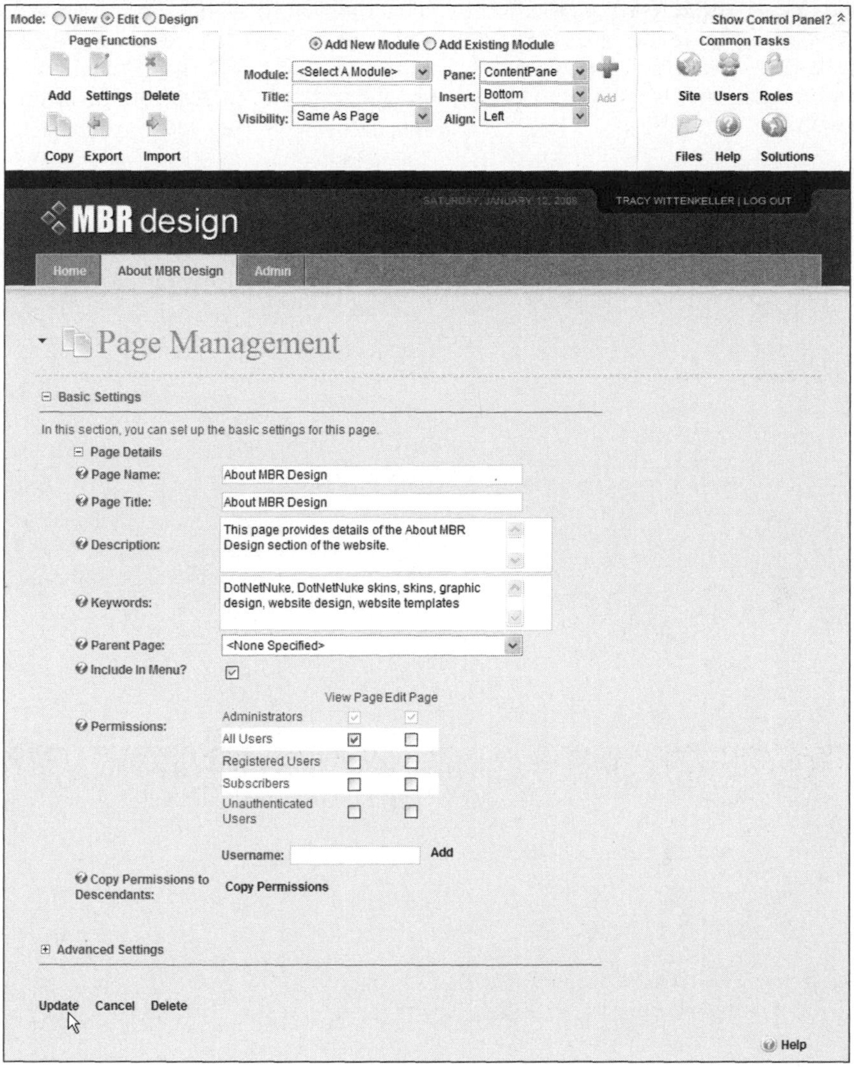

Figure 6-5

As you can see in Figure 6-5, there are many Basic Settings that can be defined, which are detailed in Table 6-1.

Table 6-1: Basic Page Functions

Function	Description
Page Name	The name of the page. The text you enter will be displayed in the menu system.
Page Title	The title for the page. The text you enter will be displayed in the browser window and in search engines.
Description	This is where you enter a description about the current page. This description appears in search engines. This is typically just a short summary about the page. 25–30 words is sufficient.
Keywords	This is where you enter keywords for the page (separated by commas). Search engines use these keywords to help index a DNN site's pages.
Parent Page	This is where you define the level of the page within the site hierarchy. The default selection is None Specified. If None Specified is selected, the page will be a top-level menu item (as shown in the menu in Figure 6-5). If you want a page to be a child page of another page on the website, you would select a page in the Parent Page drop-down menu.
Include In Menu?	This box is checked as a default. If you want a page to be hidden from the menu, clear this box. But you want "About MBR Design" to be displayed in the menu, so leave this box checked. If a page is not included in the menu, you can still link to it based on its page URL.
Permissions	This is where you choose the groups of people that can view and administer this page. By selecting the box in the "All Users" View Page column, this page will be visible to all visitors that come to the website. Roles-based security is another quite powerful feature of DNN. It allows you to define permissions at the page level and even at the module level. Chapter 9 focuses on roles-based security and defining permissions for pages and content.
Username	Using this field, you can define permissions to this page to a single user (more on this in Chapter 9).
Copy Permissions to Descendants	Copies the currently selected permissions for the page to descendant/sub pages.

Notice the question mark images in Figure 6-5. These images expand when you click them, offering a description of the type of appropriate information for each field. If you simply hover over them with your mouse, a tooltip will be displayed with the same information.

Now you will complete the Basic Settings for this page by entering the Page Title and Page Name, and selecting the All Users View Page box under Permissions, as shown in Figure 6-5. Because no other settings are required at this time, simply click Update to create the new About MBR Design page. You have successfully added the first top-level page!

Using this same process, you'll add four additional top-level pages based on the MBR Design website hierarchy: Product Solutions, Store, Portfolio, and Contact MBR Design.

Figure 6-6 displays the site with four additional top-level pages added.

Figure 6-6

Adding Sub-Level/Child Pages

To complete your initial website hierarchy, you will also add four sub-level pages: Why MBR Design, The Team, DotNetNuke Skins, and Custom Development. The process of adding sub pages is the same as adding a top-level page. However, parent pages have to be defined for them. To define a page on the website as a sub or child page, simply choose a page from the Parent Page drop-down menu within the Basic Page Management settings, as shown in Figure 6-7. You can also change the Parent for any given sub-level page at any time to change its location within the site.

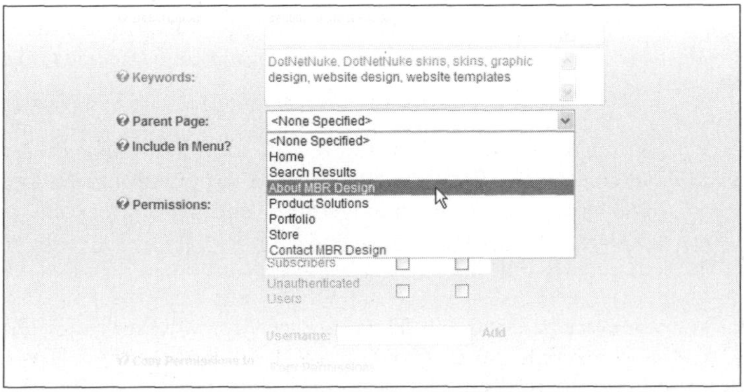

Figure 6-7

Choosing About MBR Design as the parent page for the Why MBR Design? page makes Why MBR Design a sub or child page of the About MBR Design page, as shown in Figure 6-8.

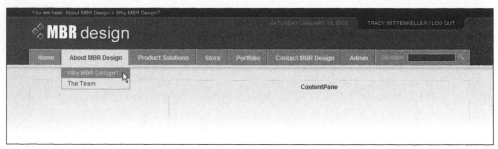

Figure 6-8

As you have learned, it is very easy to add pages to a DNN website that display as top or sub-level menu items. However, you can also add pages that are hidden from the menu. Why would you want to do this? You may have other pages of information that you want to have available to visitors or members, but not as part of the menu. A good example would be news articles or a news archive where you have perhaps hundreds of pages that you want to link to without displaying them in the menu.

Creating hidden pages or hiding pages from the menu is easy. Within Page Management settings for a given page just make sure to clear the Include in Menu option to make your page hidden to the menu, but still usable to the website.

Previewing Pages

Notice that when pages are viewed in Edit mode (above the Control Panel on the left), content pane IDs and boundaries are displayed. As previously discussed, content panes are the areas of your skin(s) that you can insert modules into. Modules enable you to add content and organize it in a manner that makes best use of the real estate on each page of your site. (Chapter 7 discusses modules in detail.) Content pane structure (the number of panes and their placement) is defined at the skin-level and cannot be changed within the DNN interface itself.

When changing skins, if DNN cannot find a matching content pane ID, modules will automatically be placed in the ContentPane. It is important to note that while the layout of a skin may change, DNN's functionality is preserved.

If you want to preview your pages as they will appear to non-administrators, you can click the View button next to Mode (above the Control Panel on the left). This simply hides all content panes and Admin functions while displaying pages as general website visitors (not logged in) would see them. If you want to view the content pane structure of your skins, while displaying module titles but hiding module content, click the Design button next to Mode. This gives you a quick look at your skin structure for adding content. However, because you can view the content pane structure easily while in Edit mode, the Design mode function is rarely, if ever, useful.

Moving Pages

We've added five top-level pages to the site. But notice, in Figure 6-6, the order is not correct. The Portfolio page is supposed to come before the Store page. Not to worry! It is quite easy to change the order of pages after they have been added to a DNN website by navigating to Admin ⇨ Pages, as shown in Figure 6-9.

Figure 6-9

By navigating to Admin ⇨ Pages, Administrators can manage all Pages (sub-level pages are signified by "...") within the portal. From this page, Administrators can create new pages, modify existing pages, delete pages, change the order of pages, and change the hierarchical page levels using the arrow icons. Clicking the pencil icon allows you to edit the selected page's settings. This comes in handy when you have hidden or disabled a page from the menu, and you need to access its settings. Clicking the magnifying glass allows you to view the selected page. Clicking the red X icon deletes the selected page.

To change the location of the Portfolio page, you must first select it from the list and then click the top green arrow to move it up one position in the current level, as shown in Figure 6-10.

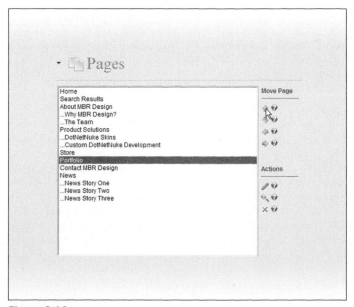

Figure 6-10

Figure 6-11 shows the result of moving the Portfolio page up one level. Notice that it is now above the Store page within the site hierarchy edit window, and its position has changed on the nav bar as well.

Using the Pages editor (Admin ⇨ Pages) you can change the hierarchical level of any page.

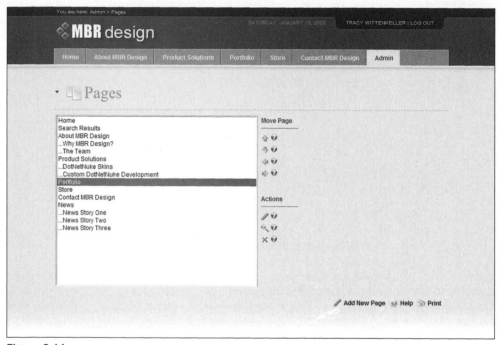

Figure 6-11

A quick way to move subpages to a different location within a DNN website is to simply select a different Parent page by first navigating to the page you want to move, and then going to Settings (under Page Functions) and selecting a different Parent page on the Page Management edit screen.

Copying Pages

Sometimes when adding content, it can be advantageous to copy pages you have already populated. This can save lots of time and come in handy when you need to add additional pages that follow a consistent content structure that has been created. This is also quite helpful when you want to add the same content to multiple pages, and you want changes in that content to be reflected everywhere it exists by editing just one instance of it.

To illustrate the options that are available to you when copying pages, I've created a hidden page called Copy Master that includes three modules on it, as shown in Figure 6-12. Again, I delve into modules in Chapter 7. For now, you'll copy the Copy Master page by clicking Copy under Page Functions in the Control Panel.

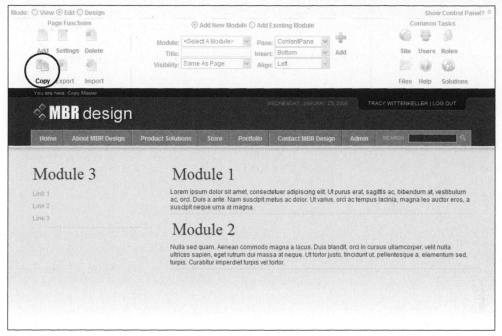

Figure 6-12

This will load the Page Management page for the new page you are creating. You'll use the same process to define the Basic Settings as when adding a page. However, as shown in Figure 6-13, if you scroll down a bit further, you can expose the additional options that are available when copying a page.

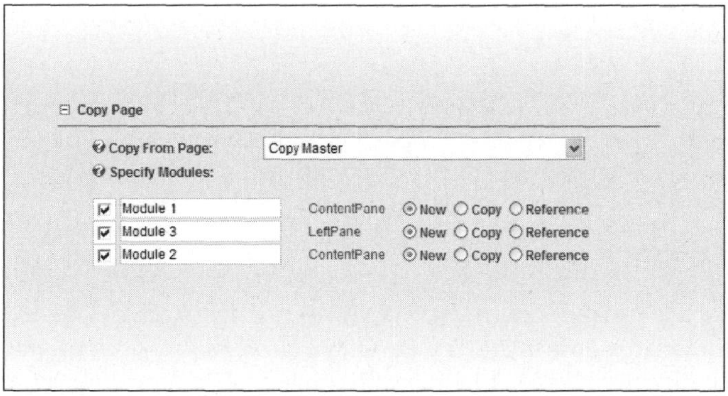

Figure 6-13

First, you need to select the page you want to copy from the Copy From Page drop-down menu. The Copy Master page is selected in the drop-down menu because it is the page you were on when you selected Copy from the Control Panel. However, you can select any page on the site to copy from the drop-down menu. You'll notice that as different pages are selected, the corresponding modules associated with them are displayed. Because you want to copy the Copy Master page, you select it from the Copy From Page menu.

Next you need to specify the modules you want to copy. As a default, all modules are selected. However, modules can be selected by checking the boxes next to their names and entering new titles for them.

When copying modules from a page, there are three options: New, Copy, and Reference. These options are defined in Table 6-2.

Table 6-2: Page Copy Options

Function	Description
New	If this option is specified, the module will be copied without content.
Copy	If this option is specified, the module will be copied with the same content. But the content will be independent of the original module.
Reference	If this option is specified, the module will be copied and the content will be shared. Changes to the content in this module will affect all instances of the module.

You'll copy the Copy Master page to a new page called Copied Module with the options specified in Figure 6-14.

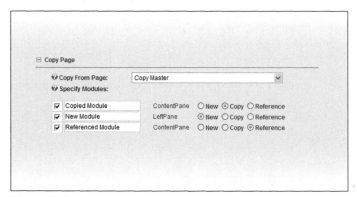

Figure 6-14

The end result, as shown in Figure 6-15, is a page with a blank New Module in the left pane (content needs to be added to it); a new Copied Module with duplicated, independent content; and a Referenced Module, which is a second instance of the Module 3 module on the Copy Master page. (Any change to this module will be reflected on all pages where it exists.)

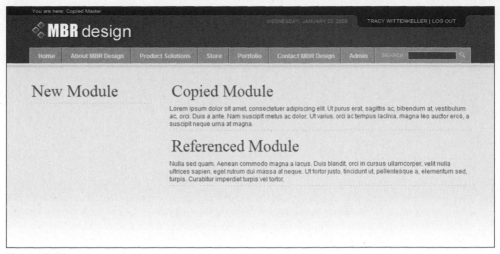

Figure 6-15

Deleting Pages

Pages can easily be deleted in one of three ways:

❑ Navigating to Admin ➪ Pages, selecting the page to delete, and clicking the red X, as shown in Figure 6-16

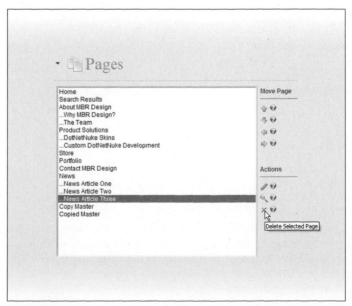

Figure 6-16

❑ Navigating to the page to be deleted and clicking Delete in the Control Panel under Page Functions, as shown in Figure 6-17

Figure 6-17

❑ After navigating to the Page Management settings for a page to be deleted, by clicking Settings in the Control Panel under Page Functions, then scrolling down and clicking Delete, as shown in Figure 6-18

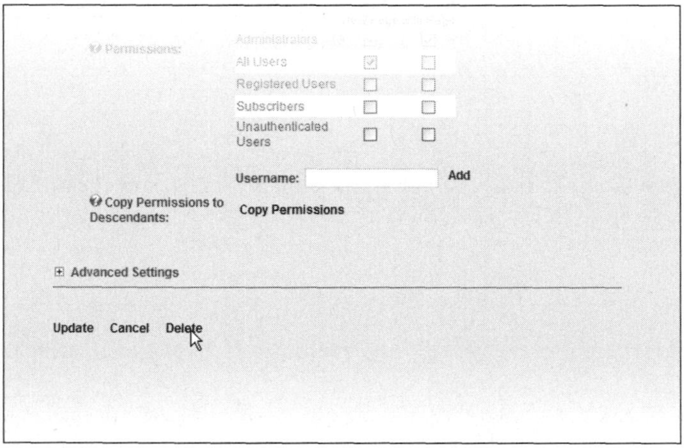

Figure 6-18

Changing Skins

As you learned in the last chapter, it is quite easy to apply skins on a global level via the Admin or Host menu. However, applying the same skin to every page on your site may not meet the requirements for every page on your site. To compensate for that fact, a single skin package may include several skins with different content structures or features for different scenarios. For example, within the MBR Design skin package, you have created an interior-page skin (MBR-IP) that has been defined as the default skin for all pages that do not have a different skin specifically applied to them. The interior-page skin includes a breadcrumb trail (see Figure 6-19) that you do not want displayed on the home page of the website. Because of this, the MBR Design skin package also includes a home page skin (MBR-HP) version that does not have a breadcrumb.

Figure 6-19

Let's apply the MBR-HP skin to the home page using the following steps:

1. Navigate to the home page and click Settings in the Control Panel under Page Functions, as shown in Figure 6-20.

Figure 6-20

2. Scroll down to the bottom of the Page Management page and click the "+" next to Advanced Settings to expose additional page settings, as shown in Figure 6-21.

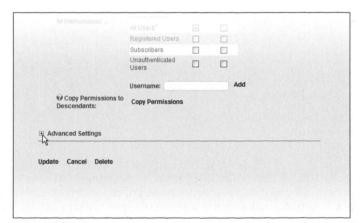

Figure 6-21

3. With the Advanced Settings expanded, scroll down to Page Skin, and then, with the Site skins loaded (make sure the Site radio button is selected), choose the MBR-HP skin from the drop-down menu, as shown in Figure 6-22.

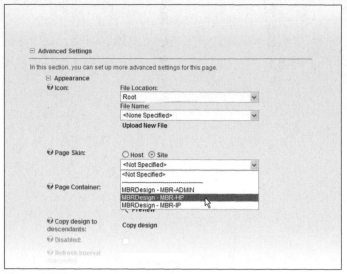

Figure 6-22

4. Scroll down and click Update, as shown in Figure 6-23.

Figure 6-23

As you can see in Figure 6-24, the MBR-HP skin does not include the breadcrumb control because it's not required for the home page.

Figure 6-24

More About Advanced Page Settings

As you have learned, there are a number of basic options that can be selected and defined for DNN pages. However, there are also some Advanced Settings that add additional features to your pages, which are detailed in Table 6-3.

Table 6-3: Advanced Page Functions

Function	Description
Page Skin	The selected skin will be applied to this page.
Page Container	The selected container will be applied to all modules on this page.
Copy design to descendants	Copies the currently selected design (skin and container) for the page to descendant pages.
Disabled	If the page is disabled, it is not available to users of the site. You can use this option to suppress content that you might wish to show at a later time.
Refresh Interval (seconds)	Enter the interval to wait between automatic page refreshes. (Example: Enter "60" for 1 minute or leave blank to disable.)
Page Header Tags	Enter any tags (i.e., META tags) that should be rendered in the HEAD tag of the HTML for this page.
Secure?	Specify whether or not this page should be forced to use a secure connection (SSL). This option will be enabled only if the administrator has Enabled SSL in the site settings.
Start Date	Enter the start date for displaying this page. You may use the Calendar to pick a date.
End Date	Enter the end date for displaying this page. You may use the Calendar to pick a date.
Link Url	If you would like this page to behave as a navigation link to another resource, you can specify the Link URL value here. Please note that this field is optional.

Many of the Advanced Page Settings are very useful, but I'll highlight a few that deserve extra attention.

The Icon feature lets you apply an icon next to the page title in the menu system. You can select an icon that has already been uploaded to the server by selecting the appropriate folder from the File Location drop-down menu and then selecting the appropriate file from the File Name drop-down menu, as shown in Figure 6-25.

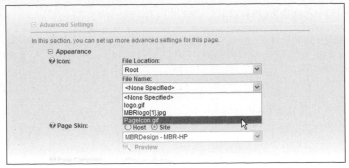

Figure 6-25

Or, if you want to use your own icons, you can upload them in seconds using the following steps:

1. Click Upload New File, as shown in Figure 6-26.

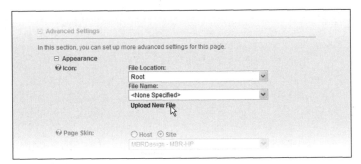

Figure 6-26

2. Click the Browse button, as shown in Figure 6-27.

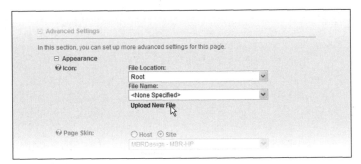

Figure 6-27

This opens a pop-up window that allows you to select an image on your local computer to upload. After you select your file and click Open, your filename path is added to the File Name field (I'm uploading a file named HomeIcon.gif). Next, click Upload Selected File, as shown in Figure 6-28. This adds your file to the File Name drop-down menu.

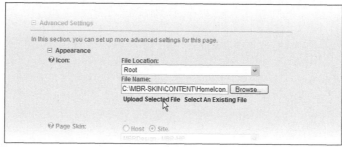

Figure 6-28

3. As you can see in Figure 6-29, after your file is uploaded, it is automatically selected in the File Name drop-down menu as the icon to apply next to Home in the navigation bar.

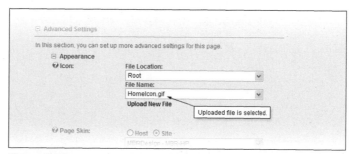

Figure 6-29

4. Scroll down to the bottom of the Advanced Settings and click the Update link to apply your settings. Figure 6-30 shows the results of adding an icon to the home page.

Figure 6-30

Page Skin is obviously at the top of my list since one of my areas of expertise is DNN skinning. As you have just learned, you can apply different skins at the page level in DNN. If you like, every page on your website can have a different skin by simply using the Page Skin feature. How cool is that?

The Disabled feature is useful when you show a menu item within the navigation, but you don't want it to be clickable.

The Start Date and End Date feature is one of those features that makes most users new to DNN say "wow!" In fact, I think I even used that term (with certain expletives) the first time I saw this feature. The ability to automatically display/remove time-sensitive content is powerful indeed. And I think most users understand the value of this feature because a) time-sensitivity is so much a part of most business operations, and b) most users can think of uses for it immediately. How about a way to announce promotions on your website? Simply create your promotional content, decide when you want the promotion to start, and define the date you want the promotional content removed from the website . . . automatically!

I really like this feature because, like many DNN options, it is easy to implement. You simply enter dates in the Start Date and End Date fields. To make it even easier, you can pop up a calendar by clicking the Calendar link next to each field and select the correct dates. It doesn't get much easier that that! Figure 6-31 displays the calendar pop-up when clicking the End Date Calendar link.

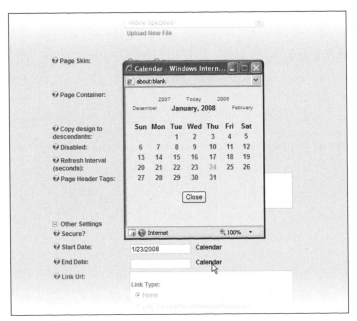

Figure 6-31

Finally, Link Url is a great feature that allows you to forward a page to another URL . . . quite useful indeed.

Summary

This chapter introduced the concept of working with pages and discussed most of the options associated with configuring them. You learned just about everything there is to know about adding, copying, and deleting pages; moving them to different locations within your site; and configuring many of the Basic and Advanced Page Settings including:

- Page
- Name, Title, Description, and Keywords
- Parent Page
- Include In Menu?
- Icon
- Page Skin
- Page Container
- Disabled?
- Start Date
- End Date
- Link URL

In this chapter you actually built your initial website hierarchy. Hopefully, you have learned that adding pages to a DNN website and applying Page Settings is fairly straightforward. Once you get the hang of it you will find that you can build entire website hierarchies, literally, in just minutes.

Now that you've created the MBR Design hierarchy, you can move on to the meat and potatoes of your website — the content. In the next chapter you are introduced to the concept of modules, and you add content by implementing several of the core modules included with a standard DNN installation.

7

Building Content — Working with Modules

So far, you've spent a lot of time readying your website solution for what I'm going to affectionately refer to as the meat and potatoes of the entire solution. Of course, I'm talking about the concept of modules, which is how content is added to a DNN website. Modules are pluggable components that present some type of functionality to the user. It is helpful to think of modules as "chunks" of content that are addressed independently within a DNN website. Typically, several modules are grouped together to create a web page, and they can easily be added, edited, deleted, moved within a page, or transferred to another page. Each module also has its own settings that can be configured, depending on the functionality it delivers. In order to add content to a DNN page you must first insert an "empty" module into a content pane. Then, you configure its settings and add content to the module, or vice versa. You can define, to a certain degree, how a module behaves and how it is displayed, but a lot has to do with how it has been coded and the features it may contain.

DNN provides several unique core modules out-of-the-box, each with its own specific functionality, such as a text editor, discussion board, feedback form, and document manager, just to name a few. Alternatively, custom modules can be created to add additional functionality to a DNN website. However, in this chapter, you learn how to implement some of the core modules built into DNN as you build and apply content to the MBR Design website.

Problem

Many users fall short when it comes to using modules effectively. There are many modules included with DNN out-of-the-box, and although DNN makes it easy to add and edit content via modules, it is not always clear which modules are the best choice for every situation. For example, do you use the Media module or the Text/HTML module to add an image? The answer is . . . it depends. The module choices you make, and the way you configure them for the website solution, will determine the level of effort required to maintain the content within your website on an ongoing basis. But, in many cases, users don't make optimal choices simply because of their inexperience with DNN.

If understanding which modules are the appropriate modules to use at any given time isn't enough, the way you configure them can make a tremendous difference in the ease and efficiency at which the content within the website can be updated and/or maintained.

Yet another problem many users face is making content look professional. Even though users may get accustomed to using the various modules included with DNN, it can be challenging to make content look great throughout the website. Of course, skin and containers can be created as needed when new presentation requirements are defined. However, in many cases, it takes more than that to present DNN content in a professional manner. You'll be happy to know that the MBR Design examples presented in this chapter will go a long way in helping you to accomplish that.

Design

This section focuses on using some of DNN's core modules that are implemented extensively with typical DNN websites. Specifically, in this chapter you learn how to make the best use of modules. You learn how to:

❑ Assign modules (turn them on)

❑ Install modules

❑ Add new modules to a page

❑ Add existing modules to a page

❑ Move modules to different locations on a single page

❑ Move modules to other pages

❑ Delete Modules

❑ Apply containers to modules

❑ Customize module settings and properties

In this chapter, you also learn how to implement the following widely used core modules:

❑ Text/HTML

❑ Media

❑ Announcements

❑ Links

❑ Survey

❑ FAQ

By the end of this chapter, you will have a good understanding of how to use many of the core modules included with DNN. This is a good thing because you'll want to use them over and over again in your future DNN projects. You'll also have a good understanding of how to install new modules and configure them to your advantage in ways you may not have even thought of. As you move through this learning process, I'm confident you'll discover how much easier your life can be when it comes to creating and maintaining DNN content using core modules.

Solution

At the most basic level, adding content to a DNN website requires you to insert a module into a content pane, and then add content to the module. DNN offers many different types of core modules that allow you to add different types of content. You are going to be using several core modules as you populate the MBR design website with content. The first module you're going to start with is the module that's used most often for adding content within DNN — the Text/HTML module. But, before we get into the nuts and bolts of the Text/HTML module, you need to learn how to work with modules in a general sense. First, this section covers how to install modules. It then explains how to add modules, configure their settings, move them around your site, and apply different containers to them. Finally, it demonstrates how to use several key core modules that are used on most DNN websites to implement content.

Installing Modules

Before you can use modules with a DNN website, they have to be installed at the Host level. Typically, when you download or buy a DNN module, it is delivered as a single packaged Zip file (commonly referred to as the Private Assembly or PA). The easiest way to install a module is to use the automated install method, which involves uploading the PA. To perform an automated install, use the following easy steps:

1. Navigate to the Host menu and select Module Definitions, as shown in Figure 7-1. This loads the Module Definitions page where you can see the list of modules (with descriptions) that are installed.

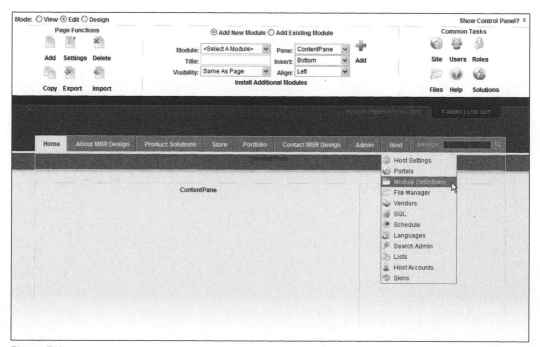

Figure 7-1

2. At the top-left corner is a downward-facing arrow (Action menu) next to the title Module Definitions. Hover over this arrow and select Install New Module from the drop-down menu, as shown in Figure 7-2. Alternatively, you can also scroll to the bottom of the page and click Install New Module.

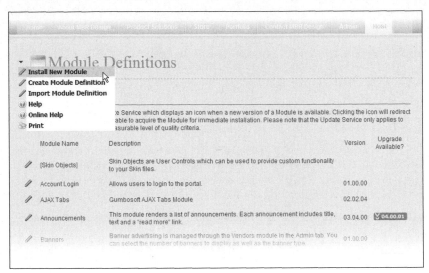

Figure 7-2

3. Browse to the folder where your module PA (Zip file) is located and select the package you want to upload to your DNN website. Then, click the Install New Module link, as shown in Figure 7-3.

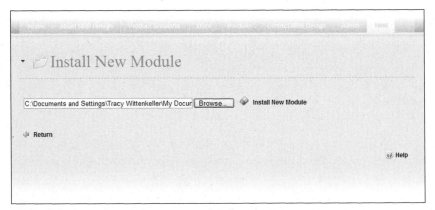

Figure 7-3

Upon installation, the resource log is displayed. If no errors are reported, you see the message "Installation Successful at the bottom of the Resource Log," as shown in Figure 7-4.

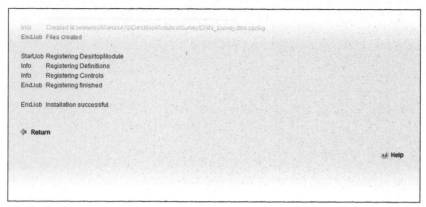

Figure 7-4

Clicking the Return link takes you back to the Module Definitions page where the newly installed module is added to the list of previously installed modules. When your module is successfully installed, it is available immediately for use on the current portal.

Learning to install new modules is a good practice because you will most likely, at some point in your DNN life, purchase at least one third-party module, or require another DNN core module that is not included with a DNN installation. Before you can use third-party modules or additional DNN modules, you have to install them.

With early DNN versions, all core modules were included with DNN and installed. However, this created a bloated application unnecessarily because most DNN users simply don't use all of the core modules. As a result, all core modules are now included with DNN, but not installed. This lets you, as the website owner or Administrator, decide which core modules you want to use for your website at any given time using a simple method to make them available (install them). And because you are using only DNN core modules with the MBR Design website solution, you only need to be concerned with the core modules that are included with the DNN application.

So, how do you choose which core modules you want to make available to your website? I'm glad you asked. The following process is very straightforward.

1. Log in as Host and navigate to Host ⇨ Module Definitions, which will display the Module Definitions page. The Module Definitions page allows the Host to set one or more modules as Premium, manage module properties, and upload new modules.

2. Scroll down to the bottom of the Module Definitions page and view the Available Modules that have been included with the DNN application, but not installed.

3. Select the modules you want to install by selecting the checkboxes next to the module names; then click Install Selected Modules, as shown in Figure 7-5.

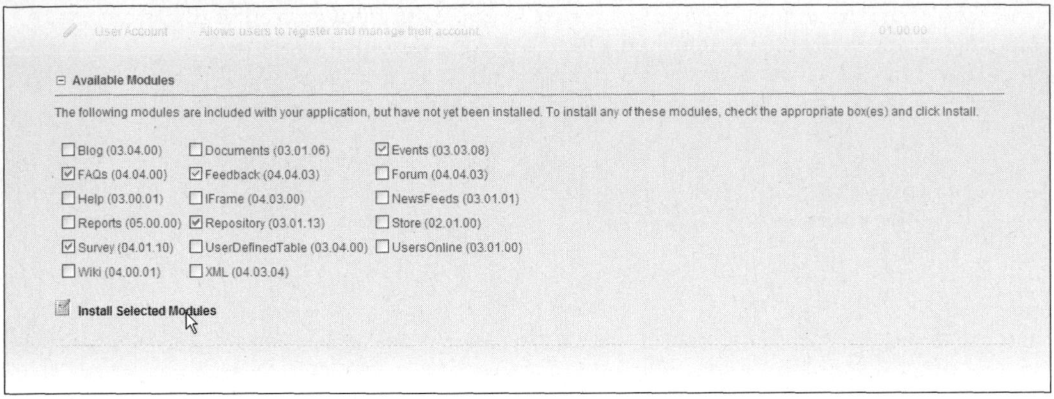

Figure 7-5

This will make the modules you have selected immediately available in the Module area of the Control Panel so they can be added to your DNN website.

Adding New Modules to a Page

The first step in understanding the concept of modules is reviewing the middle section of the Control Panel, which is viewable to administrators or users with appropriate edit permissions. There are two modes for adding modules to a page, depending on the radio option you select. The first and default option is Add New Module, as shown in Figure 7-6.

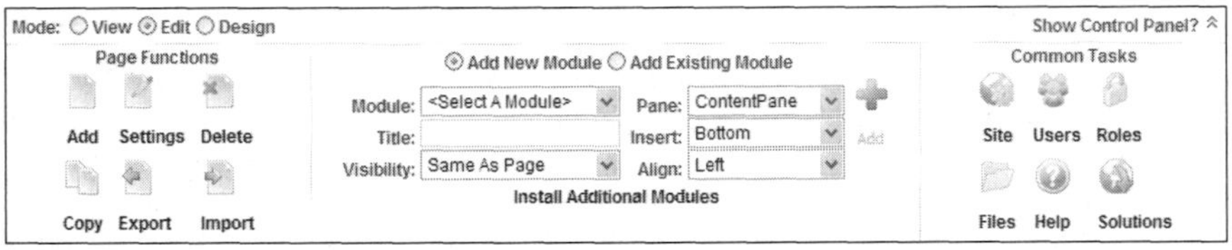

Figure 7-6

As you can probably guess, selecting this default option allows you to add a new, blank module to a page. However, when adding a module, you need to define some parameters.

First, you need to select the type of module you want to add from the Module drop-down menu. All modules you have installed will be included in this menu. Second, you need to give the module a title by entering it in the Title field. This will be the actual title displayed in the title area of the module. If you don't enter a module title, a default title, defined by the module, will be applied.

Next, you need to define the level of permissions for your new module using the Visibility drop-down menu. The default selection is Same As Page, which means the new module being added will inherit the permissions from the current page. The other option in the Visibility drop-down menu is Page Editors Only, which means the new module being added will be viewable and edited by Administrators only. If you select this option when adding a module, you will see a red border around it with the label that reads "Visible By Administrators Only." This red border and label indicate that the module is viewable only by administrators and not by general visitors. The reason for this is so administrators can add content to a page without anyone seeing it. Once finished, an administrator can assign the proper permissions to make the content visible. With the Action menu, described later in this chapter, the permissions can be changed to make the module viewable by general visitors.

Next, you need to define which content pane the new module will be placed in by making a selection from the Pane drop-down menu. The default selection is ContentPane. The Pane drop-down menu will include all content panes for the current skin defined at the skin level.

You then need to decide if the new module is going to be added at the top or bottom of a content pane by making a selection from the Insert drop-down menu. The default selection is Bottom. It is important to note that modules can only be placed above or below other modules within a content pane. Modules cannot be placed side-by-side other modules within the same content pane.

The last parameter that can be defined is the horizontal alignment of a new module being added using the Align drop-down menu. The default selection is Left. The other Align options are Center, Right, and Not Specified. It is important to note that module content alignment is usually defined at the skin level, making the Align selection usually irrelevant. After all parameters have been defined, simply click the Add icon to add your new module to a page.

Adding Existing Modules to a Page

The second option for adding modules is Add Existing Module, as shown in Figure 7-7.

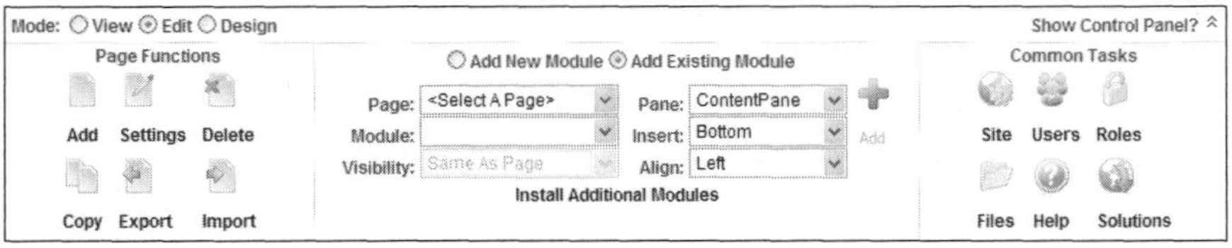

Figure 7-7

This option enables you to add an instance of a module that has already been added to another page. This is an easy way to create a single block of content that gets shared and updated across any number of pages you decide. That's right — any updates that are performed to an existing module are automatically applied globally, no matter which instance of the module you choose to update, or which page the instance is on. As you can imagine, this feature can be a huge time-saver!

The process of defining the parameters when adding an existing module is a little different than adding a new module. When you select the Add Existing Module radio button, Module and Title drop-down selections are replaced by Page and Module drop-down selections.

To add an existing module, select a page from the Page drop-down menu (this populates the Module drop-down menu with all of the modules included on the selected page). Then, choose the module you want to add from the Module drop-down menu.

Next, define the additional Visibility, Pane, Insert, and Align parameters just as you would when adding a new module. Finally, click the Add button to inject the module into the selected content pane. Now that you have learned how to add modules to a page, it's a good time to detail the available features for editing module settings (not content).

The Action Menu

The Action menu contains a number of configuration options and is similar for all modules (with the exception of one or two options being module-specific). Typically, the Action menu is located next to a module's title and is indicated by a downward-facing arrow icon. Table 7-1 outlines the general options that are available for all modules.

Table 7-1: Action Menu Options

Option	Description
Import Content	Enables you, to import a module's content from a single XML file. This option is only available with modules that support IPortable (the ability to import/export report definitions).
Export Content	Enables you to export a module's content to a single XML file. This option is only available with modules that support IPortable (the ability to import/export report definitions).
Help	Links to the configured help for each specific module, depending on the help methods module developers have implemented.
Online Help	Links to online help resources on www.dotnetnuke.com.
Settings	Enables you to edit various options of the selected module.
Basic Settings	Shown in Figure 7-8, includes the Module Title and Permissions options.
Advanced Settings	Also shown in Figure 7-8, allow you to display the module on all pages, define a header and footer for the module, and provide a start and end date for displaying the content contained in the module.
Page Settings	Shown in Figure 7-9, includes options for controlling the display of the module such as: Icon (typically in the title bar) Alignment (within the content pane) Color (content area) Border (content area) Visibility (the default visibility for the module) Additional options include: Display Container (show or hide) Allow Print (enable printing if this option has been added to the container at the skin level) Allow Syndicate (share content via RSS) Module Container (allows you to change the container applied to the module) Cache (the amount of time module is kept in cache) The Advanced section of Page Settings, also shown in Figure 7-9, allows the authorized user to define the settings of a module as the default settings for all new modules, apply the settings to all modules, and/or move the module to another page within the website.

Option	Description
	The final section, HTML Module Settings, also shown in Figure 7-9, enables you to use Token Replacement, which allows you to display information such as the username, date, and portal title directly within the text of modules.
Delete	Allows you to delete the module. Deleting the module will remove it from the page and place it in the recycle bin located under the Admin menu.
Move	Allows you to move the selected module to another content pane within the same page.

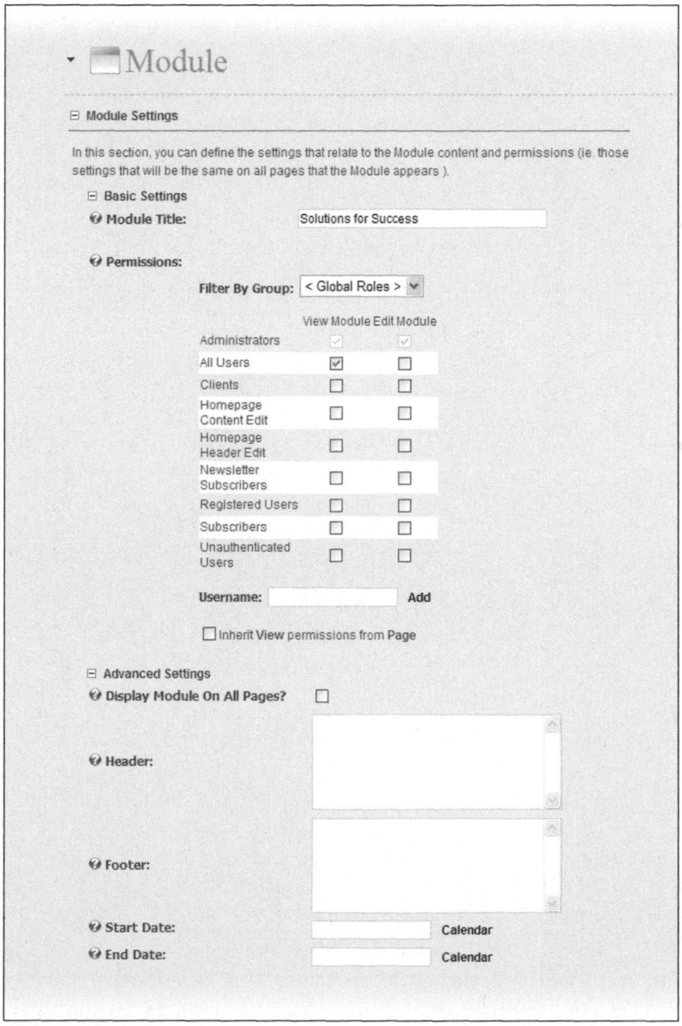

Figure 7-8

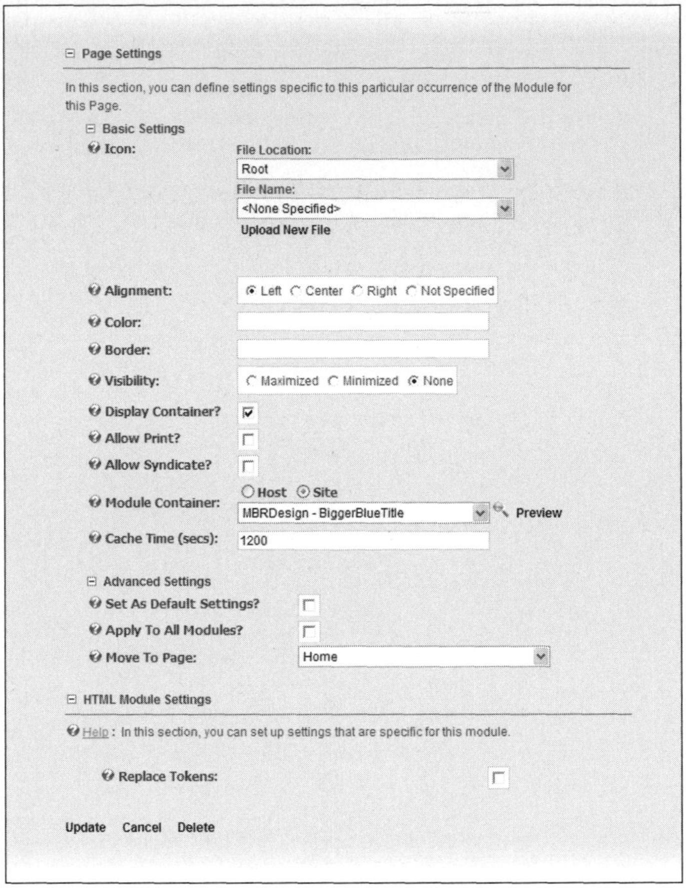

Figure 7-9

Moving Modules within the Same Page

There are two ways to move modules to different locations within the same page. The first is drag-and-drop. Just as the term suggests, drag-and-drop enables an authorized user to select a module, drag it to a new location within the same content pane or to a different content pane, and then drop it there.

To drag-and-drop a module to a new location, click and hold with your mouse on the title of a module. When the entire module is highlighted, drag it to a new location (into the same content pane above or below other modules, or into a different content pane above or below other modules). When the content pane you are dragging the module into is highlighted, as well as the area above or below modules, release your mouse button to drop the module into its new location. Figure 7-10 shows the action of moving a module from the RightPane to the top of the ContentPane using the drag-and-drop feature.

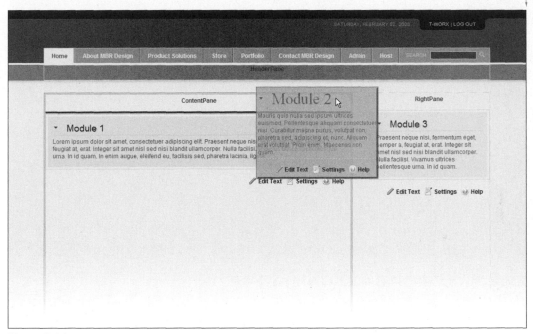

Figure 7-10

The second way to move a module to a different location within the same page is to use the Move feature located at the bottom of the Action menu. You can see the Action menu icons to the left of the module titles in Figure 7-8 and Figure 7-10. To move a module to a new location within the same page (top, up, or down within the same content pane, or to a different content pane altogether) using the Action menu, hover over the Action menu icon (the downward-facing arrow), navigate to the Move item at the bottom of the Action menu, and select an option, as shown in Figure 7-11. The Move submenu displays all content panes available on the current page, not including the pane the module is currently in.

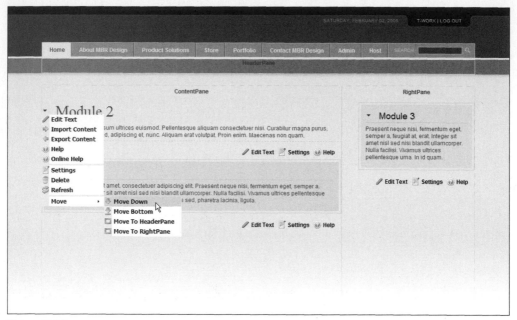

Figure 7-11

Moving Modules to a Different Page

As you have seen, moving modules within the same page is quite easy. But what if you want to move modules to a different page within the website? As you will now see, this takes almost as little effort.

First, hover over the Action menu icon and navigate to Settings or click the Settings icon/link typically located at the bottom of the module, as shown in Figure 7-12. Most skinners include a similar Settings icon/link on module containers to make navigation efficient.

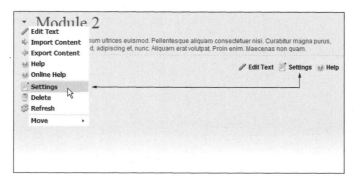

Figure 7-12

This loads the Module Settings. Similar to Page Settings, Module Settings enable you to define the settings that relate to the Module content and permissions. After navigating to this page, scroll down to expand Page Settings, and then scroll a little further to expand Advanced Settings. Next to the Move To Page option, select a page on your site from the drop-down list, as shown in Figure 7-13. Then, click the Update link at the bottom of the page to move your page to its new location.

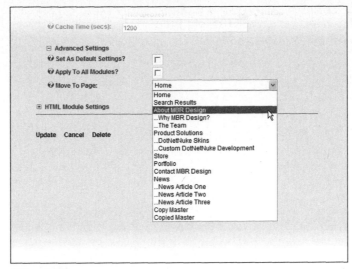

Figure 7-13

When moving a module to a different page, it is inserted into a content pane with the same ID as its original location (the content pane it resides in). If no content pane exists with the same ID on the page the module is being moved to, it is automatically inserted into the ContentPane.

Deleting Modules

To delete a module, simply select Delete from the Action menu and confirm the deletion by clicking OK.

Containers

As you learned in Chapter 5, containers can be applied globally via Admin ⇨ Site Settings. However, containers can also be applied at the module level, giving you the freedom to use different containers when applying content to your website. To apply a different container to a module, first select Settings from the Action menu to navigate to the Module Settings page. Next, scroll down and expand Page Settings. Then, next to the Module Container option, select a container from the drop-down list, as shown in Figure 7-14. Then, click the Update link at the bottom of the page to apply the new container.

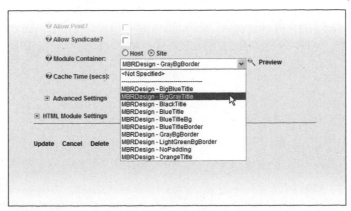

Figure 7-14

When the Site radio button is selected next to the Module Containers option, only the containers available to the current portal will be listed in the drop-down menu. Select the Host radio button to display the containers available to all portals on the same DNN instance.

The Text/HTML Module

As mentioned in the beginning of this chapter, there are several core modules included with DNN that allow you to add specific types of content providing a solid base of tools for professional content implementation. As you use them over and over and get accustomed to configuring them, you'll be able to deploy content with very little effort. However, there is one module in particular that has become one of the most important tools when talking about online content editing. Of course, I'm talking about the Text/HTML module, and it deserves some special attention.

As I mentioned earlier, the Text/HTML module is the most widely used and essential module for adding content to a DNN website, as you can use it to extend your site's capabilities without the need for a great deal of additional modules. The Text/HTML module provides a ton of flexibility when adding content because it has an integrated Microsoft Word–like interface that most people are familiar with. This allows you to add all types of content without knowing much, if any, HTML code. However, you also have the option to paste your own HTML code directly in the editor while in Source mode (great for all of you designer/developer types that prefer to create content locally and simply paste your code in the editor — just don't forget to upload your images!).

The Text/HTML editor that is now part of the core set of DNN modules is the FCKeditor, which is one of the best free online rich text editors on the Internet. The FCKeditor's rich set of features is well known and is the reason it has become very popular among DNN users. In fact, it is a big step up from the text editors that were part of the DNN core set of modules early on, as it provides much more capabilities for adding and editing content easily.

Synching CSS Styles to the Text/HTML Module

Before you add content using the Text/HTML module, I highly recommend you make a simple update to the module's Custom Editor Options. As a default, when editing content inside the Text/HTML module, the CSS styles are displayed via the Static mode, which means the content will not be displayed using the same CSS styles that were created with the skins. This default mode uses a generic set of CSS styles to display content within the editor. The update I am referring to will allow you to view and edit content using all the same CSS styles that were created in the skin.css and displayed throughout the site. This will make your life much easier when editing content inside the Text/HTML module. To update the Custom Editor Options, use the following steps:

1. Add a Text/HTML module to a page by selecting the Text/HTML Module from the Module drop-down list (the Add New Module radio button will be selected as a default), as shown in Figure 7-15. After you select the Text/HTML Module from the drop-down list, define the Title, Visibility, Pane, Insert, and Align parameters. Then click the Add button to add your module to a page.

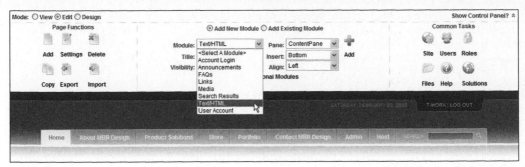

Figure 7-15

2. Select Edit Text from the Action menu or from the Action button at the bottom of the module container, as shown in Figure 7-16.

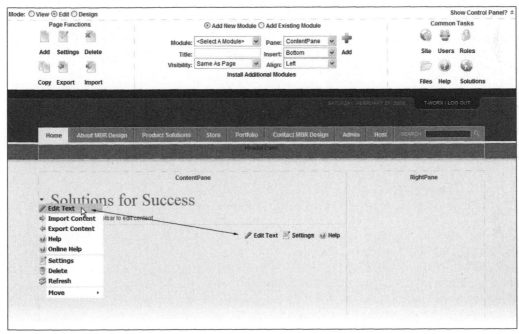

Figure 7-16

This launches the Text/HTML FCKeditor, as shown in Figure 7-17.

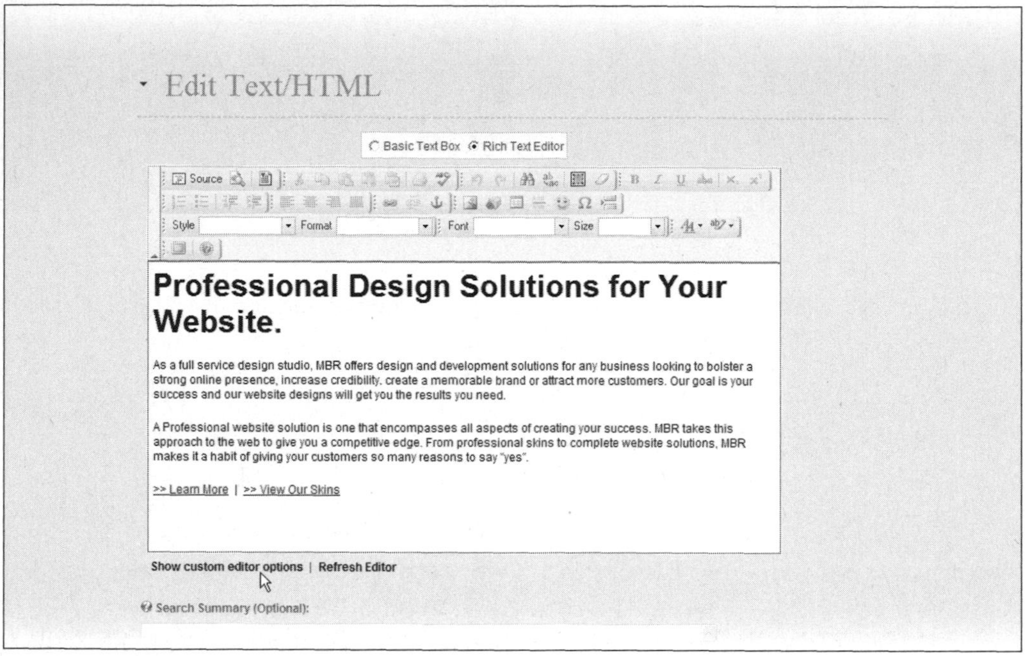

Figure 7-17

As you can see, a few lines of text were added in the editor. However, notice the generic formatting of the content. If you click Update at this point, the editor closes, your page refreshes, and you would see the content applied in the correct CSS styles as defined in the skin.css. But that doesn't really help while creating content inside the editor itself because you can't see the correct styles while editing. Therefore, to see the correct CSS styles in the editor, you need to make a change to the custom editor options.

3. Click Show custom editor options to launch the FCKeditor custom options pop-up window, as shown in Figure 7-18.

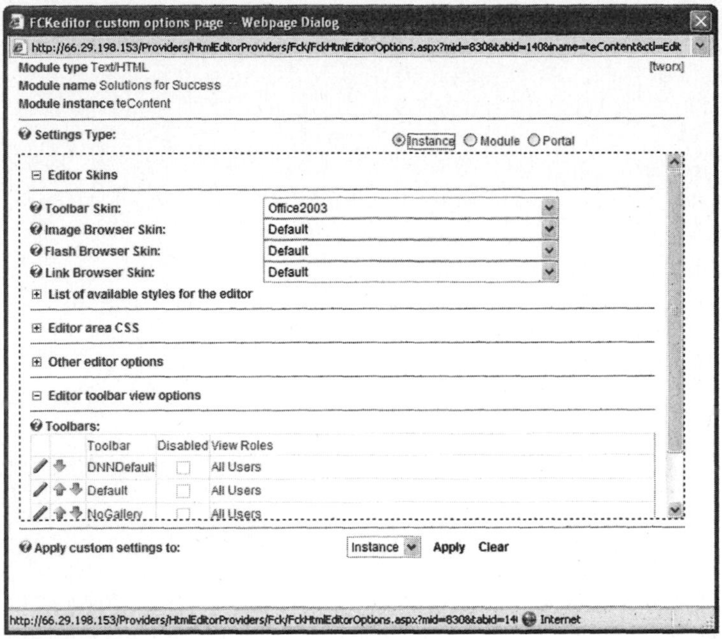

Figure 7-18

There are just a few settings you need to change to get all of the correct CSS styles to display in the editor. Figure 7-18 shows the default settings of the FCKeditor custom options page. As a default, Instance is selected as the Settings Type. This needs to be changed.

4. Change the Settings Type to Portal, as shown in Figure 7-19.

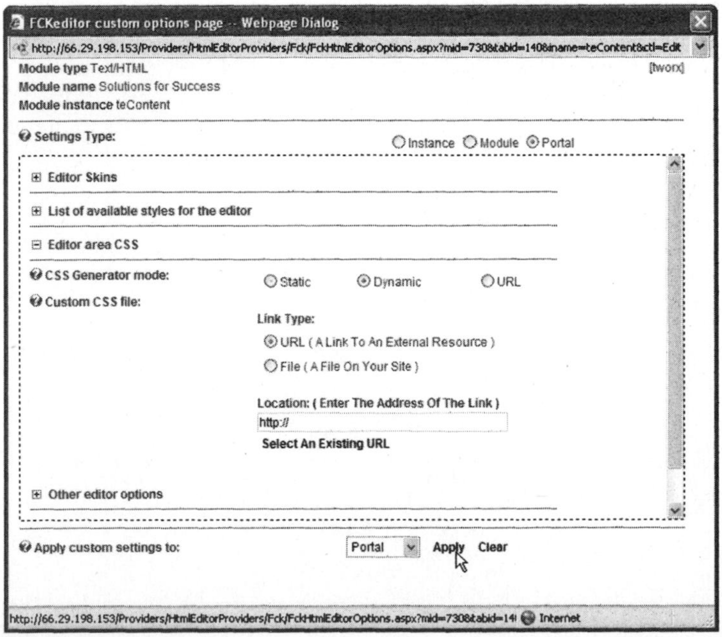

Figure 7-19

5. The only other settings you need to change involve the Editor Area CSS, so in Figure 7-19, I've collapsed all other settings and exposed only the Editor Area CSS settings. As another default, Static is selected as the CSS Generator Mode. As shown in Figure 7-19, this needs to be changed to Dynamic.

6. To get the correct CSS styles to display in the editor, simply click Apply, as shown in Figure 7-19.

7. After clicking Apply and confirming the custom values change, close the FCKeditor custom options page.

8. Click the Refresh Editor link under the editor window, as shown in Figure 7-20.

Figure 7-20

After clicking the Refresh Editor, notice how the content in the editor changes to match the site, as shown in Figure 7-21. The CSS styles have now been synched with the skin.css, which is the overriding CSS stylesheet for the entire site.

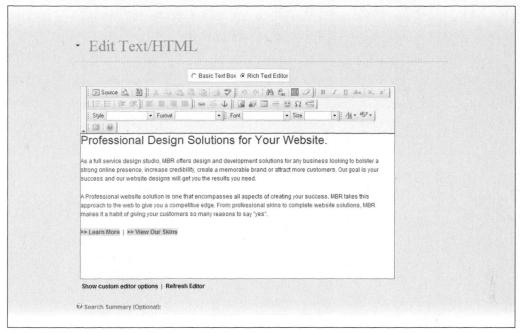

Figure 7-21

Customizing CSS Styles for Use within the Text/HTML Module

Now, because the CSS styles have been synched with the skin.css (which again, is the overriding stylesheet for the site), wouldn't it be nice if the same CSS styles designed for the site were available directly within the editor via a simple drop-down list? You would think this would happen automatically, but unfortunately, it doesn't. (If you look at the styles in the Style drop-down list, you see just a few default CSS styles that don't match the styles available in the skin.css.) But the good news is that you can define the specific CSS styles that are available via the Style drop-down list using a single XML file. This makes it easy for administrators to edit content directly using the CSS styles created for the site. As you can imagine, this makes editing very intuitive for administrators who may have little-to-no experience with HTML.

In the custom editor options, you have the ability to define the list of available CSS styles to be used by the FCKeditor. In some cases, you may have to follow specific style guidelines defined as part of a client's brand. Therefore, you'll want to have a limited list of styles for use among different administrators to ensure consistency and integrity of content style from page to page on your website. To define the list of styles available for use within the FCKeditor, use the following steps:

1. Click the Show custom editor options once again to launch the FCKeditor custom options window. By doing so, you have the ability to define the List of available styles used by the editor. Because you only want to show these custom options, you'll expand the List of available styles for the editor and collapse all of the other options, as shown in Figure 7-22.

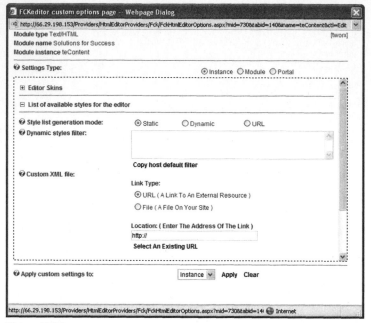

Figure 7-22

The default Setting Type is Instance and the default setting for the Style list is Static. However, because you want to generate your own custom list of styles using a file you specify, these options need to be changed.

2. Change the Setting Type to Portal by selecting the Portal option (see Figure 7-23).

3. Next to the Style list generation mode, select the URL option (see Figure 7-23). This URL will be a file on the website you define in the next step.

4. Select the File (A File On Your Site) option next to Custom XML file. Selecting the File option allows you to choose a file that already exists on the website or upload a new file. Also shown in Figure 7-23, you can see that a CustomStyles.xml stylesheet file has been selected.

5. Click the Apply link to apply these settings to the website, also shown in Figure 7-23.

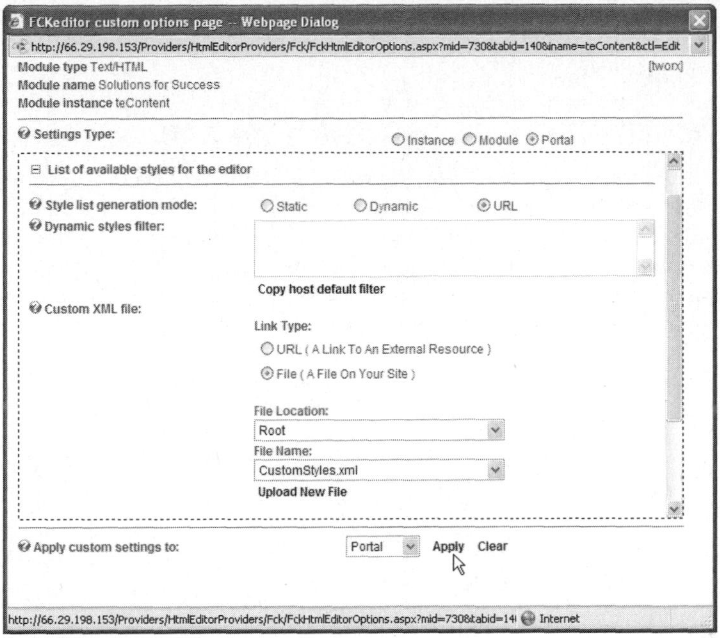

Figure 7-23

After your settings are applied successfully to the website, you can close the FCKeditor custom options window and update the editor by clicking Refresh Editor. And now, if you look at the Styles drop-down list within the editor (see Figure 7-24), you can see it contains styles (being pulled from the skin.css) you have specified using a CustomStyles.xml file, which I'll detail next.

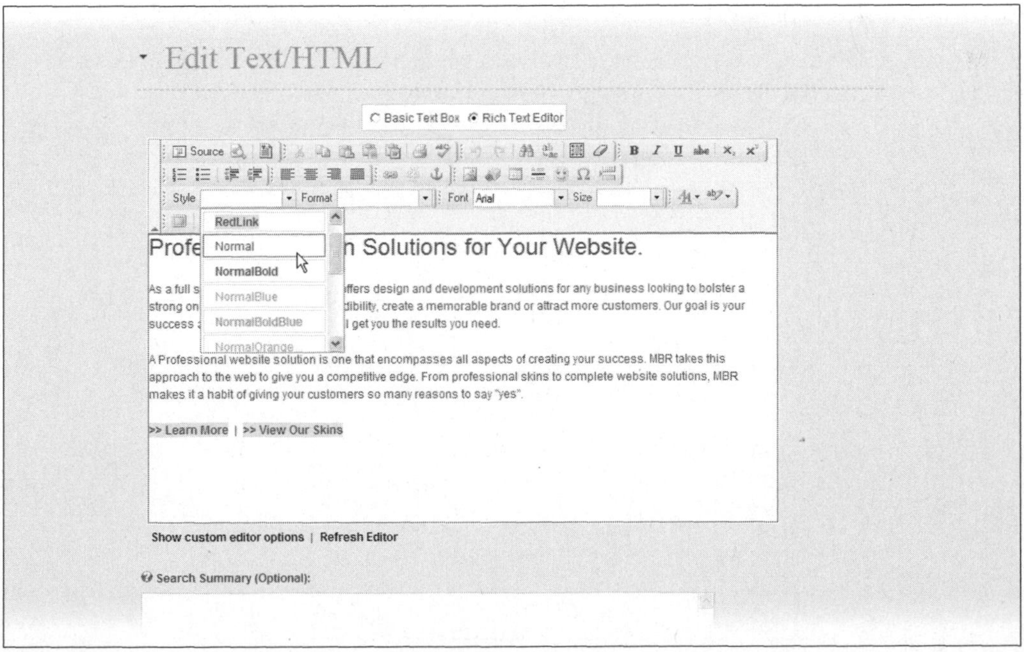

Figure 7-24

You can now easily apply specific CSS styles that were created for the website to content within the Text/HTML editor by simply selecting or highlighting an element in the editor and choosing a CSS style from the Style drop-down list.

Customizing Text/HTML Module CSS Styles via XML

You just learned how to make custom CSS styles available in the Text/HTML module by defining a custom XML file. And about now you're probably telling yourself, "That's great, but how do I define the CSS styles used in the custom XML file, and how hard is it to implement?" Let me answer the first question by explaining how to edit the XML file to include the specific CSS styles you want to pull from the skin.css for display in the editor. As I answer the first question, I think the answer to the second question will be obvious to you. But let me give you a hint . . . it's easy!

The first thing required in the CustomStyles.xml file (you can name this file whatever you want) code, is a Root element called Styles:

```
<Styles>

</Styles>
```

Inside this root Styles element, each Style is defined with a Style name and the type of element that is being affected:

```
<Style name="Link" element="span">

</Style>
```

Within each Style, CSS class attributes are defined:

```
    <Attribute name="class" value="RedLink" />
```

Attribute values specifically correlate to the styles located in the skin.css file, which in this case is a custom link style created for the MBR Design sample website.

Now let's look at all the code contained in the CustomStyles.xml file:

```
<?xml version="1.0" encoding="utf-8" ?>

<Styles>
  <Style name="Link" element="span">
    <Attribute name="class" value="Link" />
  </Style>
  <Style name="RedLink" element="span">
    <Attribute name="class" value="RedLink" />
  </Style>
  <Style name="Normal" element="span">
    <Attribute name="class" value="Normal" />
  </Style>
  <Style name="NormalBold" element="span">
    <Attribute name="class" value="NormalBold" />
  </Style>
  <Style name="NormalBlue" element="span">
    <Attribute name="class" value="NormalBlue" />
```

```
      </Style>
      <Style name="NormalBoldBlue" element="span">
        <Attribute name="class" value="NormalBoldBlue" />
      </Style>
      <Style name="NormalOrange" element="span">
      <Attribute name="class" value="NormalOrange" />
      </Style>
      <Style name="NormalBoldOrange" element="span">
        <Attribute name="class" value="NormalBoldOrange" />
      </Style>
      <Style name="NormalRed" element="span">
        <Attribute name="class" value="NormalRed" />
      </Style>
      <Style name="NormalBoldRed" element="span">
        <Attribute name="class" value="NormalBoldRed" />
      </Style>
      <Style name="SubHead" element="span">
        <Attribute name="class" value="SubHead" />
      </Style>
      <Style name="Title H1" element="h1" />
      <Style name="Title H2" element="h2" />
      <Style name="Title H3" element="h3" />
    </Styles>
```

You can see that not all of the CSS styles found in the skin.css are included, as this would be too much for Administrators to sift through each time they want to apply a style via the Style drop-down list from inside the text editor. Only certain CSS styles deemed applicable to website administrators have been included in the XML file. Also note that H1, H2, and H3 styles have no attributes defined for them because they are HTML tags for formatting and not classes.

You have now learned how to totally customize the CSS styles used within the FCKeditor, and how to link them to the Text/HTML module. I trust you will find the information in this lesson to be quite valuable, as you will use the Text/HTML module extensively with your own DNN projects.

Adding Basic Content Using the Text/HTML Module

Now that you have set up the Text/HTML module with the correct styles for the MBR Design website, let's take a look at some of its key features as you add content to a page. Figure 7-25 shows a Text/HTML module with content that has been added to it. As you can see, the H1 style has been applied to the first line (simply using the Style drop-down list). And because no other formatting has been applied, the other content is displayed, by default, using the Normal CSS style.

Figure 7-25

Here's what the HTML looks like so far:

```
<h1>Professional Design Solutions for Your Website.</h1>
<p>As a full service design studio, MBR offers design and development solutions for
any business looking to bolster a strong online presence, increase credibility,
create a memorable brand or attract more customers. Our goal is your success and
our website designs will get you the results you need.</p>
<p>A Professional website solution is one that encompasses all aspects of creating
your success. MBR takes this approach to the web to give you a competitive edge.
From professional skins to complete website solutions, MBR makes it a habit of
giving your customers so many reasons to say "yes".</p>
<p>&gt;&gt; Learn More | &gt;&gt; View Our Skins</p>
<p></p>
```

Now, let's apply a link to >>Learn More by highlighting the text and clicking the Link icon, as shown in Figure 7-26.

Figure 7-26

This launches the Link dialog box. Within this window, click the Browse Server button, as shown in Figure 7-27.

Figure 7-27

This opens the Link Gallery, as shown in Figure 7-28.

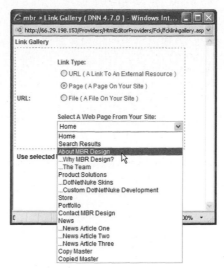

Figure 7-28

The default Link Type is URL, which provides a simple text field to enter an address for the link. However, because you want to link the selected >>Learn More text to a page on the MBR Design site, you'll select the Page radio button under Link Type. After a quick refresh, you'll have the option to select the About MBR Design from all the pages with the website hierarchy. After the About MBR Design page is selected from the drop-down list, click Use selected link to close this window, as shown in Figure 7-29.

Figure 7-29

Next, click OK in the Link dialog box to apply the link to the >>Learn More text, as shown in Figure 7-30.

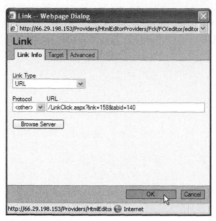

Figure 7-30

Figure 7-31 shows the >>Learn More text, which now links to the About MBR Design page when clicked, displayed in the default CSS link style. As you can see, you have also applied a link to the >>View Our Skins text using the same linking method described previously.

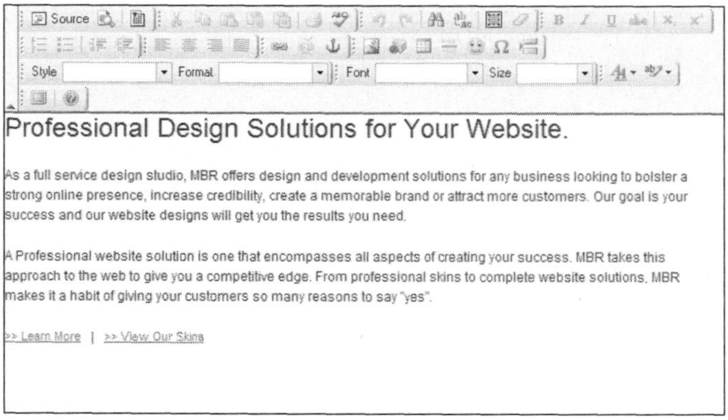

Figure 7-31

Here's a look at the HTML with the links applied:

```
<h1>Professional Design Solutions for Your Website.</h1>
<p>As a full service design studio, MBR offers design and development solutions for
any business looking to bolster a strong online presence, increase credibility,
create a memorable brand or attract more customers. Our goal is your success and
our website designs will get you the results you need.</p>
```

```
<p>A Professional website solution is one that encompasses all aspects of creating
your success. MBR takes this approach to the web to give you a competitive edge.
From professional skins to complete website solutions, MBR makes it a habit of
giving your customers so many reasons to say "yes".</p>
<p><a href="/LinkClick.aspx?link=158&amp;tabid=140">&gt;&gt; Learn More</a> | <a
href="/LinkClick.aspx?link=180&amp;tabid=140">&gt;&gt; View Our Skins</a></p>
<p></p>
```

Next, add an image to your module. The first thing you need to do is place your cursor in the text where you want the image to be inserted (before the first paragraph) and click the Image icon to launch the Image Properties dialog box, as shown in Figure 7-32.

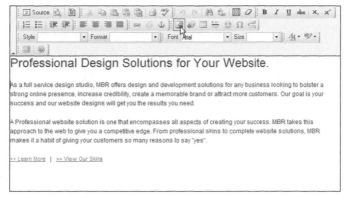

Figure 7-32

Next, click the Browse Server button, as shown in Figure 7-33, to launch the Image Gallery.

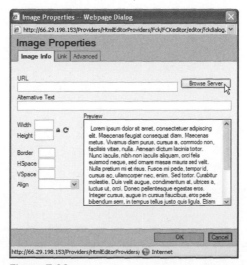

Figure 7-33

The Image Gallery, as shown in Figure 7-34, displays all of the images that have been uploaded to the site that are available to insert/use as content. However, because the image you want to use isn't available to the site yet, you have the option to upload a single image from within the Image Gallery by clicking the Browse button, also shown in Figure 7-34.

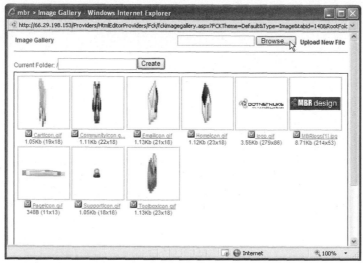

Figure 7-34

After you have uploaded a new image, it is displayed in the Image Gallery and available to add to the Text/HTML module by simply clicking on it to select it, as shown in Figure 7-35.

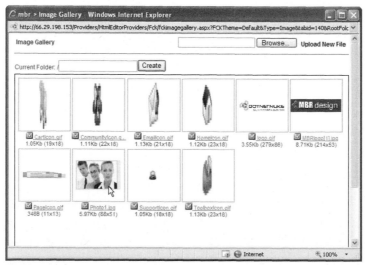

Figure 7-35

Selecting the image will close the Image Gallery window and display image formatting options in the Image Properties dialog box, as shown in Figure 7-36. The actual height and width of the image is applied automatically, but this can be changed. However, I don't recommend ever changing the dimensions of an image after it has been uploaded to the site because pixel degradation is a distinct possibility, resulting in reduced image quality.

Among the image options, you'll want to define the Alternative Text with something descriptive, so visitors using screen readers will have an idea of what the image is. You also have the option to apply a border and define horizontal and/or vertical space around the image.

Setting the alignment of an inserted image is important, and DNN makes it easy to determine which setting works best for a specific image using the Preview window. As you change the settings in the Align drop-down menu, the Preview window is updated, giving you a very good idea of how the image will be inserted into your content.

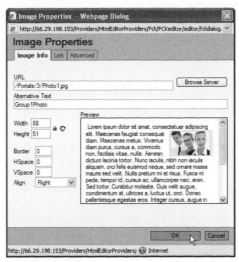

Figure 7-36

After clicking OK and returning to the editor, you can see your image as it has been placed within the content based on the properties you defined. However, what if you change your mind about the alignment of the image in relation to the content? No worries. Simply right-click on an image and select Image Properties from the drop-down menu, as shown in Figure 7-37, to easily change image alignment or any other image property. This opens the Image Properties dialog box, enabling you to make any changes you like.

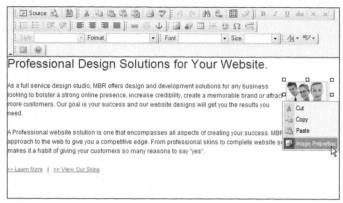

Figure 7-37

Here's the completed HTML for the content you just added:

```
<h1>Professional Design Solutions for Your Website.</h1>
<p><img height="70" alt="" hspace="0" width="88" align="left" border="0"
src="/Portals/3/Photo1.jpg" />As a full service design studio, MBR offers design
and development solutions for any business looking to bolster a strong online
presence, increase credibility, create a memorable brand or attract more customers.
Our goal is your success and our website designs will get you the results you
need.</p>
<p>A Professional website solution is one that encompasses all aspects of creating
your success. MBR takes this approach to the web to give you a competitive edge.
From professional skins to complete website solutions, MBR makes it a habit of
giving your customers so many reasons to say "yes".</p>
<p><a href="/LinkClick.aspx?link=158&amp;tabid=140">&gt;&gt; Learn More</a> | <a
href="/LinkClick.aspx?link=180&amp;tabid=140">&gt;&gt; View Our Skins</a></p>
<p></p>
```

In order to apply the content you just added in the Text/HTML module to your page, there is but one thing left to do. And that, of course, is to click the Update link. Figure 7-38 shows the result of adding the newly populated Text/HTML module to the home page.

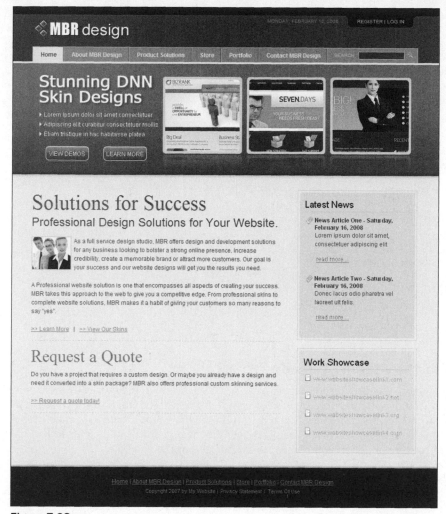

Figure 7-38

As you can see, the home page also includes a few other modules with content applied to them. Next, we'll focus on the Media module, which I've used to apply the image in the HeaderPane.

There's no question that you'll use the Text/HTML module for adding most of the content within your DNN website. There are many options within the editor, and I've only touched on a few key features that make it easy to create professional-looking content in minutes with simple formatting. As you gain more experience using the Text/HTML module, you'll discover many additional features that make it easy to add content and control its format consistently.

The Media Module

When you need to add images, video, or other types of media to a DNN page, you can turn to the Media module for help. The Media module replaces the Image module that was used in early versions of DotNetNuke and now includes support for the following additional file types:

- Audio Interchange File Format (AIFF)
- Audio Video Interleave (AVI)
- Moving Pictures Expert Group (MPEG)
- MP3 (Audio aspect of MPEG)
- Musical Instrument Digital Interface (MIDI)
- QuickTime (MOV)
- Real Video (RM, RAM)
- Shockwave Flash (SWF)
- Waveform (WAV)
- Windows Media Formats (ASF, ASX,WMA,WMV)
- And, of course, images

Configuring the Media Module

I'm going to show you how to add the image to the header, shown in Figure 7-38, with very little effort. First, add a Media module to the page by selecting it from the Module drop-down list in the Control Panel, adding a Title, selecting the HeaderPane from the Pane drop-down list, and clicking the Add icon, as shown in Figure 7-39. This places an instance of the Media module in the HeaderPane with the default BigBlueTitle container applied (as defined in the Site Settings).

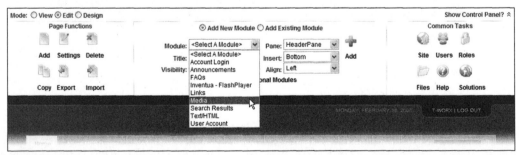

Figure 7-39

Because you don't want the container title to be visible, you need to hide the container by selecting Settings from the module Action menu, maximizing the Page Settings, clearing the box next to Display Container and finally, clicking Update, as shown in Figure 7-40.

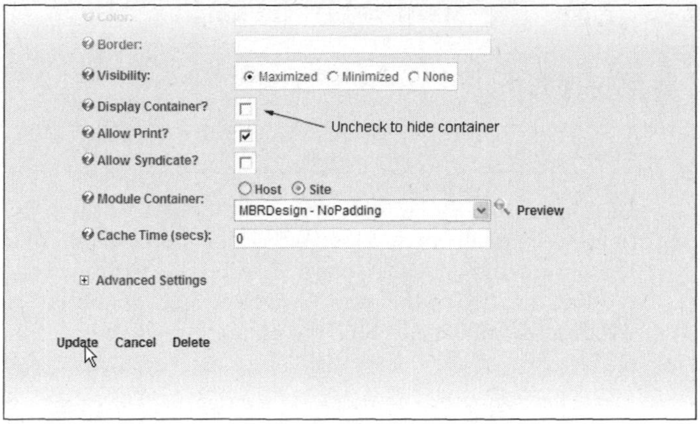

Figure 7-40

Next, add the header image to the Media module by selecting Edit Media Options from the top of the module Action menu. This will open the Edit Media page where you can define the options, shown in Figure 7-41, for this specific instance of the Media module.

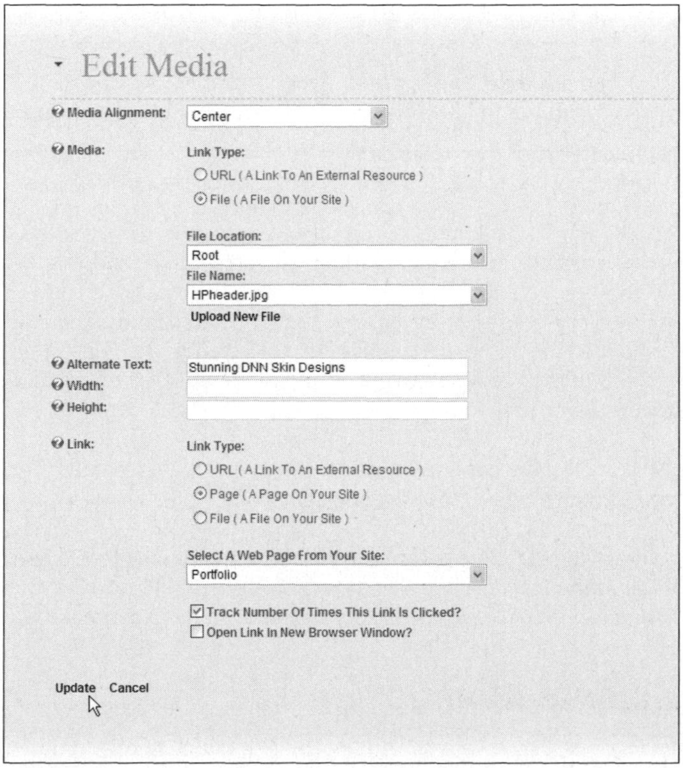

Figure 7-41

The various options for configuring the Media module are detailed in Table 7-2.

Table 7-2: Media Module Setting

Function	Description
Media Alignment	Use this setting for better control over the alignment of the Media module. The default option is to Use Module Settings Value. This will align the module using the settings that are applied within the Control Panel at the time the module is added to the page. Other available alignment options within the drop-down list are None (no alignment will be specified), Left, Center, and Right.
Media	Select the media file you wish to display. Selecting URL allows you to select the location of the media file. Selecting File allows you to select a file directly within your DNN website.
Alternate Text	This is the text that will be displayed by browsers that are not able to display the actual Media. Alternate Text is required.
Width	This is where you enter a width (in pixels) for the Media. If no value is entered, the width will match the actual image width.
Height	This is where you enter a height (in pixels) for the Media. If no value is entered, the height will match the actual image height.
Other Options	You also have the option to Track Number Of Times This Link Is Clicked And Open Link In New Browser Window by simply selecting the checkboxes.

As you can see in Figure 7-41, an Alignment of Center has been selected from the Media Alignment drop-down list. This ensures that the Media module will be center-aligned within the HeaderPane.

The HPheader.jpg image has already been uploaded to the site. Therefore, the File Link Type radio button has been selected and the HPheader.jpg has been selected in the File Name drop-down list. If an image has not been added to the site, you can click Upload New File to upload a new file and choose it from the File Name drop-down list.

Next, Stunning DNN Skin Designs has been added in the required Alternative Text field and the Portfolio page was selected as the link from this image.

The only thing left to do is click Update to add the HPheader.jpg image to the Media module. This adds the Media module to the HeaderPane exactly as it is shown in Figure 7-38 when in View mode or when logged out. To delete a module, simply select Delete from the Action menu.

The Announcements Module

The next module I focus on is also used extensively. The Announcements module is used for displaying news items on your site; it's very handy for making your website visitors aware of content that may have links to additional information, such as case studies or news articles (one Announcements module can contain many announcements). It's also a module that makes great work of one of my favorite features of the DNN application — the ability to define, publish, and expire dates on pages, or in this case, a module. And it happens to work quite well for content such as news articles because you may want only current articles being displayed at any given time. It also works quite well for promotional content when you have a special offer that has a specific timeframe.

When contemplating using the Announcements module to link to additional content, it's quite helpful to think in reverse. Let me explain what I mean. When used for a news article, you add an Announcements module to a page that includes a title, short lead-in or summary, and a Read More link that links to a complete article/page. When configuring the module, you define the actual link within the settings for the Announcements module. If you don't have the complete article already created on your website, you have nothing to link to. So working in reverse, you first add the complete article by creating a new hidden page on the website (if you forgot how to create a hidden page, refer to the last chapter or keep reading through Step 1 in the list that follows) and add the article content. Then, you would add an announcement and link to the completed article. Even if the article content isn't complete, at least you already have the page created and linked to from the Announcements module, so the only remaining task is to edit the article content. This makes perfect sense because typically, the short lead-in or summary is derived from a full article anyway.

Configuring the Announcements Module

Without further ado, let's add the Latest News module to the right pane shown in Figure 7-38 and link its two contained announcements to hidden pages using the following steps:

1.   Add two new hidden pages to the website and apply content to them. Remember, to make a page hidden from the navigation, simply clear the box next to Include In Menu? on the Page Management page, as shown in Figure 7-42. A page will be automatically hidden from the menu if it is added under a Parent page that is defined as hidden.

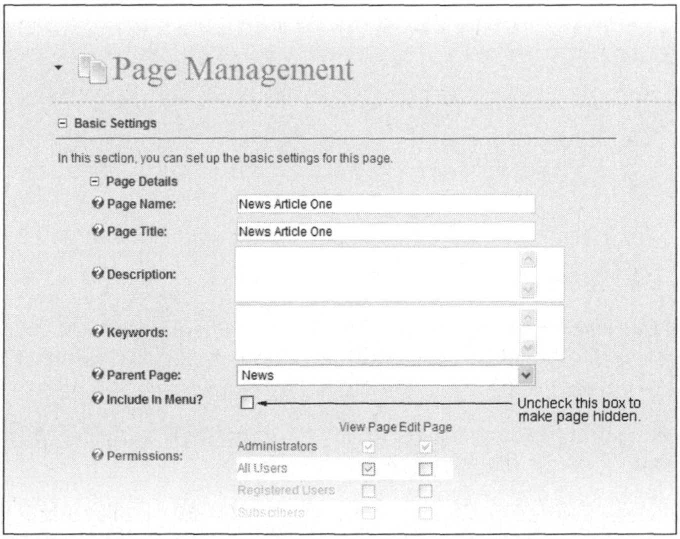

Figure 7-42

2. Add an instance of the Announcements module to a page (you should have a good handle on how to select and add a module by now).

3. Select Add Announcement from the top of the Action menu. This will launch the Edit Announcements page, as shown in Figure 7-43, allowing you to define the options for this specific instance of the module.

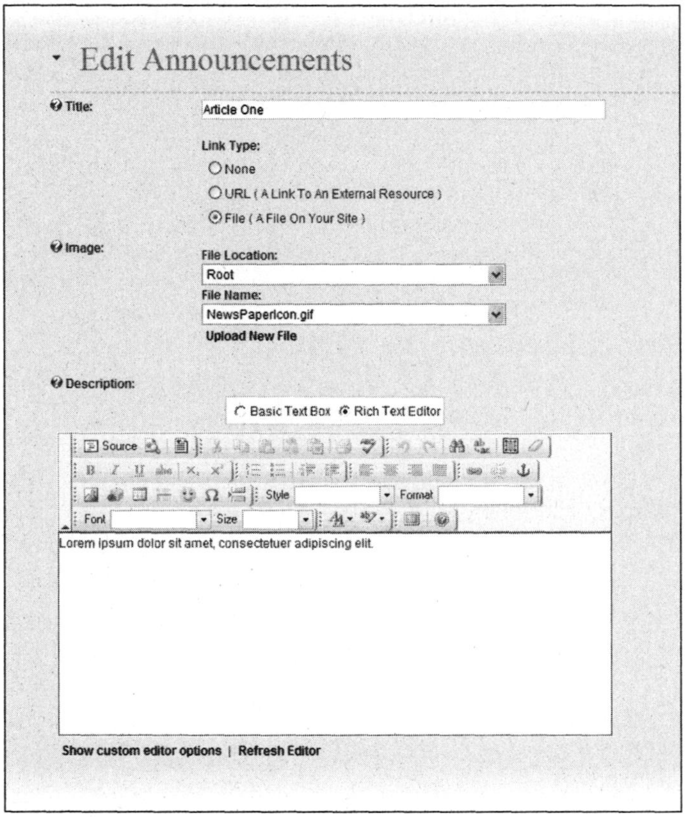

Figure 7-43

4. Enter a title for the announcement.

5. If you want to display an image next to the announcement, select a URL location or a file directly on your website using the Link Type option. Again, you can select a file that has already been uploaded to your site, or you can upload a new file.

6. Enter a short lead-in or summary in the text editor under Description. You can include images or any other content you wish.

7. Scroll down a bit further under the Description (see Figure 7-44), and choose the Link Type for the complete article. In this case, the complete article is the News Article One page within your website. However, you can link to an external source (URL) or a File on your site (PDF, for example), or you can specify a single user to view the information by selecting User and entering a username.

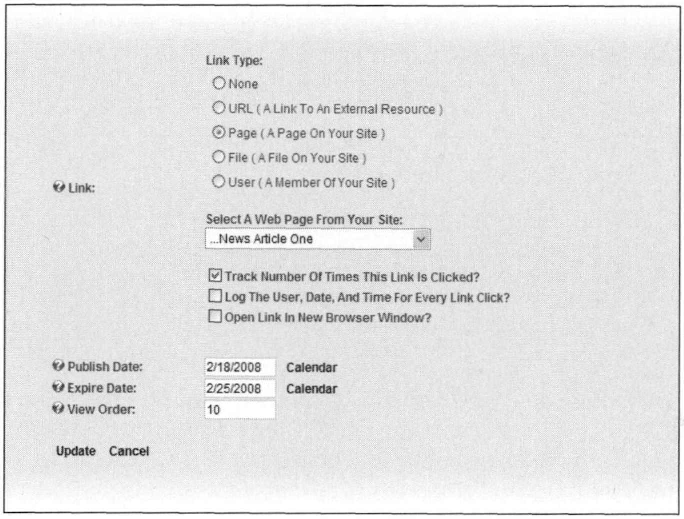

Figure 7-44

8. Next, you have a couple of additional options. You can Track the number of times the link is clicked, log the user date and time for every link click, and even open the link in a new browser, simply by checking the boxes next to these items.

9. This step includes one of my favorite features of the DNN application — the ability to define Publish and Expire dates on pages or modules. And it happens to work quite well for content, such as news articles, since you may want only current articles being displayed at any given time. It also works quite well for promotional content when you have a special offer that has a specific timeframe. Enter Publish and Expire dates in the correct default format shown in Figure 7-44, or simply click on the Calendar links to select dates from a calendar pop-up window.

10. Enter a view order for the announcement. As several announcements can be listed in descending order within the same Announcements module, DNN provides the ability to update the order using this simple function. Starting with a View Order of 10, easily gives you room to add 9 more announcements above the first one. And continuing to add additional announcements starting at 20, then 30, then 40, and so on, gives you a lot of flexibility to add announcements and change the order as you are required to do so. Allowing enough room between announcements using the View Order option provides flexibility to change the order of your announcements painlessly.

11. Click Update to add the announcement to the Announcements module on your page, as shown in Figure 7-38. As you can see, a second announcement titled Article Two was also added. You should easily be able to add this additional announcement to your module now that you understand how to add announcements! To edit announcements, click the Edit Pencil icon next to them. This loads the Edit Announcements page. To delete an Announcement, simply click Delete from the bottom of the Edit Announcements page.

The various options for configuring the Announcements module are detailed in Table 7-3.

Table 7-3: Announcement Options

Function	Description
Title	Enter a Title for the announcement.
Image	Allows you to select an image to display with the announcement. Selecting URL allows you to select the location of the image file. Selecting File allows you to select a file directly within your DNN website. You can also upload a new file.
Description	Enter the short lead-in or summary using the text editor to add any content you wish.
Link	Choose where you want the announcement to link to. Options are None (no link), URL (link to an external resource), Page (a page on your site), File (a file on your site), and User (a member of your site).
Other Options	You also have the option to Track Number Of Times This Link Is Clicked And Open Link In New Browser Window by simply selecting the checkboxes.
Publish Date	Enter the date you want an announcement to start being displayed.
Expire Date	Enter the date you want an announcement to automatically be hidden.

Customizing the Layout of the Announcements Module

The Announcements module provides a lot of flexibility when adding news-related (or other) content to a website. What's more, you can change the layout of the Announcements module by modifying a template that consists of simple HTML and tokens. Tokens are placeholders that represent some type of dynamic content. In this case, for example, the description or image associated with an Announcement is a Token.

The first thing to do to customize the display of the Announcements module is apply an Icon and/or specific Container to be used with the module. Select Settings from the Action menu, scroll down on the Module page, and maximize Page Settings. Within the Page Settings options, you can define an Icon and a specific Container of your choice.

Next, a little further down the Module page, expand the Announcement Settings to expose the options, as shown in Figure 7-45.

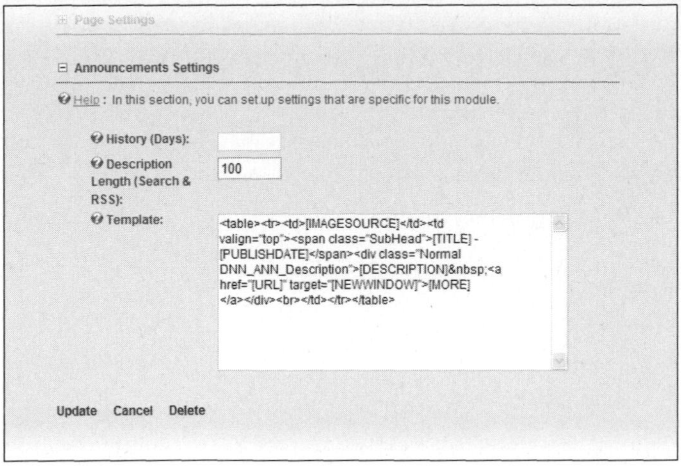

Figure 7-45

As you can see in Figure 7-45, there are a few options. You can define the number of days to display the Announcement and the Description Length — the number of characters in the description used for search results and RSS feeds. (Tip: Use 0 to use the maximum text length — 2000 characters.) But our current focus is on the Template. As you can see, the template code is simple HTML with [TOKENS]. The default template code shown in Figure 7-45 results in the following layout in Figure 7-46 with the default container applied.

Figure 7-46

You can see that the display is not terrific for a couple of reasons. First, the date is displayed in the same bold type style as the Announcement titles. Second, the date starts on the same line as the title and wraps to the next line. This presentation just doesn't look polished.

However, by making the following simple changes to the template HTML, a much more professional presentation is applied to the Announcements module, as shown in Figure 7-47. Note that I also selected (within Page Settings) a newspaper.gif icon to display beside the Announcements and applied a different Container. Also note that clicking on Module Help will provide detailed information about the available [TOKENS] and their definitions.

```
<table>
  <tr>
    <td align="left" valign="top">[IMAGESOURCE]</td>
    <td valign="top"><span class="SubHead">[TITLE]<br /></span>
      <span class="Normal">[PUBLISHDATE] -</span>
      <div class="Normal DNN_ANN_Description">[DESCRIPTION]<a href="[URL]"
target="[NEWWINDOW]">[MORE]</a></div><br />
    </td>
  </tr>
</table>
```

Figure 7-47

The Links Module

Now let's take a look at another widely used DNN module, the Links module. Quite simply, the Links module is designed to display text links in a couple of different styles and formats — period. Even though it's a module with simple functionality, that is exactly what makes it so popular and usable for maintaining links.

Configuring the Links Module

Let's add the Links module, shown in Figure 7-38, to a page. First, add an instance of the Link module to the page by selecting it from the Modules drop-down menu in the Control Panel, entering a title, selecting the RightPane as your target pane, and clicking the Add icon. This adds the Link module to the bottom of the RightPane.

Next, configure the display of the links within the Links module by selecting Settings from the Action menu. This loads the Module Settings page. When on the Module Settings page, scroll down if necessary, and expand the Links Settings. This exposes Edit Link options, shown in Figure 7-48.

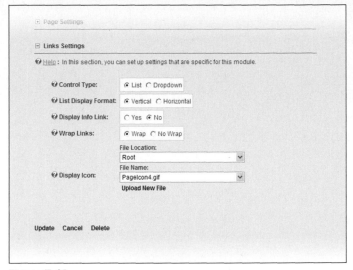

Figure 7-48

Choose a Control Type. The default Control Type is List, which displays the links as simple text items. The Dropdown List Type displays the links in a drop-down list, just as you would expect. Next, select a List Display Format. Vertical is the default selection. The List Display Format is irrelevant if Dropdown is selected as the Control Type.

Next, make a selection next to Display Info Link. The default selection is No. Choosing Yes displays an ellipsis (. . .) hyperlink that allows an optional brief text description of the link to display when the ellipsis is clicked. Unfortunately, the current version of the Links module does not use a template with tokenized text like the Announcements module. Therefore, at the time of this writing, it is not possible to change the layout of the Links module without changing the source code of the module, which I do not recommend.

Next, choose to have your links wrap to more than one line (Wrap) or force links to a single line (No Wrap). The last option is Display Icon. You can select an image that already exists on the website, upload a new image, or choose not to use an image at all by selecting None in the drop-down list.

Click update to apply the Link Settings and go back to the page containing the module.

Adding Links to the Links Module

Now that you have configured the display of the Links module, it's time to add some links. Let's start by selecting Add Link from the top of the Links module Action menu. This loads the Edit Links page, as shown in Figure 7-49, exposing the various options for adding a link.

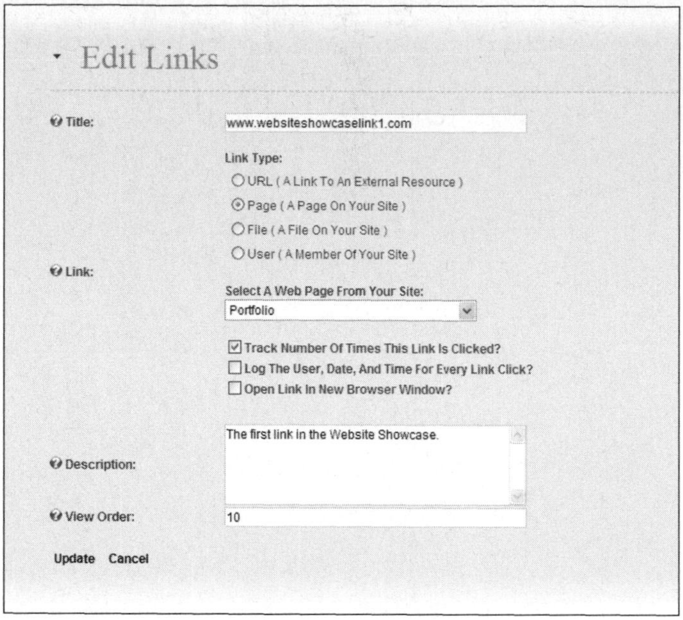

Figure 7-49

First, enter a Title for the link. Then, choose the location of the link by selecting a Link Type. Next, you can choose to track the number of times the link is clicked, log the user date and time for every link click, and open the link in a new browser.

Then, you can enter a description. This is the description that will be displayed when clicking the ellipsis to the right of the links if the Display Info Link has been activated by selecting Yes in the Links Settings. You also have the ability to define the link order for links within the Links module. Again, this makes it very easy to change the view order of links.

Finally, clicking Update results in a Links module that looks similar to the one shown in Figure 7-38.

I'm quite sure most DNN users will use the Links module a great deal because it is easy to configure (like many DNN modules) and easy to implement. It's also an easy way to provide intuitive navigation on your DNN pages.

The Survey Module

The next module we'll examine is the Survey module, shown in Figure 7-50 below. It's a great tool to get all types of feedback from your clients, customers, and users because you can create customized surveys whenever you like, which can consist of one or more survey questions that can have single or multiple choice answers. It also includes a results chart, so authorized users can quickly view the results of surveys. To keep users from submitting answers to the same survey more than once, the module uses cookies to record if a computer has already been used to submit a survey.

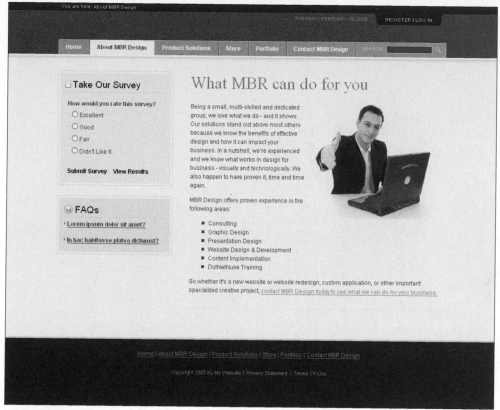

Figure 7-50

Configuring the Survey Module

Figure 7-50 displays the example Survey module (Take Our Survey), which has been added via the following steps:

1. Add the Survey module to a page by selecting it from the Module list in the Control Panel, entering an appropriate Title, selecting the LeftPane as the target pane, and clicking the Add icon.

2. Before applying module-specific settings, now is a good time to define the icon that will be displayed next to the title, if you like, and the container that will be applied to the Survey module. Therefore, select Settings from the Action menu. After the Module Settings page loads, scroll down and expand the Page Settings. Then, select the Icon and container you wish to use, as shown in Figure 7-51.

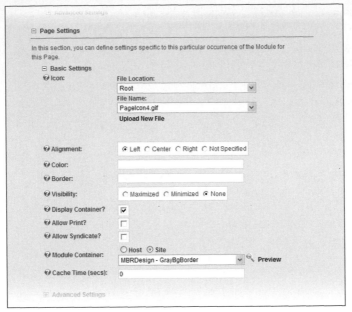

Figure 7-51

3. Now you need to configure the Survey module. Scroll a bit further down and expand the Survey Settings to expose the specific options for the Survey module, as shown in Figure 7-52.

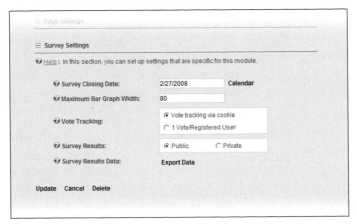

Figure 7-52

4. Select a Survey closing date by clicking the Calendar link to launch a pop-up calendar.

5. Enter an amount for the Maximum Bar Graph Width (the width, in pixels, of the results displayed by the module).

6. Choose an option for tracking votes. The default is Vote tracking via cookie (to remember which computers have already submitted a response to the survey).

7. Make a Survey Results selection (choose whether the results are made public or are available only to Administrators and/or authorized users).

Authorized users also have the ability to export the Survey Results Data at any time by clicking Export Data, but this isn't a step in the configuration process. This is an Administrative reporting function.

8. Click Update.

Adding Questions and Answers to the Survey Module

Now that the Survey module has been configured, you can add survey questions using the following steps:

1. Select Add Question from the top of the Action menu to load the Create Survey page, as shown in Figure 7-53.

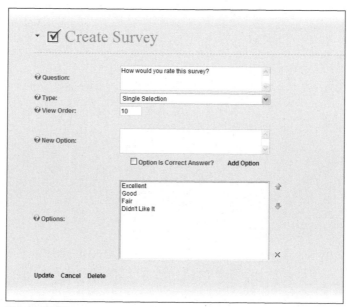

Figure 7-53

2. Enter the question for your Survey.

3. Select the type of question (Single Selection or Multiple Selection).

4. Define the View Order of the question as it is displayed within the Survey module.

5. Add possible answers for the question by typing them, one at a time, in the New Options field and clicking the Add Option link. If an answer is the correct answer, select the checkbox and

click the Add Option link. As you add answers, they will be displayed in the Options area. To change the order of their display, select an answer and click the green (up) arrow or the orange (down) arrow to change the hierarchical position.

6. Click the Update link to add your Survey to a page, as shown in Figure 7-49.

After a Survey module has been populated with questions and answers, and it is ready for public consumption on the website, users have two initial options. They can answer the questions and click Submit Survey, or they can click View Results, as shown in Figure 7-54.

Figure 7-54

Figure 7-55 shows the results of a user submitting the survey.

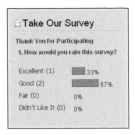

Figure 7-55

Figure 7-56 displays the Survey module to a returning user that has already taken the survey. As you can see, there is no option to submit the survey again. However, the user has the option to view the original Survey without the results being displayed.

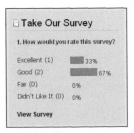

Figure 7-56

As I said previously, the Survey module is a great way to get instant feedback from visitors to your website, which is invaluable to website owners and administrators who want to keep visitors coming back for more.

The FAQ Module

The FAQ module allows you to create a list of questions. The questions are links, and when clicked, they expand to show answers. However, the FAQ module doesn't have to be used just for questions and answers, as you have a great deal of flexibility to display content for a couple of reasons. First, you use the FCKeditor to create the question and answer content. Therefore, you can insert images or anything else you like. Second, the FAQ module uses templates with tokenized text, similar to the Announcements module, so you can easily customize the appearance of the module.

As you get accustomed to using the FAQ module, I'm confident you'll find other great uses for it to show/hide additional information on your website. And now that the FAQ module utilizes AJAX technology, the way it displays answers (or whatever content you choose to display) is really slick. When you're done with this section, you will have added a nicely formatted FAQ module like the one previously shown in Figure 7-50.

Configuring the FAQ Module

1. Start by adding an FAQ module to a page by selecting it from the Module list in the Control Panel. Then enter a Title, choose a target pane, and click the Add icon.

2. Apply the Container and Icon of your choice by selecting Settings from the Action menu. Then, scroll down on the Module page and expand Page Settings to expose the module Page Settings options. For a recap on applying Icons and Containers to modules, review the beginning of this chapter.

3. While on the Module Settings page, scroll down and expand the FAQ Module Settings to expose the specific default options for the FAQ module, as shown in Figure 7-57.

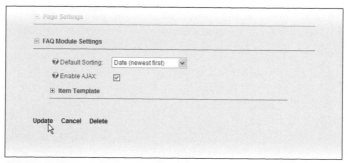

Figure 7-57

4. Select your desired Sort order from the Default Sorting drop-down list. The default setting is Date (newest). This will place the newest-added/edited FAQ at the top of the list in the module. The other options are Date (oldest first), Popularity (highest first), and Popularity (lowest first).

5. Select the checkbox to enable AJAX. When this box is checked, the page does not Postback to the server (the page does not have to refresh). So there is very little, if any, delay when displaying answer content.

In order to use AJAX, AJAX support must be enabled at the Host level by selecting the Enable AJAX checkbox under Host ⇨ Host Settings ⇨ Advanced Settings ⇨ Other Settings.

6. These are the only options you need to define at the moment. So click the Update link to apply the basic configurations to the FAQ module.

Now, let's add a couple of questions and answers and view the FAQ module. Start by selecting Add New FAQ from the Action menu (or click the Add New FAQ link below the module). This will load the Add/Edit Faqs page, as shown in Figure 7-58.

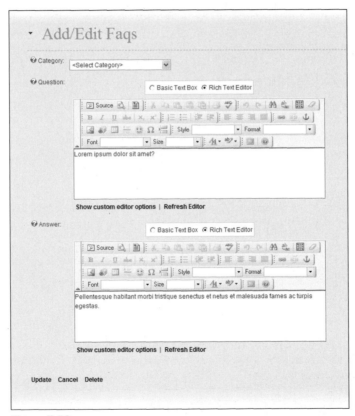

Figure 7-58

The first option available is Category, which allows you to define categories for your FAQs. As a default, no categories are available in the drop-down list because they must first be created. I'll come back to this feature a little later in the chapter.

The next options are Question and Answer. This is where you enter an actual question and answer for the FAQ. As shown in Figure 7-58, simply enter some sample question and answer text using the text editors and click Update to add the FAQ. Then, add a second FAQ via the Action menu. Your FAQ module should now look very similar to Figure 7-59 (in View mode).

Figure 7-59

You'll notice that the FAQs are ordered with the most recently added/edited FAQ at the top of the list. When you click on one of the questions, the page refreshes, and the answer is displayed below the selected question, as is Figure 7-60.

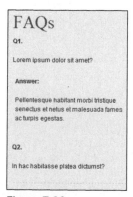

Figure 7-60

Even though you've added an FAQ module with the content you specified, the layout is far from optimal. Luckily, you can easily change the layout and the style of the FAQ module in a similar fashion as the Announcements module.

Customizing the Layout of the FAQ Module

To customize the layout of the FAQ module, select Settings from the Action menu. Then, scroll down on the Module settings page, expand FAQ Module Settings, and then expand Item Template as shown in Figure 7-61. This will expose the templates used by the FAQ module for display.

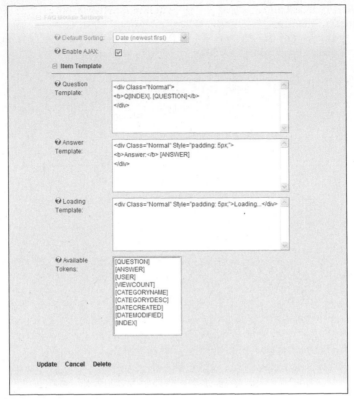

Figure 7-61

First, at the bottom of the page, notice the list of Available Tokens. These can easily be inserted in the template code to customize the display of the FAQ module.

Now, in the first box you see the Question Template. Notice that the style used to display the text is the Normal CSS class, which is also the default text style used by all Text/HTML modules. You then see a Q and the [INDEX] token, which will display the number of the FAQ. Together, these will display as Q1. in the FAQ. Following the [INDEX] token, you see the [QUESTION] token, which displays the actual question.

If you look at the Answer template, you'll see that it also uses the Normal CSS class for display. You'll also see the text Answer: followed by the [ANSWER] token. This results in the word "Answer:" being placed before the actual answer when loaded.

Also notice the Loading template (displayed when the user clicks on a Question until the Answer is fully loaded and displayed — in AJAX mode only).

The FAQ module in Figure 7-62 shows the results of making just a couple of simple changes to the configuration of the FAQ module.

Figure 7-62

What did I do? I used a couple of simple steps to customize the display of the FAQ module.

First, I selected Settings from the FAQ module's Action menu and maximized Page Settings to apply an icon (the small arrow) to be shown next to each FAQ. I also applied a different container to the FAQ module with Page Settings. Then, I simply scrolled down the page a bit, expanded the FAQ Module Settings, and modified the template code, as shown in Figure 7-63.

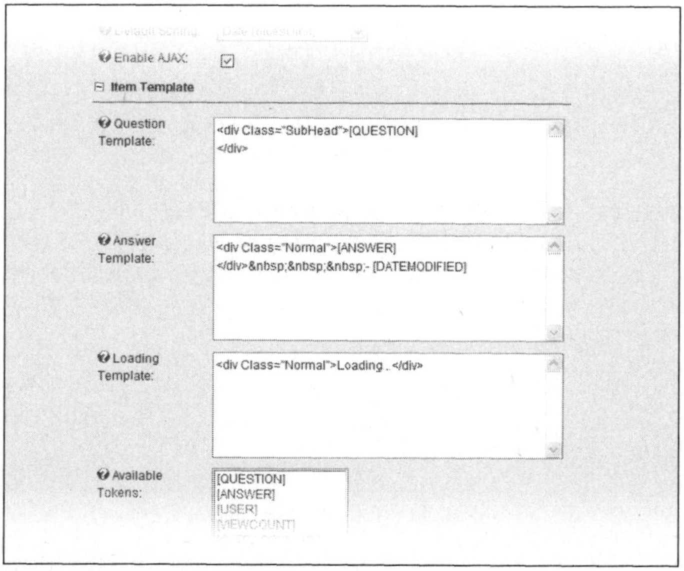

Figure 7-63

As you can see, I changed the code ever so slightly. I removed the <b>(bold) tags because the CSS Class attributes will define the display style of the text. I also removed the padding because I do not want padding around the answers. And finally, I added some spaces, a hyphen, and the [DATEMODIFIED] token, so a date is displayed under the Answer when loaded.

The FAQ looks pretty good. However, there is some extra space between each FAQ that is inadvertently caused by the FCKeditor when entering the content for the FAQs. To fix the spacing, follow these steps:

1. When logged in, click the edit pencil icon for an FAQ, as shown in Figure 7-64. This will take you to the Add/Edit FAQ page.

Figure 7-64

2. Click on the Question Source icon within the FCKeditor, as shown in Figure 7-65.

Figure 7-65

After you click the Source icon, you will see that the FCKeditor has automatically inserted paragraph (<p></p>) tags around the content within the source code, as shown in Figure 7-66.

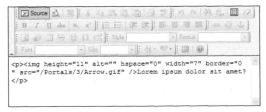

Figure 7-66

3. Remove these paragraph tags from the source, as shown in Figure 7-67, but do not click on the Source tab again to go back to design view. If you do, the FCKeditor will place the paragraph tags back in the source code around the content.

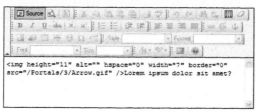

Figure 7-67

4. While still in Source mode within the Question editor, scroll down and click the Answer Source icon within the FCKeditor to remove the paragraph tags from the Answer source. The source code I used for this FAQ's Answer is as follows:

```
<table height="11" cellspacing="0" cellpadding="0" border="0">
  <tbody>
   <tr>
    <td valign="top" align="left" width="7"> </td>
    <td>Pellentesque habitant morbi tristique senectus et netus et malesuada
fames ac turpis egestas.</td>
   </tr>
  </tbody>
</table>
```

You can see I added a table to achieve the alignment I wanted for display of the Answer. I could have easily designated a CSS style directly within the Answer template to achieve the same padding. But I actually made an important discovery while implementing the table source for the Answer. I found that the FCKeditor doesn't place paragraph tags around tables within the source code like it does with text. So if content is placed within the FCKeditor in a table, the spacing issue goes away. Spooky . . . I know. But it's actually one of the very few faults I find with the FCKeditor.

5. The only thing left to do is to click the Update link to apply your changes to the FAQ. Because you want to make the same changes to any additional FAQs, simply complete this same process for the other FAQs. Figure 7-68 shows the results of removing the paragraph tags from the FAQs.

Figure 7-68

As you can see, the FAQ module now has a much more polished and professional layout. It also requires a minimal amount of real estate on our site.

Adding FAQ Categories

To create FAQ categories, you must select Manage Categories from the FAQ module's Action menu. This will take you to the Categories page displayed in Figure 7-69.

Figure 7-69

Click the Add New link to add a new category, as shown in Figure 7-70.

Figure 7-70

Simply enter a Category Name and Category Description, and click Update to add a new category, as shown in Figure 7-71.

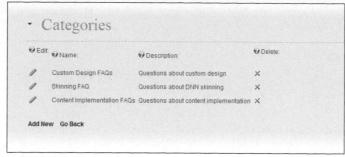

Figure 7-71

As you can see, I've added three categories. To edit a category, click the pencil icon to the left of the category. To delete a category, click the red x to the right of the category. Click the Go Back link to exit the Category Manager.

Summary

This chapter introduced modules, the lifeblood of any DNN website. There are many types of core modules that have their own unique functionality included with a DNN installation. However, I believe you can accomplish the majority of the implementation required for most websites if you have a thorough knowledge of the key core modules. This chapter highlighted many of their not-so-obvious features. If you understand how to get the most out of these key core modules, and master them, you will quickly build a solid foundation for building your own DNN website solutions. And quite possibly, once you get used to using some of the advanced features, you may find that you can accomplish far more with this base set of modules than you thought possible.

Some of the key information you learned from this chapter:

❑ How to add modules and move them throughout the site easily.

❑ How to synch the skin.css file to the Text/HTML module.

❑ How to customize the CSS styles available directly inside the FCKeditor for editing — I believe this knowledge alone is worth the cost of this book many times over!

❑ How to customize the layout of the Announcements and FAQ module.

I hope the knowledge you gain from this chapter goes a long way in helping you make good decisions when using modules to implement content, and I hope this chapter empowers you to do more with the modules you have at your fingertips.

In the next chapter, I show you how to make extensive CSS changes throughout the website. You learn how to make style changes to containers, skins, content, and the DNN interface itself by making simple CSS changes.

8

Customizing with CSS

Now that you've become more familiar with the DNN interface and adding content to the MBR Design website using a variety of modules, you're probably wondering, "How can I customize the look and feel of content, modules, skins, or even the overall DNN environment?" *Cascading style sheets* (CSS) is the answer.

CSS is used to format the layout of web pages and gives both website designers and developers a great deal of control over web page presentation. Designers and developers use CSS to define colors, fonts, layout, and other aspects of web pages. It is designed primarily to enable the separation of document content (HTML) from document presentation (CSS). This separation can improve content accessibility, provide more flexibility and control of presentation characteristics, and reduce complexity and repetition in the structural content. CSS can also allow the same page and content to be presented in different styles. CSS specifies a priority scheme to determine which style rules apply if more than one rule matches against a particular element, hence the term "cascading." With "cascading," priorities or weights are calculated and assigned to rules, so that the presentation results are predictable.

CSS addresses many of the problems of HTML. Some of the older tags, especially the notorious <FONT> tag, clutter web page source code and make for inflexible sites. With CSS, style information is centralized, leading to increased power and flexibility. This helps web designers and developers create a uniform look and feel across the pages on their DNN website. Instead of defining the style of each table and each block of text within a page, commonly used styles need only be defined once in a CSS document (typically the skin.css file). Once a specific style is defined in CSS, any page that references the CSS file can use it. Plus, CSS makes it easy to change styles globally. For example, a web developer may want to increase the default Normal text size from 10pt to 12pt for all the pages on a DNN website. Because the site references the skin.css style sheet, the text size only needs to be changed in the skin.css file so all pages show the larger text.

While CSS is great for creating text styles, it is also helpful for formatting other aspects of the MBR Design web page layout as well. For example, CSS can be used to define the cell padding of table cells; the style, thickness, and color of a table's border; and the padding around content panes, images, or other objects. CSS gives web designers and developers more exact control over how web pages will look than standard HTML does. This is why most web pages today incorporate CSS. The MBR Design website is no exception.

Problem

Using CSS is a great way to achieve a high level of control over the presentation of a DNN website. However, because many DNN users don't understand the relationship between the DNN application and the different CSS files that are read and interpreted, they are often not even aware of the additional CSS styles that allow you to customize certain administration areas of a DNN website, such as the Control Panel, File Manager, and wizard. As a result, they are not able to customize these areas to match the skin package they are using.

Yet another problem is that users don't know how to edit existing CSS styles or add new CSS styles and apply them to their website. This lack of knowledge limits their ability to make customizations to DNN skins, containers, and the display of general content site wide. There are many default styles used by DNN to display different elements, such as common text, subheads, titles, and command links (when logged in as an administrator). Users who aren't familiar with the various CSS styles that affect certain elements are severely limiting their ability to tweak things the way they want. They quickly become frustrated when adding or editing CSS styles that don't have any impact on their site because they don't understand the way skins inherit settings from the different CSS files used by DNN.

Design

This section focuses on customizing many aspects of a DNN website using CSS. In this chapter you learn about the CSS hierarchy and how CSS files are read and interpreted by DNN. In particular, you learn how to:

❑ Edit existing default CSS styles and eliminate unnecessary CSS code

❑ Customize skin CSS attributes

❑ Customize container CSS attributes

❑ Add custom CSS styles and apply them to elements within the site

By the end of this chapter, you will have a good understanding of how DNN utilizes CSS and you'll be very familiar with the default CSS styles used by DNN to define the look and feel of elements throughout a DNN website. You'll also have a good understanding of how to tweak certain aspects of skins and containers to your liking. And finally, you should be able to create custom CSS styles and apply them to your content comfortably.

Solution

Because a number of CSS stylesheets are in play when a DNN website is loaded, it is important to understand the order (hierarchy) at which DNN loads and interprets them.

DotNetNuke reads the CSS code from files in the following order:

- **default.css:** The default stylesheet created by DotNetNuke upon installation, stored in the Portals/_default/ directory.

- **skin.css:** The stylesheet created with the skins loaded by the current page skin.

- **container.css:** The stylesheet loaded by the current page container (a separate container.css file may or may not exist, as the container CSS styles may be optionally included in the skin.css file).

- **portal.css:** The stylesheet generated by DotNetNuke for each portal in your installation. A default portal.css file template is located in the Portals/_default/ directory and copied to each portal folder. If your portal is a parent portal, the portal.css file is found in the Portals/0 directory. If your portal is a child portal, the portal.css file is found in the Portals/X directory, where X is the number of your portal (1, 2, 3, and so on).

As you can see, potentially four different CSS files are read by DNN when a page is loaded, with the portal.css file being the ultimate overriding stylesheet. Why is this important to understand? Because of the way DNN inherits the settings from each CSS file. Let me explain this further.

As each style sheet is read, its styles are applied to various elements within your DNN website. If two style sheets contain CSS styles that have attributes for the same element, the last style sheet to be read contains the CSS attributes that get applied, thus the term "cascading." So if your skin.css style sheet defines the Normal CSS style with a 10pt attribute, but the portal.css style sheet defines the Normal CSS style with a 14pt attribute, portal.css is the style sheet that gets applied and your Normal text will be 14pt.

CSS Inheritance

When a DNN page is loaded, the skins inherit the attributes from each of the CSS files listed in the preceding section, unless the attributes are overridden by another CSS file. To illustrate this, see the following example.

In the default.css file, let's add attributes to the Normal CSS class:

```
.Normal {
  color: #374953;
  font-family: Arial, Verdana, Tahoma, sans-serif;
  font-size: 10pt;
  font-weight: normal;
  line-height: 15pt;
}
```

If Normal CSS class attributes are not specified in any of the other CSS files, the display of the Normal CSS class will be defined with the attributes contained in the default.css file.

Add the following Normal CSS class attribute to the skin.css file:

```
.Normal {
  color: #000000;
}
```

The color attribute from the skin.css file overrides the color attribute in the default.css file. Therefore, the skin now displays a font color of #000000 (black) rather than #374953 (dark teal). However, the skin still uses the font-family, font-size, font weight, and line-height Normal CSS class attributes that are specified in the default.css file because the attributes in the skin.css file do not override them.

Now add the following attributes to the portal.css file:

```
.Normal {
  color: #FFFFFF;
  font-family: Trebuchet, Tahoma, sans-serif;
  font-size: 11pt;
  font-weight: bold;
  line-height: 12pt;
}
```

These CSS attributes override all of the attributes in the default.css file, skin.css file, and container.css file displaying the Normal CSS class in white, Trebuchet, 11 point, bold text with a line height of 12 points.

Now you should have a good idea how DNN CSS styles are inherited. During the course of updating the skin.css file, if you experience unexpected styling with elements being displayed on your DNN pages, check your CSS code in the default.css file to make sure you are not inheriting undesirable attributes. If you are, then you simply need to override them using the same methods discussed in the preceding section.

Best Practices

Although several CSS stylesheets are referenced by DNN, you don't have to use all of them. In fact, it doesn't make sense to override a lot of styles if you don't have to, as this can cause unnecessary duplicate code. When creating skins, I recommend you use the skin.css file to edit or add the CSS styles you want to use for your DNN website. Therefore, it's a good idea to remove any CSS code from the default.css file that you are going to specify in your skin.css file. (As a general rule, you should remove all styles from the default.css file except those needed by the Admin interface, such as Control Panel styles, File Manager styles, and wizard styles — all other styles should be defined at the skin level in the skin.css file.) This will eliminate the possibility of undesirable CSS results within your DNN website. However, keep in mind that in cases when you do not have access to edit the default.css file, you will have to override the CSS attributes in the default.css file using the skin.css file.

The portal.css File

The best use of the portal.css file is to create, edit, or override CSS style attributes that are specific to an individual portal on a single DNN instance, where the first portal installed with DNN has a portal ID of 0 (zero), and all other portals are numbered subsequently 1, 2, 3, and so on. So, for example, when Portals/1 is created, a default portal.css file is generated in the Portals/1 folder.

Under this scenario, all portals in the instance may share a consistent set of styles defined in the default.css file and skin.css file. However, each portal may also require attributes specifically styled for that portal — either by updating existing styles or by adding new styles. And there are a couple of easy ways to update the portal.css file independently for each portal.

CSS Updates via the Stylesheet Editor

For users that don't have FTP access to their DNN website, the preferred method for updating the portal.css file is directly from the Admin ⇨ Site Settings menu. Updating the portal.css file using this method provides an easy way for users to edit the CSS stylesheet simply using only their browser.

First, log in and navigate to Admin ⇨ Site Settings and scroll down to maximize the Stylesheet Editor, as shown in Figure 8-1.

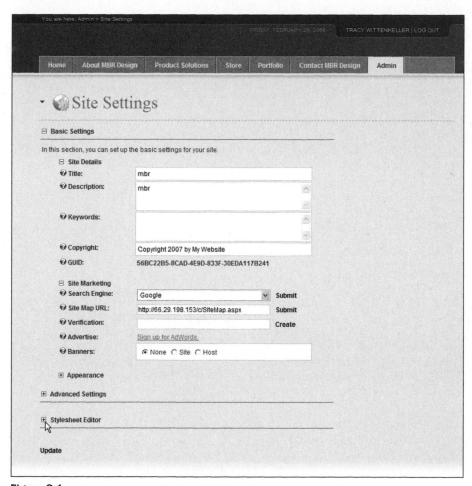

Figure 8-1

This will expose the Stylesheet Editor, as shown in Figure 8-2.

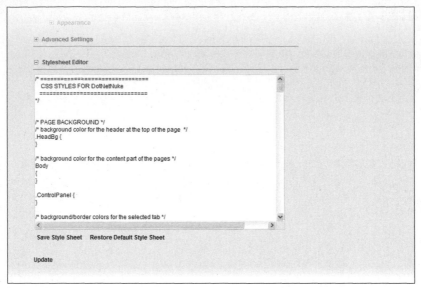

Figure 8-2

The Stylesheet Editor displays the portal.css file (shown here) for editing with default CSS styles used by the DNN application, also possibly found in the default.css file and/or skin.css files.

```
/* ================================
    CSS STYLES FOR DotNetNuke
   ================================
*/

/* PAGE BACKGROUND */

/* background color for the header at the top of the page  */
.HeadBg {
}

/* background color for the content part of the pages */
Body {
}
.ControlPanel {
}

/* background/border colors for the selected tab */
.TabBg {
}
.LeftPane {
}
.ContentPane {
}
.RightPane {
}

/* text style for the selected tab */
```

```
.SelectedTab {
}

/* hyperlink style for the selected tab */
A.SelectedTab:link {
}
A.SelectedTab:visited {
}
A.SelectedTab:hover {
}
A.SelectedTab:active {
}

/* text style for the unselected tabs */
.OtherTabs {
}

/* hyperlink style for the unselected tabs */
A.OtherTabs:link {
}
A.OtherTabs:visited {
}
A.OtherTabs:hover {
}
A.OtherTabs:active {
}

/* GENERAL */

/* style for module titles */
.Head {
}

/* style of item titles on edit and admin pages */
.SubHead {
}

/* module title style used instead of Head for compact rendering by QuickLinks and
Signin modules */
.SubSubHead {
}

/* text style used for most text rendered by modules */
.Normal {
}

/* text style used for textboxes in the admin and edit pages, for Nav compatibility */
.NormalTextBox {
}
.NormalRed {
}
.NormalBold {
}

/* text style for buttons and link buttons used in the portal admin pages */
```

(continued)

(continued)

```css
.CommandButton {
}

/* hyperlink style for buttons and link buttons used in the portal admin pages */
A.CommandButton:link {
}
A.CommandButton:visited {
}
A.CommandButton:hover {
}
A.CommandButton:active {
}

/* button style for standard HTML buttons */
.StandardButton     {
}

/* GENERIC */
H1 {
}
H2 {
}
H3 {
}
H4 {
}
H5, DT {
}
H6 {
}
TFOOT, THEAD {
}
TH {
}
A:link {
}
A:visited {
}
A:hover {
}
A:active {
}
SMALL {
}
BIG {
}
BLOCKQUOTE, PRE {
}
UL LI {
}
UL LI LI {
}
UL LI LI LI {
}
```

```
OL LI {
}
OL OL LI {
}
OL OL OL LI {
}
OL UL LI {
}
HR {
}

/* MODULE-SPECIFIC */
/* text style for reading messages in Discussion */
.Message {
}

/* style of item titles by Announcements and events */
.ItemTitle {
}

/* Menu-Styles */

/* Module Title Menu */
.ModuleTitle_MenuContainer {
}
.ModuleTitle_MenuBar {
}
.ModuleTitle_MenuItem {
}
.ModuleTitle_MenuIcon {
}
.ModuleTitle_SubMenu {
}
.ModuleTitle_MenuBreak {
}
.ModuleTitle_MenuItemSel {
}
.ModuleTitle_MenuArrow {
}
.ModuleTitle_RootMenuArrow {
}

/* Main Menu */
.MainMenu_MenuContainer {
}
.MainMenu_MenuBar {
}
.MainMenu_MenuItem {
}
.MainMenu_MenuIcon {
}
.MainMenu_SubMenu {
}
```

(continued)

241

(continued)

```
.MainMenu_MenuBreak {
}
.MainMenu_MenuItemSel {
}
.MainMenu_MenuArrow {
}
.MainMenu_RootMenuArrow {
}

/* Login Styles */
.LoginPanel {
}
.LoginTabGroup {
}
.LoginTab {
}
.LoginTabSelected {
}
.LoginTabHover {
}
.LoginContainerGroup {
}
.LoginContainer {
}
```

As you can see in the preceding code, no attributes have been added or defined in the portal.css file. This provides a clean slate to work with. You can add attributes to existing styles to change their display, add new classes altogether, or delete any of the existing styles. As you can see in Figure 8-3, attributes have been added to the Normal CSS class that will result in black, Trebuchet, 11 point, Normal text with a line height of 12 points.

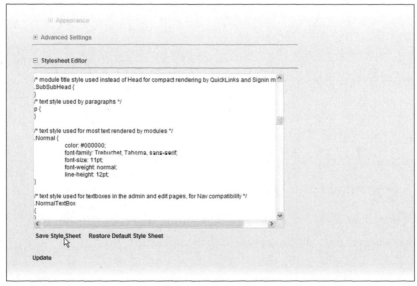

Figure 8-3

To update the portal.css file with your changes, simply click the Save Style Sheet link and refresh your browser to see the updates.

Remember that the portal.css stylesheet is the overriding stylesheet of your DNN website. So any updates you make to styles that exist in the default.css file or skin.css file will be overridden by the attributes you define in the portal.css file.

CSS Updates via FTP

Another way to easily update the portal.css file is via *FTP* (File Transfer Protocol). In order to use FTP, you must have an FTP client application for uploading/downloading files from your DNN website server. I use Bulletproof by Digital Candle, but there are many FTP clients available for free and for purchase. FileZilla is also excellent and free to download from SourceForge.com.

When you use FTP, you simply connect to your server, navigate to the appropriate folder, upload (replace) a new portal.css file, and refresh your browser to see the changes. But where is the appropriate folder located? The answer depends on the ID of your portal, which is defined when your website is created.

If your DNN website is the default portal with an ID of 0 (zero), the correct path would be as follows:

```
/InstanceName/Portals/0/portal.css (where InstanceName is the name of your DNN
instance.)
```

If your website is a different portal on the DNN instance, the ID of your portal will be a sequential number higher than 0, depending on when your portal is created in relation to other child portals.

So if your website is a child portal with an ID of 3, the correct path to the portal.css file is as follows:

```
/InstanceName/Portals/3/portal.css (where 3 is the sequential number of the portal ID.)
```

Because you know where the correct portal.css file is located for your DNN website, it's very easy to edit it locally and replace this file via FTP.

CSS Updates via the File Manager

Many developers use FTP to update their websites. But what if you don't have FTP access to your DNN site? Depending on your website host, you may or may not have FTP access. Not to worry! There is yet another way to update the skin.css file associated with your skins/website.

The File Manager is a simple and intuitive way to update files and directories on your DNN website and is a pretty good replacement for FTP. The File Manager gives you many options to upload, edit, and delete files in your DotNetNuke website, including:

❑   **Folder management:** Option to create, rename, and delete folders.

❑   **File management:** Option to upload, rename, and delete files, and copy files to folders.

❑ **File decompression:** Option to automatically extract a Zip file upon upload (this is especially useful for uploading several images in one Zip file).

❑ **Security Role Permissions:** Option to select which users get access to files and folders.

❑ **Synchronizing files:** This ensures that the list of all folders/files within the File Manager is updated to show all current folders/files.

For now, we're going to focus on synchronizing files. Figure 8-4 shows the File Manager with the Portal Folder expanded within the Folders pane. This is the main directory for the current portal/website. As a default, all files are uploaded into the Portal Root directory.

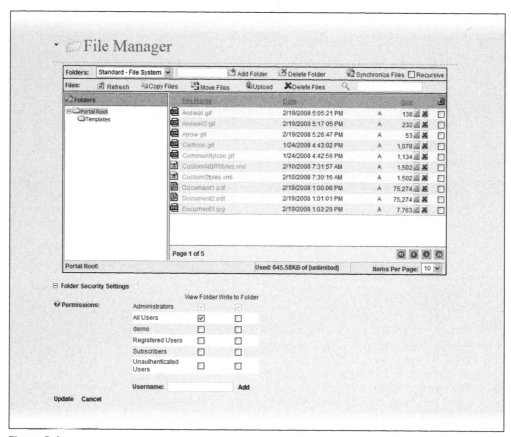

Figure 8-4

As you can see, only one Templates folder is currently displayed in the Portal Root directory. In order to access the skin files via the File Manager, or any other files that have been uploaded to the site, you must select the Recursive checkbox and then click Synchronize Files at the top of the File Manager, as shown in Figure 8-5.

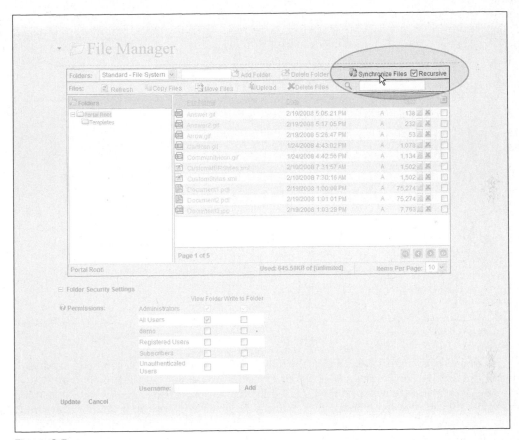

Figure 8-5

This will update the list of folders/files displayed in the File Manager, as shown in Figure 8-6.

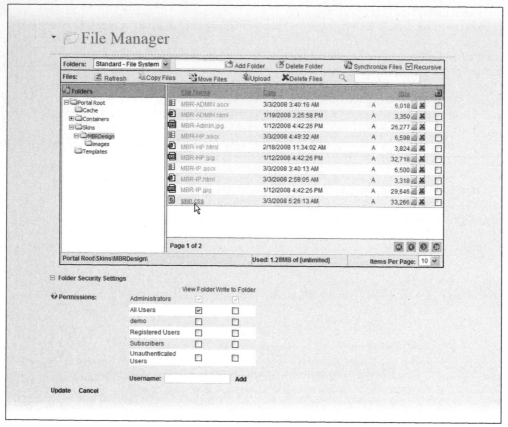

Figure 8-6

Now, when the list of folders is expanded, the full tree of site folders is displayed in the Folders pane, including the Skin folder where the MBRDesign skin files are located. Clicking on the MBRDesign folder within the Folders pane will display the list of files within the skins folder (on the right), including the skin.css file. All you need to do now is click on the skin.css file to download it. After making updates with your favorite CSS or text editor, you simply select the MBRDesign folder in the Folders pane, click the Upload link near the top of the File Manager, and browse your local computer for the updated skin. css file. Then, just refresh your browser to see your changes.

Now that you have a general understanding of how to manage the CSS files associated with DNN, it's time to learn how to make specific CSS customizations to your DNN website. First, we'll make a few typical customizations to skins and containers. Then you'll create a few custom styles and apply them to content within the MBR Design sample website. Finally, you'll customize certain aspects of the Admin interface, including the Control Panel and the File Manager, to give these areas a more consistent look and feel with the MBR Design website.

Locating the skin.css File

Over the past few years I have personally created custom skin packages for many, many clients all over the world. And during this time period I learned quite a lot. Above all, I learned that it is important to deliver skin packages that offer a great deal of flexibility for implementing customizations. The easiest way to accomplish this is by using CSS extensively when developing the HTML for your skins. With a little forward thinking, it's actually quite easy to build skins that allow you to alter their appearance, simply by changing a few CSS attributes. But before we get into updating CSS code, you should become familiar with the location of the skin.css file after a skin package has been uploaded and applied to a DNN website.

Remember, the skin.css file is typically created as part of a skin package with several other related files. When a skin package is uploaded, the location of the files (including the skin.css file) on the server is different for a Host-level install than that of an Admin-level install. If you want to make CSS updates after a package has been installed, it's important to know the difference, since you need to know where the correct skin.css file exists in order to make changes to your site.

When a skin package is installed at the Host-level (via the Host ⇨ Skins menu), a new skin folder is created with the same name as the skin package (in this case MBRDesign) in the Portals_default directory. For the MBRDesign skin package, the correct path is the following:

```
/MBRdev/Portals/_default/Skins/MBRDesign
```

When the MBR-Skins are installed at the Admin-level (via the Admin ⇨ Skins menu), the new skin folder is created in a different directory. The correct path is:

```
/MBRdev/Portals/3/Skins/MBRDesign (where 3 is the sequential number of the portal ID.)
```

If, at some point in the future, you don't remember whether your skins were installed at the Host or Admin level, it's easy to decipher. Simply go to Admin.Site Settings and scroll down to expand the Appearance section. This will expose the current Skins and Containers that are applied to the website, as shown in Figure 8-7.

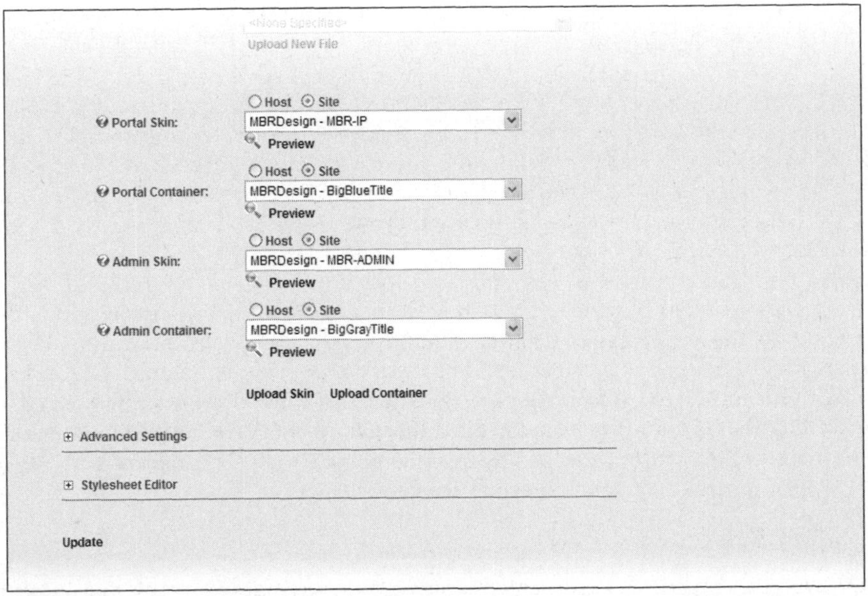

Figure 8-7

If the current skins were installed at the Host level (via the Host ⇨ Skins menu), the Host radio buttons next to Portal Skin, Portal Container, Admin Skin, and Admin Container would be selected. But, as you can see in Figure 8-7, the Site radio buttons are selected, meaning the current skins were installed at the Admin level (via the Admin-Skin menu) with a specific portal ID.

All you need to do now is find the portal ID of the current skins that are loaded so we can make sure we are working with the correct skin.css file to perform customizations. As I said earlier, when additional portals are added to a DNN instance, they are numbered sequentially. Therefore, the actual folder names on the server are 1, 2, 3, 4, and so on. If you have many different portals created, it would be time-consuming to look inside several folders because their names are not indicative of the skins they contain. Luckily, there is an easy way to find the current portal ID without having to open several non-descript folders to find the skin name. Simply right-click on the logo image within your website and select Properties from the bottom of the list (the logo is applied via Admin ⇨ Site Settings in the current portal). This will open a pop-up window similar to the image shown in Figure 8-8.

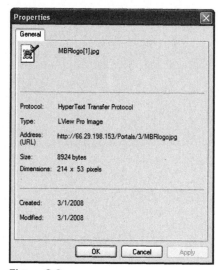

Figure 8-8

Next to the Address (URL), you can see that the path to this image is:

```
http://66.29.198.153/Portals/3/MBRlogo.jpg
```

Therefore, you know the correct portal ID is 3.

So now, you can use an FTP client to navigate to the /InstanceName/Portals/3/Skins folder that contains the MBRSkins folder. And when you open this folder, you'll find all of the skin package files, including the skin.css file, which is the file you are now going to edit. This makes it easy to update the skin.css file, upload it (replace it), and refresh to see your changes.

Customizing Existing skin.css Attributes

As I said earlier, it is a good practice to include all CSS styles used to control your website's look and feel, except certain Admin interface styles, in your skin.css file. This gives you one centralized location for editing most of the attributes associated with the presentation layer of your website. One of the first CSS styles I recommend is one that controls the width of your pages like the following code:

```
/* Width of Skin */
.MainTable { width: 780px; }
```

When developing your skins with tables, the preceeding code provides instant flexibility for changing the minimum width of your skins if your HTML is coded properly. For example, using this method, you can easily change the width of your skins by making the following simple edit to the MainTable CSS class:

```
/* Width of Skin */
.MainTable { width: 100%; }
```

Changing the width to 100 percent will make your page expand and contract as you stretch your browser window. This is what is called a *fluid width*.

Another way to provide flexibility in terms of your content structure (content pane layout) is to use CSS styles to control the width of content panes. As you can see in Figure 8-9, the MBR home page skin provides a two-column structure (ContentPane and RightPane) for the main content area.

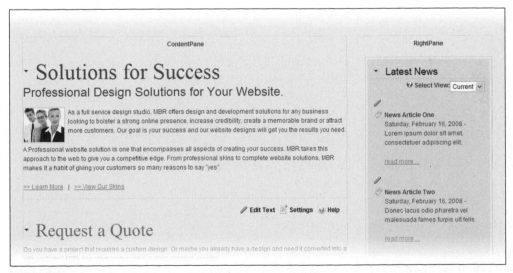

Figure 8-9

As you can see in Figure 8-9 and in the CSS attributes in the code that follows, the RightPane has a width of 250 pixels and a left-padding of 35 pixels.

```
.RightPane {
font-family:  Arial, Verdana, Tahoma,sans-serif;
  font-size: 11px;
  font-weight: bold;
  text-align:left;
  color: #034681;
  vertical-align:top;
  vertical-align:top;
  padding-left: 35px;
  width: 250px;
  padding-top: 5px;
}
```

Therefore, 250 pixels is the current minimum width of the RightPane (although placing an image in the RightPane that is wider than 250 pixels would make it expand beyond 250 pixels). However, because you can easily change the width and the padding of the RightPane, it's very easy to change the content structure by editing just those two CSS attributes shown in the following code:

```
.RightPane {
  font-family:  Arial, Verdana, Tahoma,sans-serif;
  font-size: 11px;
  font-weight: bold;
  text-align:left;
  color: #034681;
  vertical-align:top;
  vertical-align:top;
  padding-left: 15px;
  width: 50%;
  padding-top: 5px;
}
```

This simple CSS code change results in the RightPane having a width of 50 percent, equal with that of the ContentPane, and just 15 pixels of left-padding, as shown in Figure 8-10.

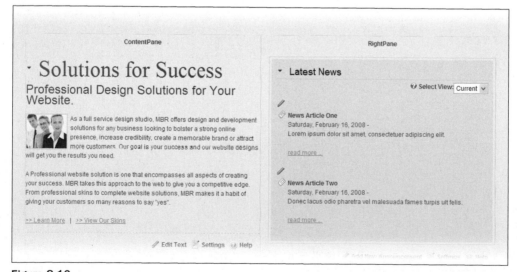

Figure 8-10

When CSS has been used properly, it is also easy to change the various text styles used by DNN. For example, the current Normal (used by default to display text), P (anything wrapped in paragraphs tags), H1, and SubHead CSS styles have the following attributes:

```
.Normal {
  color: #374953;
  font-family: Arial, Verdana, Tahoma, sans-serif;
  font-size: 12px;
  font-weight: normal;
  line-height: 18px;
}
P {
  color: #374953;
  font-family: Arial, Verdana, Tahoma, sans-serif;
  font-size: 12px;
  font-weight: normal;
  line-height: 18px;
}
H1 {
  color: #374953;
  font-family: Arial, Verdana, Tahoma,sans-serif;
  font-size: 18pt;
  font-weight: normal;
}
.SubHead {
  color: #034681;
  font-family: Arial, Verdana, Tahoma,sans-serif;
  font-size: 12px;
  font-weight: bold;
  text-decoration: none;
  line-height: 18px;
}
```

The display of these styles is highlighted in Figure 8-11.

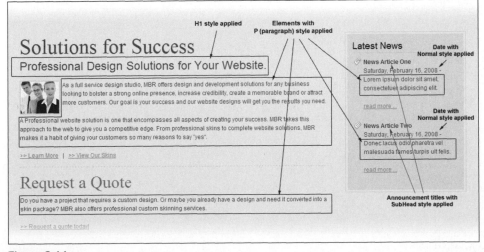

Figure 8-11

Let's make a few simple CSS edits to change the display of the Normal, P, and H1 styles. You'll change the font-size of the Normal and P styles; the color, font-family, and font-size of the H1 style; and the font-size of the SubHead style.

```
.Normal {
    color: #374953;
    font-family: Arial, Verdana, Tahoma, sans-serif;
    font-size: 14px;
    font-weight: normal;
    line-height: 18px;
}
P {
    color: #374953;
    font-family: Arial, Verdana, Tahoma, sans-serif;
    font-size: 14px;
    font-weight: normal;
    line-height: 18px;
}
H1 {
    color: #374953;
    font-family: Tahoma,sans-serif;
    font-size: 23pt;
    font-weight: normal;
}
.SubHead {
    color: #034681;
    font-family: Tahoma,sans-serif;
    font-size: 14px;
    font-weight: bold;
    text-decoration: none;
    line-height: 18px;
}
```

Figure 8-12 shows the results of the simple CSS edits applied in the preceeding code.

Figure 8-12

Creating and Applying Custom CSS Styles

CSS edits are not only limited to text styles. If a skin package has been coded correctly, you have the ability to change just about every aspect of the look and feel of your DNN website using the same principles mentioned in the previous section, including entire color schemes, backgrounds, and images. You can also add custom CSS styles and easily apply them to content with your DNN website. Figure 8-13 shows two custom CSS styles that were created and applied to the Solutions for Success module - the style applied to the words "Reasons to Say Yes" and the style applied to the Learn More and View Our Skins links.

Figure 8-13

First, you'll create the custom styles, and then you'll apply them to the content with the Solutions for Success module.

The first step in creating a custom CSS style is to open the skin.css file. To make sure you're always using the latest version of the skin.css file, I recommend you download the latest version from your server via the File Manager or via FTP, as previously discussed in this chapter. Once you have the skin.css file open, add the following new styles:

```
.NormalBoldBlue {
  color: #4d9fd7;
  font-family: Arial, Verdana, Tahoma,sans-serif;
  font-size: 18px;
  font-weight: bold;
  line-height: 18px;
}
.RedLink {
  color: #A50000;
  font-family: Arial, Verdana, Tahoma,sans-serif;
  font-size: 12px;
  font-weight: bold;
```

(continued)

(continued)

```
    text-decoration: none;
    background-color: #E7DDD9;
}
A.RedLink:Link, A.RedLink:Visited, A.RedLink:Active {
    color: #A50000;
    font-family: Arial, Verdana, Tahoma,sans-serif;
    font-size: 12px;
    font-weight: bold;
    text-decoration: none;
    background-color: #E7DDD9;
}
A.RedLink:Hover {
color: #A50000;
    font-family: Arial, Verdana, Tahoma,sans-serif;
    font-size: 12px;
    font-weight: bold;
    text-decoration: underline;
}
```

After the styles have been added to the skin.css file, it needs to be saved and uploaded to the server via the File Manager or via FTP, so the new styles are available to apply to elements within the site.

After the new skin.css file has been successfully uploaded, select Edit Text from the Solutions for Success module Action menu. This opens the FCKeditor. When it opens, add the Reasons to Say Yes text, as shown in Figure 8-14.

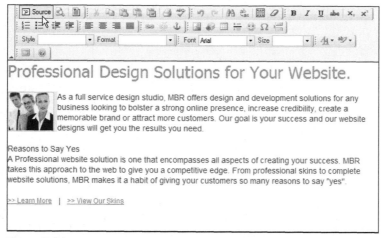

Figure 8-14

Next, click the Source link in the top-left corner of the FCKeditor, also shown in Figure 8-14. This shows the HTML source of the content in the Text/HTML module, as shown in Figure 8-15.

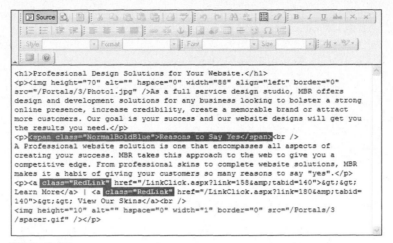

Figure 8-15

While in Source view, you need to apply the new CSS styles you just created. So first, to apply the NormalBoldBlue style, you need to wrap the Reason to Say Yes text in a <span> tag, as shown in Figure 8-15.

Next, to add the custom RedLink class, you need to add class="RedLink" to the Learn More and View Our Skin href link tags, also shown in Figure 8-15.

After you add the simple code for your new styles, click the Source link again, which takes you back to Design view, as shown in Figure 8-16.

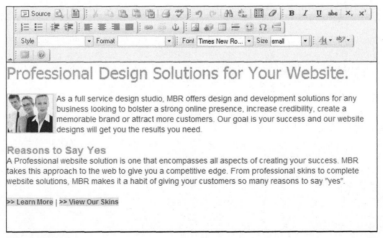

Figure 8-16

As you can see, because the skin.css file has been linked to the FCKeditor (this was covered in Chapter 7), the new styles you added to the skin.css file are previewed directly within the FCKeditor while in Design view. The only thing left to do is click the Update link to apply the changes to the Solutions for Success module, as displayed in Figure 8-13.

Let's recap this simple process. First, you downloaded the latest skin.css file. Then, you added a few new styles. Next, you uploaded the new skin.css file to the website, overwriting the old file. Then, you selected Edit Text from the Action menu of a Text/HTML module. Next, you applied your new custom styles within Source view to content with the Text/HTML module (you added large, bold, blue text, and customized the display of the links). After that, you previewed your updates in Design view within the Text/HTML module. Finally, you clicked Update to apply the new CSS styles to the content.

When you break the process down, it's really not complicated. A little CSS knowledge is definitely helpful. But just about anyone can create custom styles and apply them within minutes to their DNN website.

Customizing Container CSS

The great thing about using CSS to control the display of elements on a DNN website is that it's easy to customize the skin.css file. However, making CSS changes to containers (content wrappers) is even easier because containers typically are associated with very little code and few CSS styles. But like skins, before you can edit container files, you just need to be aware of the location of the proper container CSS file(s) after a skin package has been uploaded, so you can ensure you are updating the correct container files.

In the case of the MBRDesign skin package, a separate container.css file has been created for each container (in some cases container CSS styles are included in the skin.css file, but this tends to make the skin.css file quite large). Therefore, the MBRDesign container.css files are found in the following folder on the server:

```
/MBRInstance/Portals/3/Containers/MBRDesign
```

Updating a container.css file is different from updating a skin.css file because you can only control the display of CSS styles within a single container and not site-wide. Common container customizations include changing the font, color, and/or size of titles and the border and/or backgrounds applied to containers. However, you can also use CSS styles within the container.css file to override general CSS styles in the skin.css file. For example, you can define the Normal style font-color attribute as red for a given container when it's applied to a module placed in the LeftPane and green when it's applied to a module in the RightPane.

First, you would define DIV ID's in the skin.css file like this:

```
.LeftPane #BlackTitle .Normal {
color: #FF0000;
}
.RightPane #BlackTitle .Normal {
color: #00FF00;
}
```

And then reference these styles by wrapping a container in a div with the ID name like this:

```
<div id="BlackTitle">ContainerHTML</div> (where ContainerHTML is the container
HTML code)
```

All you're doing here is automatically changing the Normal style when it's applied in the LeftPane or RightPane. This type of styling can also be accomplished by including all container CSS styles in the skin.css file and referencing DIV ID's in the HTML skin files. But the simple method I just described allows you to create so-called "smart containers" whose attributes change based on the content pane they are added to.

Customizing the Control Panel

So now you're feeling pretty good. You have this great skin design, and you're able to control the style of the content within your DNN website, comfortably, with CSS. Now, if only the Control Panel matched the rest of your site. Actually . . . it can! In fact, with CSS, you also have the power to customize the Control Panel. All it takes is a little knowledge of the styles that exist (and others you can create) to customize it to match your website design.

Figure 8-17 shows the display of the default Control Panel in all its splendor.

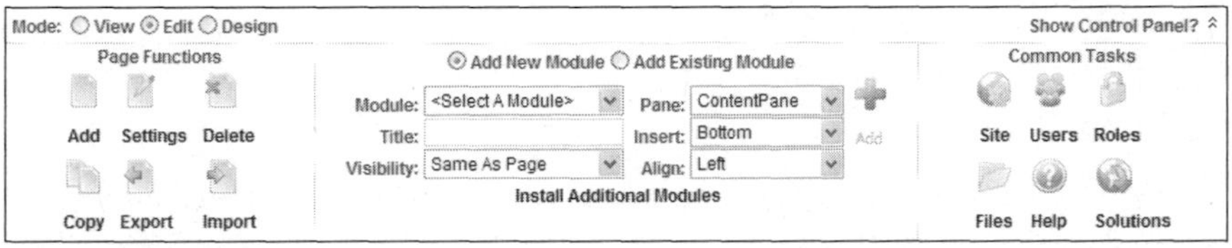

Figure 8-17

As you recall, in the default.css file, the only code for the Control Panel is as follows:

```
.ControlPanel, .PagingTable
{
  width: 100%;
  background-color: #FFFFFF;
  border-right: #003366 1px solid;
  border-top: #003366 1px solid;
  border-left: #003366 1px solid;
  border-bottom: #003366 1px solid;
}
```

However, Figure 8-18 shows you what can be accomplished with just a few simple CSS changes and a couple of new images (Users and Files).

Figure 8-18

I'm not going to show you how I did it (you'll have to work for this one), but I'll give you a hint. Here are the CSS styles I added to the default.css file to make it happen (the images can be found in the admin/ControlPanel/images folder inside your root directory):

```
/* ********** Control Panel Style ************** */
.controlpanel {
}
.controlpanel IMG {
}
.controlpanel TD TD TD TD IMG {
}
.controlpanel TD TD TD {
}
.controlpanel DIV {
}
.controlpanel TD.SubHead {
}
.controlpanel TD TD TD .SubHead {
}
.controlpanel TD TD TD input {
}
.controlpanel TD TD TD select {
}
.controlpanel A.CommandButton {
}
.controlpanel A.CommandButton:link {
}
.controlpanel A.CommandButton:visited {
}
.controlpanel A.CommandButton:active {
}
.controlpanel A.CommandButton:hover {
}
.CommandButton,A.CommandButton:link,A.CommandButton:visited,A.CommandButton:active {
}
A.CommandButton:hover {
}
```

Just add your own attributes until you're satisfied with your results!

Summary

This chapter focused on performing customizations to a DNN website using CSS. You learned about the CSS hierarchy, and how DNN inherits settings from the different CSS files described in this chapter. This chapter gave you a glimpse of what can be accomplished — there are some standards worth noting again that you may wish to adopt.

First, use only the skin.css file to add CSS styles you want to apply to content in your DNN website. Second, delete any CSS code from the default.css file that you are going to specify in your skin.css file, so you don't have unnecessary, duplicate code. Third, remove all styles from the default.css file except those needed by the Admin interface, such as Control Panel styles, File Manager styles, and wizard styles. This will eliminate the possibility of undesirable CSS results within your DNN website.

You gotta love the power of CSS and the ease with which you can control so much with so little effort! In the next chapter, you discover even more to love about DNN as you explore one of DNN's most powerful features: Roles-Based Security. You learn how to create security roles and define permissions as you lock content down to specific users. After this next chapter, don't be surprised if you feel like trying to leap tall buildings in a single bound.

9

Working with Security

One of the most important functions of the DNN framework to understand is roles-based security. Why? Because you have the ability to manage access to privileged content through the use of Security Roles, giving you the power to secure your content by defining permissions at the page level and at the module level. This makes it possible for some users to have access to standard content that is available to the general public, while other users have access to content that isn't available to just anyone that comes to your website.

When users register on your site, they are automatically added to the Registered Users role, which gives them access to all general content. However, after they register, they can be granted access to more secure content or website functionality by an administrator.

Sound complicated? Fortunately, just like many of the other features of DNN you've discovered throughout this book, it isn't rocket science. True, having this kind of control over the members of your website is one of the most powerful features of the DNN framework, but that doesn't mean it has to be difficult. As you will soon see, DNN provides very flexible options for configuring secure areas within your website. And if you take a systematic approach to setting up the permission levels for your site, applying them to different registered users is relatively painless.

Problem

The process of securing content on a DNN website can be a little tricky, depending on the outcome that is desired. And many DNN users don't understand the proper way to apply Security Roles to get the results they are trying to achieve. As a result, DNN's built-in security is sometimes not used to its full advantage. However, the MBR Design examples in this chapter will clearly show you how to implement DNN Security Roles and Permissions and get results fast.

Design

This chapter introduces the membership provider and explains methods for creating and deleting users, verifying login credentials, changing passwords, and more. This chapter goes in-depth, teaching you how to set up and define user roles, add new User Accounts, and define permissions at every level. In this chapter, you learn how to:

❏ Define the type of registration for your site

❏ Specify fields for registration

❏ Create/edit User Accounts

❏ Create Security Roles and security role groups

❏ Apply Security Roles to User Accounts

❏ Define permissions at the page level

❏ Define permissions at the module level

By the end of this chapter, you will be able to create Security Roles and apply them to User Accounts with the appropriate permissions you define. In doing so, you will be able to create secure content that is locked down and available only to users with the correct permission levels.

Solution

Site registration is the first step in managing access to privileged content. But before we get into the details of registration, it is important to define the term "user." A *user* is someone who has access to all of the content on your website or just a portion of it. Based on permission levels you define, a user can have different types of access to do the following:

❏ View all of the general content displayed to all website visitors

❏ View secure areas that are not available to the general public

❏ Administer content within the website

DNN includes the option to allow general website visitors to register on your website. This allows the website owner to create secure, private areas that are available only to users that have specific access permissions, such as registered users, administrators, or other users that require private access. DNN also has built-in functionality that enables you to require users to register and pay for access to private areas of your website.

Registration Options

Registration is the first step for managing access to secure content. DotNetNuke gives you four options for allowing users to register on your website, summarized in Table 9-1.

Table 9-1: Registration Options

Option	Description
None	Registration is not available to users. The login link remains visible so administrators can access the site. However, the registration link is not displayed. Sites that utilize this option typically have the login link in a less-prominent location than sites that actively seek registered Users. This option is appropriate for sites that do not contain secure information. New users can only be added to the website by administrators manually.
Private	Users apply for secure access to the site. Registration and login links are displayed. Upon registration, an administrator has to approve the user before the user will be granted secure access. This option is appropriate for sites that require the approval of registration requests. Upon registration, an e-mail is sent to the user letting them know the site is private. An e-mail confirmation is sent to the user upon approval/authorization.
Public	Registration is automatically approved/authorized. This is the default setting for DNN websites. Registration and login links are displayed. This option is appropriate for sites that do not require validation of contact information. Upon registration, a confirmation e-mail is sent to the user.
Verified	Registration generates a verification code. Registration and login links are displayed. Upon registration, a user receives a welcome e-mail that includes his or her verification code as part of the registration process. Authorization is granted after the user logs in for the first time and provides the correct verification code. Once a user is verified, he or she doesn't need to enter the verification code again. This option is appropriate to ensure that all users have provided a valid e-mail address upon registration.

Depending on the registration option you choose (Public or Verified), DNN displays the appropriate text message when a User registers. For Public registration, it displays: *Note: Membership to this portal is Public. Once your account information has been submitted, you will be immediately granted access to the portal environment. All fields marked with an asterisk (*) are required.*

For Verified registration, it displays: *Note: Membership to this portal is Verified. Once your account information has been submitted, you will receive an email containing your unique Verification Code. The Verification Code will be required the first time you attempt to sign in to the portal environment. All fields marked with an asterisk (*) are required.*

Selecting Registration Options

Just like many other functions of the DNN framework, defining the registration option for a DNN website is straightforward and takes just a few easy steps:

1. Log in as an administrator.

2. After logging in, go to Admin ⇨ Site Settings and scroll down to Advanced Settings, as shown in Figure 9-1.

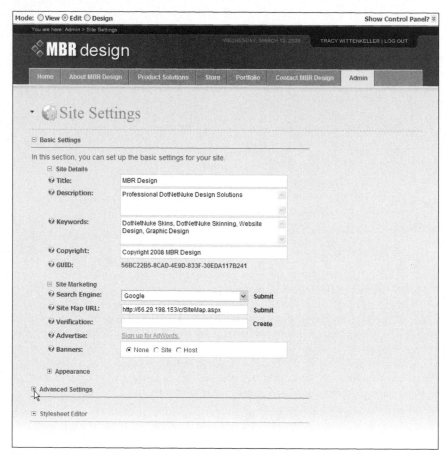

Figure 9-1

3. Expand the Advanced Settings by clicking on the plus sign to expose the User Registration options under Security Settings, as shown in Figure 9-2.

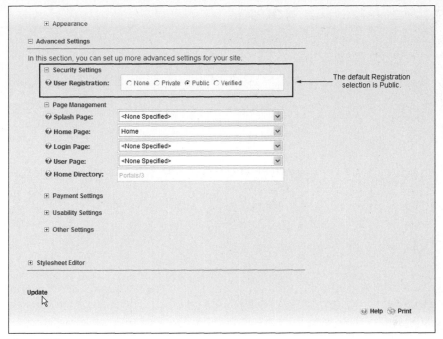

Figure 9-2

4. Select the User Registration option you require. Notice that the Public User Registration option is the default option.

5. Scroll down and click the Update link to apply your changes.

If you select the Verified option, you must configure your SMTP e-mail settings via Host-level access (Host ⇨ Host Settings ⇨ Advanced Settings ⇨ SMTP Server Settings) so that DNN can e-mail the verification code to you. If you don't have Host access, this will have already been done for you. You can check to make sure your SMTP settings work by logging out, clicking the Login link, and then clicking the Forgot Password link. If your SMTP settings are configured correctly, DNN will send you an e-mail that includes your password. If your SMTP settings are not configured correctly, you will need to contact your Host administrator to get it done.

Specifying Fields for Registration — Working with User Profiles

After you have enabled the appropriate registration option for your DNN website (for the MBR Design sample website you'll use the default Public option), you can decide the information you want to collect from users as part of the registration process.

As a default, DNN displays the list of required fields, shown in Figure 9-3, that Users must complete as part of the registration process.

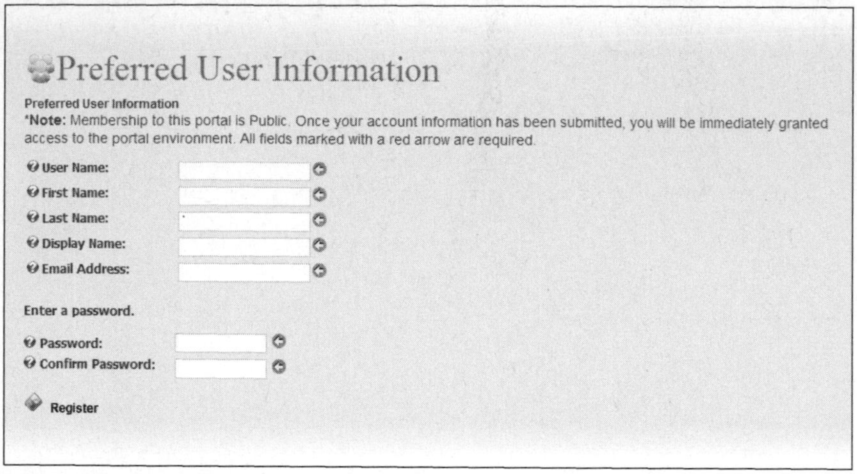

Figure 9-3

However, you can define additional fields you want to display, and which of those fields are required for registration (signified by the red circles with white arrows). This is done by customizing the Profile Properties. But first, we need to make a change to the User Settings so DNN will display additional Profile Properties within the registration form.

To accomplish this, navigate to Admin ⇨ User Accounts and click User Settings, as shown in Figure 9-4.

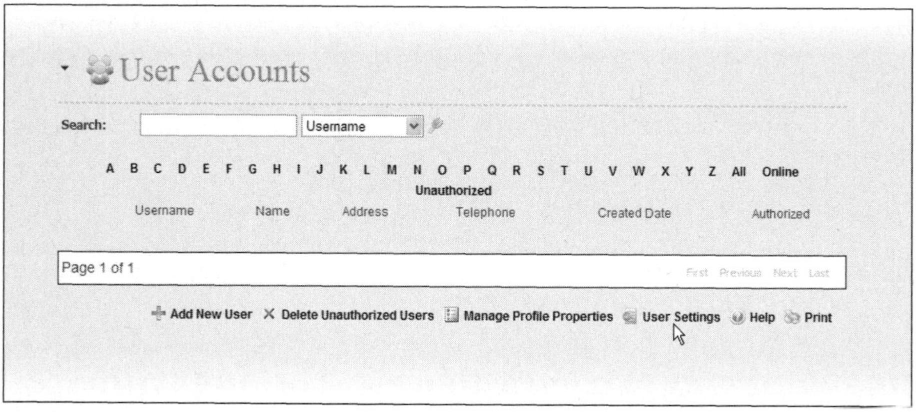

Figure 9-4

After the User Settings page loads, scroll down towards the bottom of the page and select the checkbox next to Require a valid Profile for Registration, and then click Update, as shown in Figure 9-5.

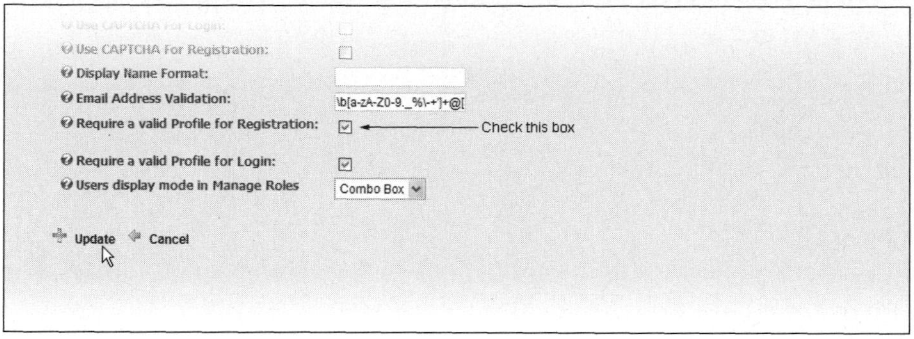

Figure 9-5

This will allow you to add additional fields to be displayed as part of the DNN registration form. Now, you can add fields using the following steps:

Navigate to Admin ⇨ User Accounts and click Manage Profile Properties, as shown in Figure 9-6.

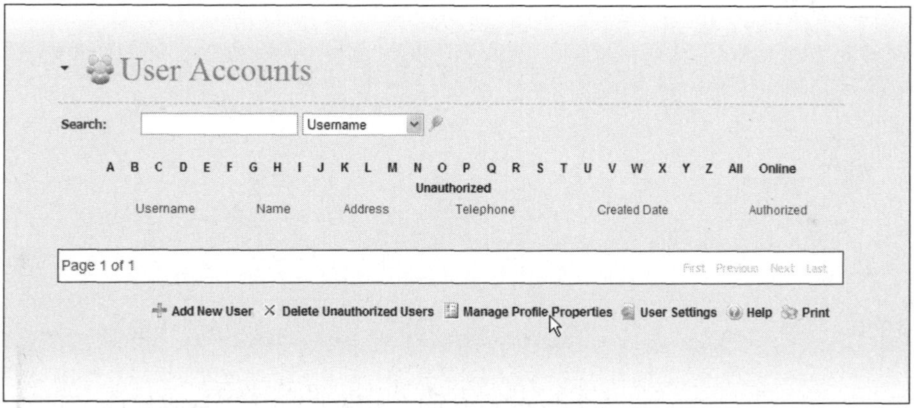

Figure 9-6

This displays all of the default Profile Properties that are available for a User's profile, shown in Figure 9-7.

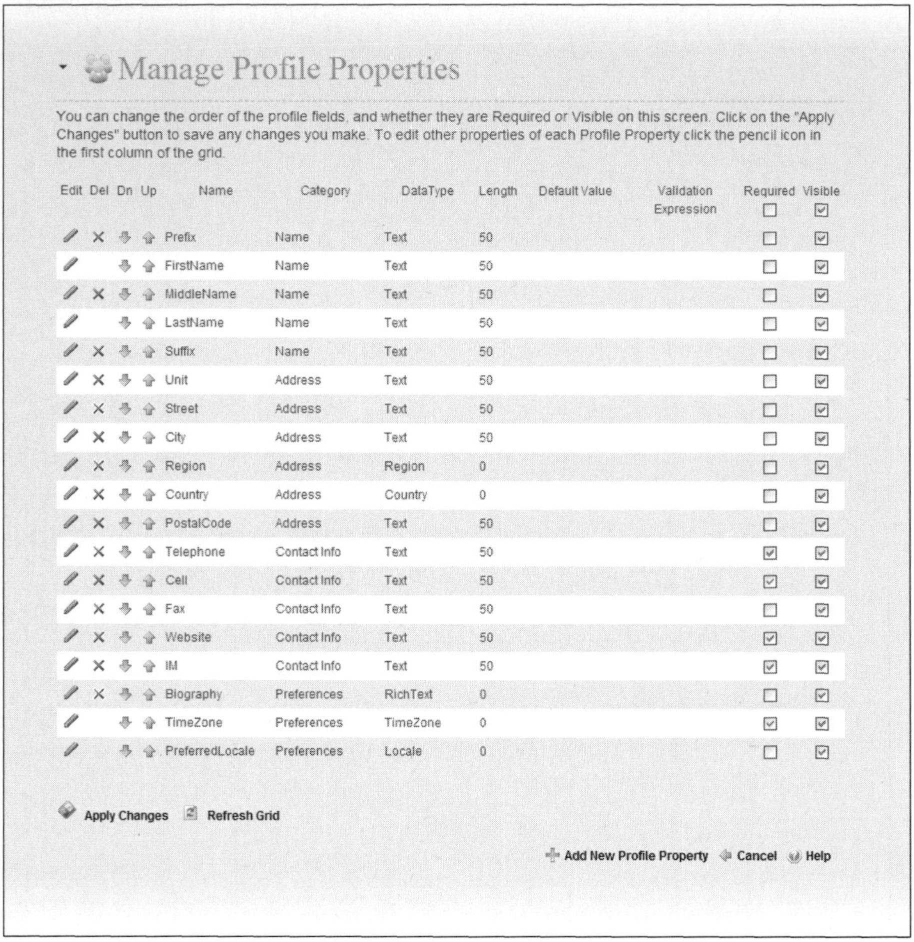

Figure 9-7

As you can see, this includes personal profile items such as first and last name, address, website, biography, time zone, and others, some of which I have selected as required items. You'll also notice on the right that all of the profile items are selected as visible. Un-checking an item in this column would remove it from the registration form displayed when a user clicks the Register link, and allow Administrators to store the extra "hidden" info about a user, which would be useful for integrating DNN with other systems. You can also add additional profile properties by clicking the Add New Profile Property link.

If you log out now and click the Register link, all of the profile properties selected as Visible in Figure 9-7 are displayed in the registration form, shown in Figure 9-8, and not just the default properties previously shown in Figure 9-3 because you now require a valid profile when you register (refer to Figure 9-5).

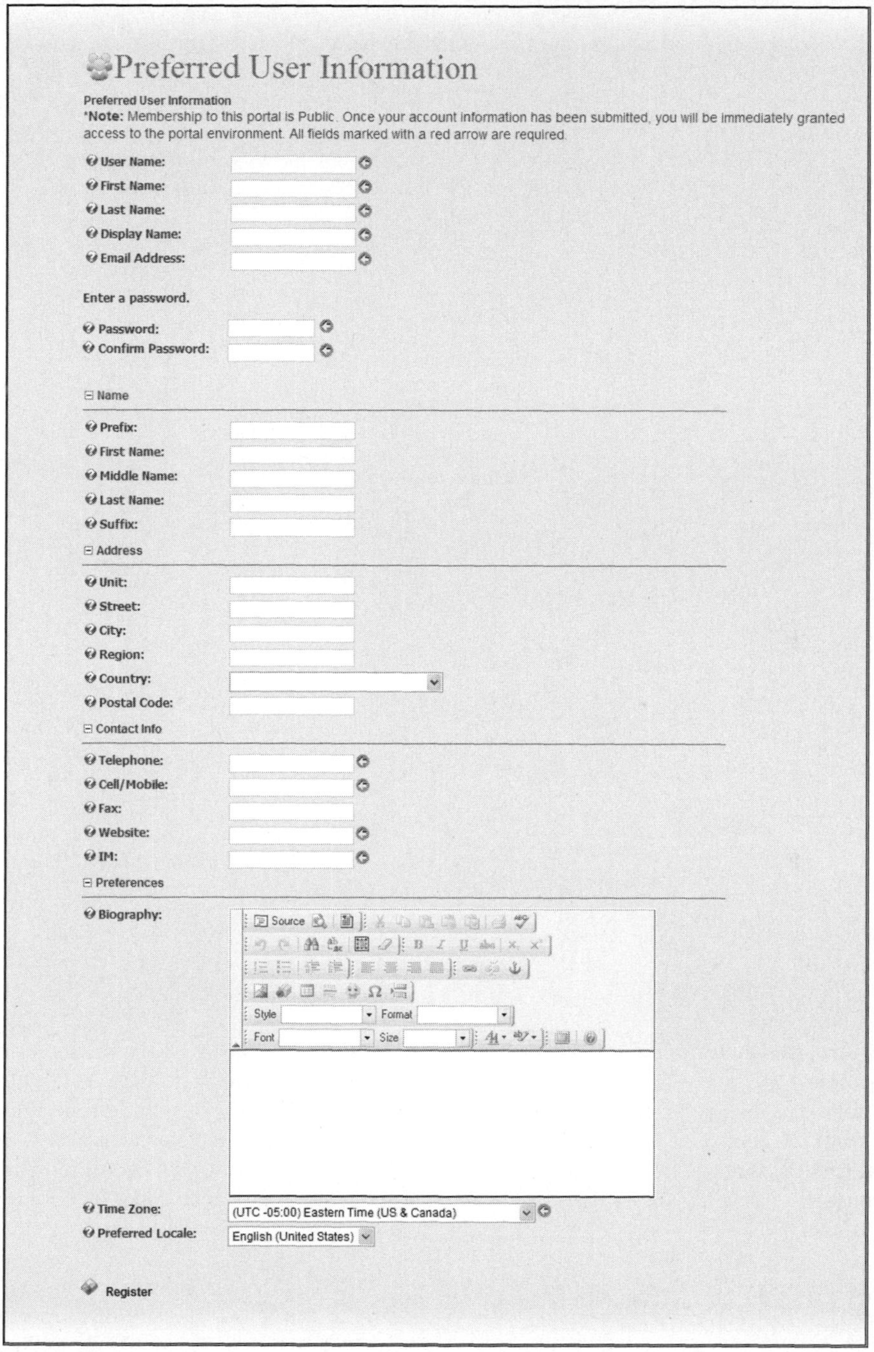
Preferred User Information
Preferred User Information
*Note: Membership to this portal is Public. Once your account information has been submitted, you will be immediately granted access to the portal environment. All fields marked with a red arrow are required.
User Name:
First Name:
Last Name:
Display Name:
Email Address:
Enter a password.
Password:
Confirm Password:
Name
Prefix:
First Name:
Middle Name:
Last Name:
Suffix:
Address
Unit:
Street:
City:
Region:
Country:
Postal Code:
Contact Info
Telephone:
Cell/Mobile:
Fax:
Website:
IM:
Preferences
Biography:
Source
Style
Format
Font
Size
Time Zone:
(UTC -05:00) Eastern Time (US & Canada)
Preferred Locale:
English (United States)
Register

Figure 9-8

You'll notice the default required fields and the additional fields you selected as required for registration in Figure 9-7 previously, indicated by the circle with the arrow.

As I said previously, un-checking profile items in the Visible column within the Manage Profile Properties page makes them hidden from the registration page. Therefore, if you wanted to show fewer items in the registration form, simply select fewer items as Visible, as shown in Figure 9-9.

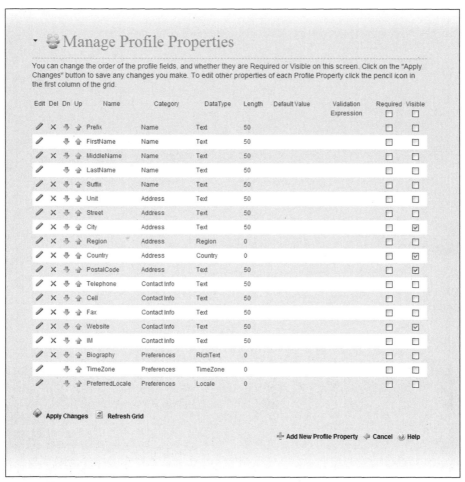

Figure 9-9

This would result in a simpler registration form as shown in Figure 9-10.

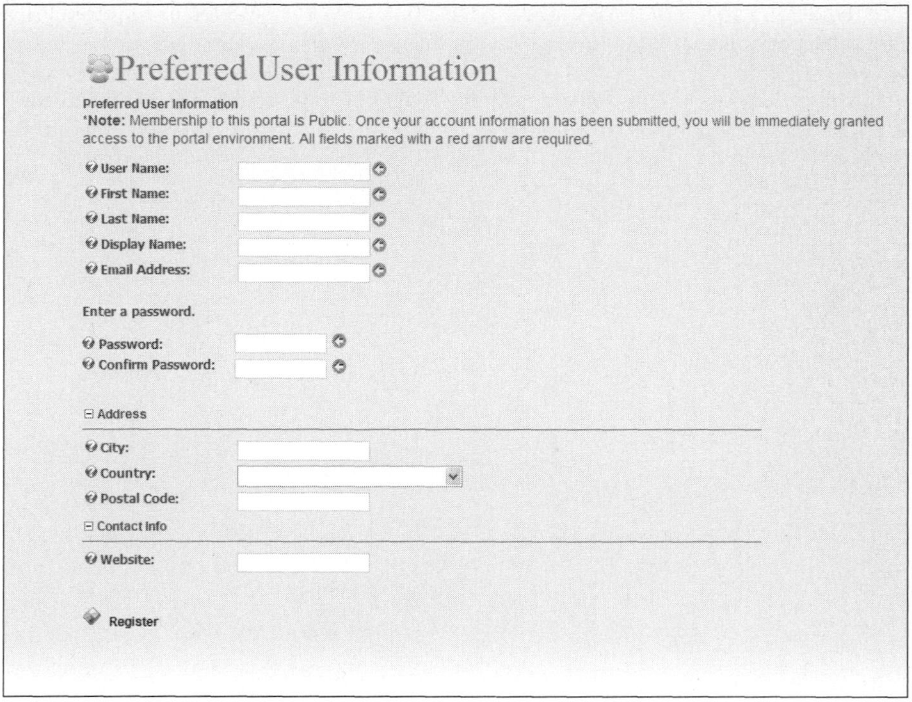

Figure 9-10

In the previous example, all the profile properties are not being displayed in the registration form for users to fill out as part of the registration process. However, registered users can update their complete profiles (and other account information) using the following steps:

1. Log in and click the user display name, as shown in Figure 9-11.

Figure 9-11

2. Click the Manage Profile link on the Manage Profile page, as shown in Figure 9-12.

This will display all of the profile properties for the user, as shown in Figure 9-13.

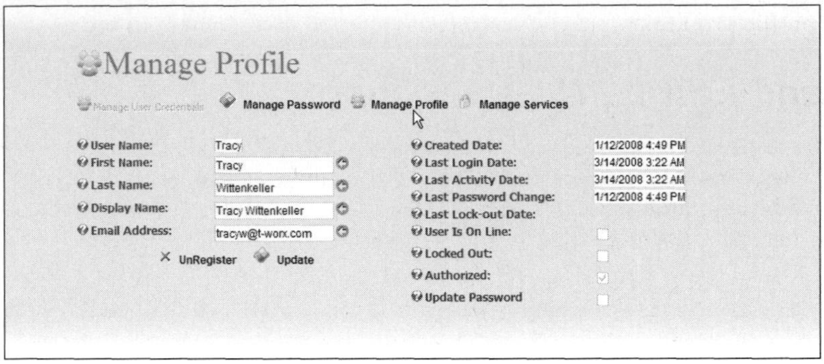

Figure 9-12

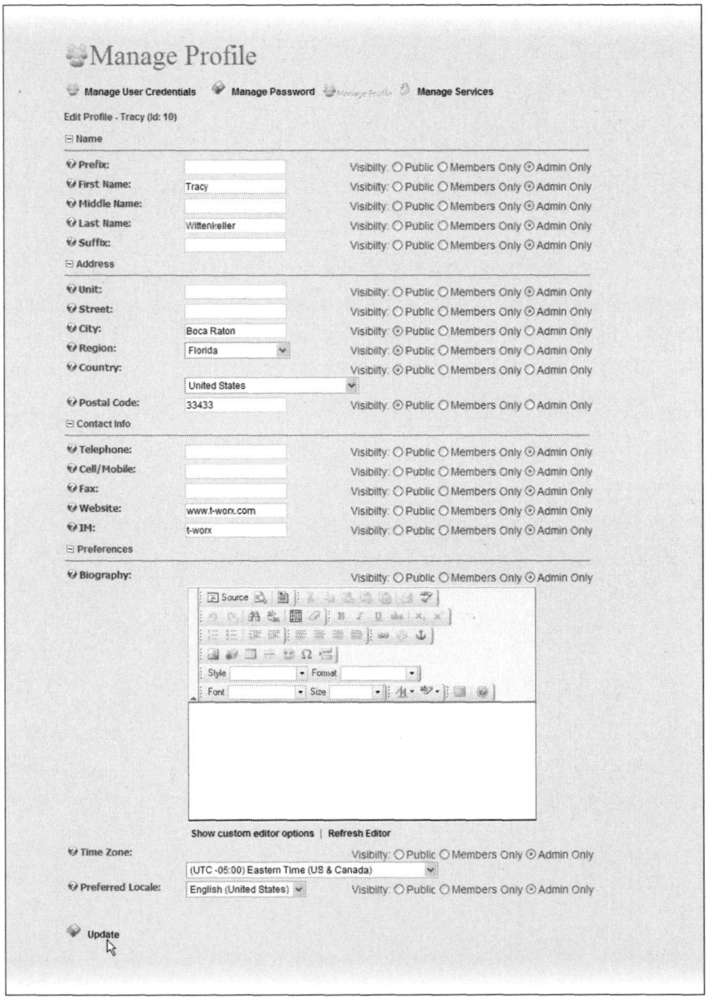

Figure 9-13

3. Edit profile properties and click the Update link to save changes to the User profile.

Creating and Editing User Accounts

User accounts are created when a user registers on the website by clicking the Register link and completing the registration form. This type of User Account is automatically added to the Registered Users role. An administrator manually creates User Accounts. To create a new User Account as an administrator, use the following steps:

1. Log in as an administrator and navigate to Admin ⇨ User Accounts, as shown in Figure 9-14.

Figure 9-14

2. On the User Accounts page, click the Add New User link, as shown in Figure 9-15.

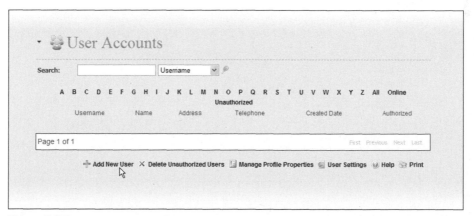

Figure 9-15

3. Complete the form and click Add New User, as shown in Figure 9-16.

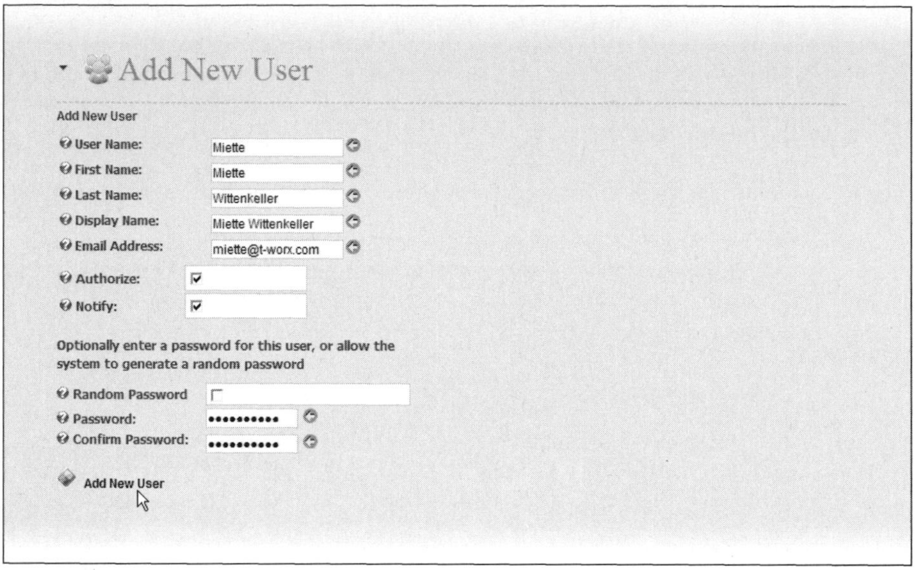

Figure 9-16

This displays the User Accounts page once again. By clicking All, it also allows you to confirm that the User Account has been created, as shown in Figure 9-17.

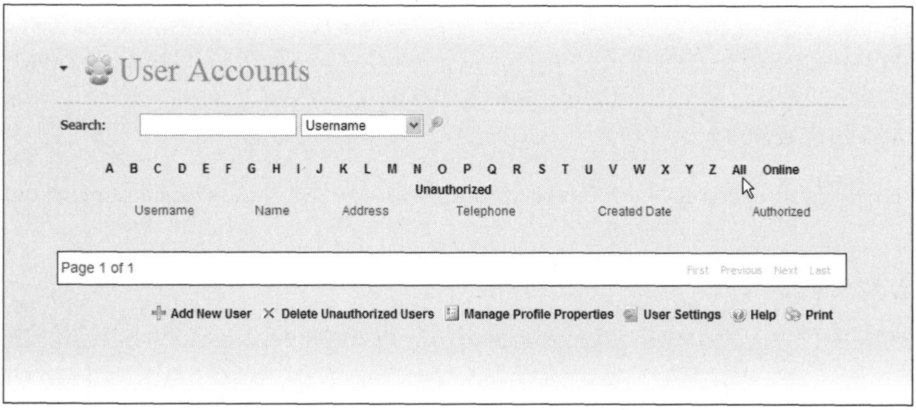

Figure 9-17

This displays all the User Accounts on your website. As you can see in Figure 9-18, a new account has been created for a user named Miette.

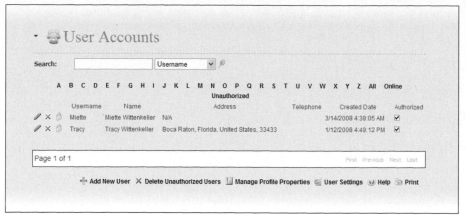

Figure 9-18

Notice the N/A next to Miette's name under the Address column. The N/A appears because no profile properties were defined for Miette, since an administrator created her account manually. However, because a confirmation e-mail was sent to Miette at the time her account was created, she can now log in and update her profile using the same process you stepped through earlier.

Editing User Accounts

After a User Account is created, users have the ability to update some of their account settings, including the ability to:

❑ **Manage User Credentials:** Change first and last name, display name, and e-mail address.

❑ **Manage Password:** Change password.

❑ **Manage Profile:** Complete additional properties that have been added (made visible) by an administrator.

❑ **Manage Service:** Subscribe to website services, if any are available.

To edit his account, a user must log in and click his display name to access his account information (refer to Figure 9-12).

Administrators

After a user has registered, administrators can edit User profiles and update other User Account properties including the ability to:

❑ **Manage User Credentials:** Change first and last name, display name and e-mail address, unauthorize Users (removing access to the website), force a password change.

❑ **Manage Password:** Change password, reset password.

❑ **Manage Profile:** Complete all available properties for a specific user.

❑ **Manage Profile Properties:** Edit list of available profile properties.

Administrators also have the ability to manage one of the most important features of the DNN framework, Roles-Based Security, which is the focus of this chapter.

Creating Security Roles

As I said in the beginning of this chapter, Roles-Based Security gives you the power to secure access to your website content via Security Roles. This allows you to make areas of your website available to users based on the Security Role(s) they belong to.

DotNetNuke provides the following flexible options for configuring the areas of our website:

❑ Each user of your website is assigned to a security role.

❑ A user can be assigned to several security roles at the same time.

❑ A Security Role can have several users assigned to it.

DNN includes the following three default Security Roles:

❑ Administrators

❑ Registered Users

❑ Subscribers

The Security Roles required for the sample MBR Design website are outlined in Table 9-2.

Table 9-2: Security Roles for MBR Design

Security Role Name	Type of Website Access
Administrators	Access for high-level administrators, add skins, modules, and so on
Registered Users	Access to all general areas of the website and downloads
Content Admin	Staff member access to manage all website content
Newsletter Subscribers	Users that wish to receive a monthly newsletter
Clients	Client access to see project updates

Now that I have defined the appropriate Security Roles for the MBR Design website, we need to add them. Because the Administrator and Registered User Security Roles exist by default, we only need to create the Content Admin, Newsletter Subscriber, and Client roles. You add the Content Admin Security Role using the following steps:

1. Log in with Admin or Host access and navigate to Admin ⇨ Security Roles, as shown in Figure 9-19.

Figure 9-19

This loads the Security Roles page displayed in Figure 9-20.

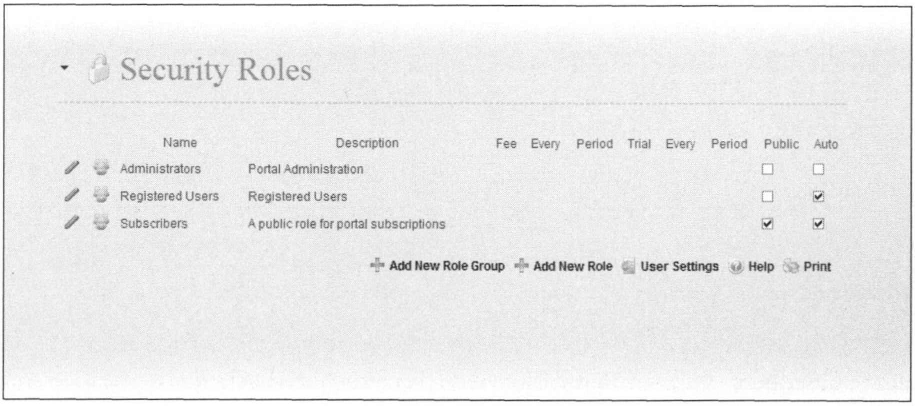

Figure 9-20

On the Security Roles page, you can see the Name and Description of the current roles. Also notice the Public and Auto columns on the right. These columns serve the following functions:

❑ **Public:** If the Public checkbox is selected, users are able to view details of this role and subscribe to it. It is important to note that users can subscribe to, or unsubscribe from, these roles when they manage their profile. Clear the Public checkbox if the role is Private.

❑ **Auto:** If the Auto checkbox is selected, users are automatically assigned to this role. Clear the Auto checkbox if users must be manually added to the role.

2. Select Add New Role to open the Edit Security Roles page shown in Figure 9-21.

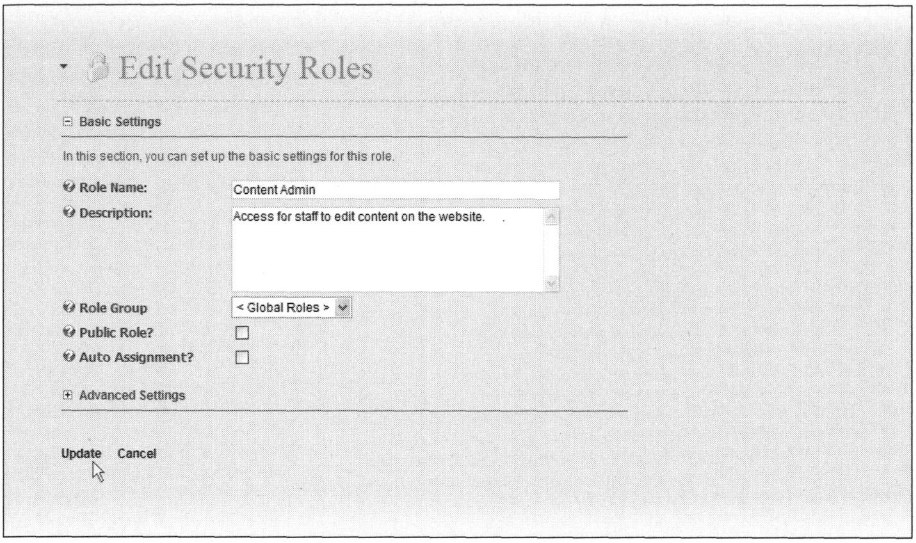

Figure 9-21

3. Enter the name for the new security role and the description. As you can see in Figure 9-21, other options are available. But for now, just click the Update link.

Figure 9-22 displays the Security Roles page with the new Content Admin Security Role added. As you can see, the Clients Security Role and the Newsletter Subscribers Security Role have also been added. If you want to edit the settings of a Security Role, simply click on the edit pencil to the left of the Role Name.

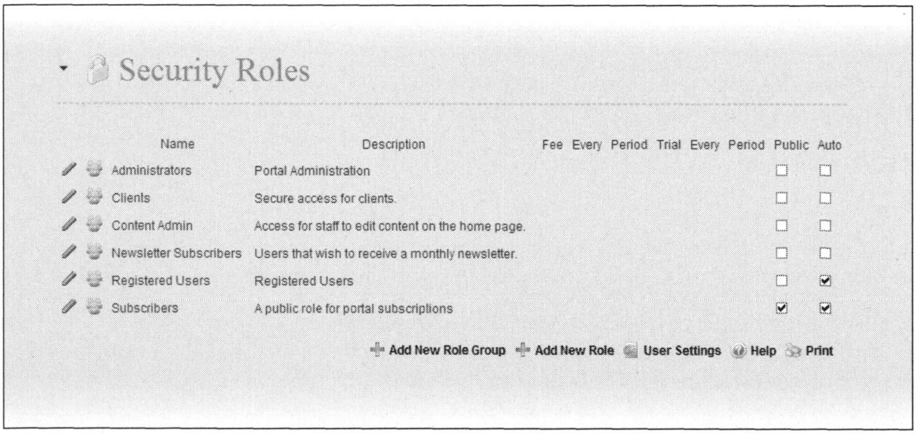

Figure 9-22

That's all there is to the creation of Security Roles. We'll apply the new roles to Users shortly. But first, we'll examine Role Groups.

Creating Security Role Groups

As a matter of convenience, in situations where you have a large number of roles, grouping them together creates a more manageable administration experience because roles can be applied to entire groups of users at the same time.

To create a new Role Group, select Add New Role Group on the Security Roles page. This will open the Edit Role Group page shown in Figure 9-23.

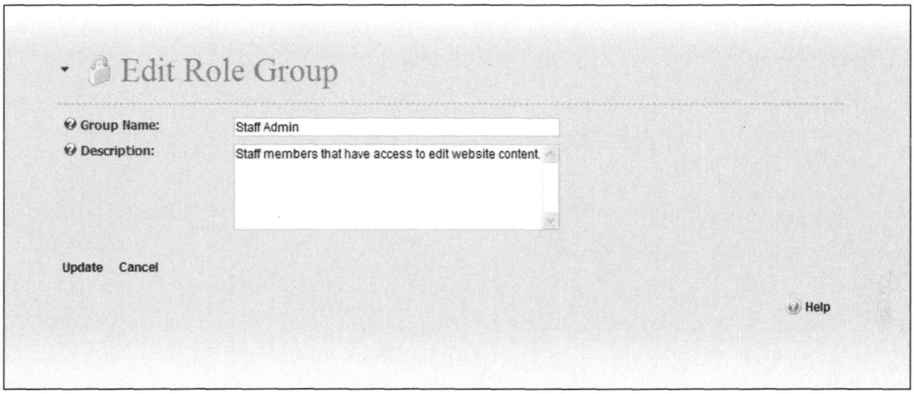

Figure 9-23

For this example, you create a Role Group to provide access to all staff members that can edit website content. After you enter the Group Name and Description, click Update to create the Role Group. Because the new Staff Admin Role Group has been created, you'll notice the Filter By Role Group drop-down list on the Security Roles page, as shown in Figure 9-24. However, if we were to select the Staff Admin Role from the drop-down list, no Roles would be displayed because no Roles have been added to the Staff Admin Role Group yet. So let's add the Content Admin Role to the Staff Admin Role Group by first clicking on the edit pencil icon next to Content Admin, also shown in Figure 9-24.

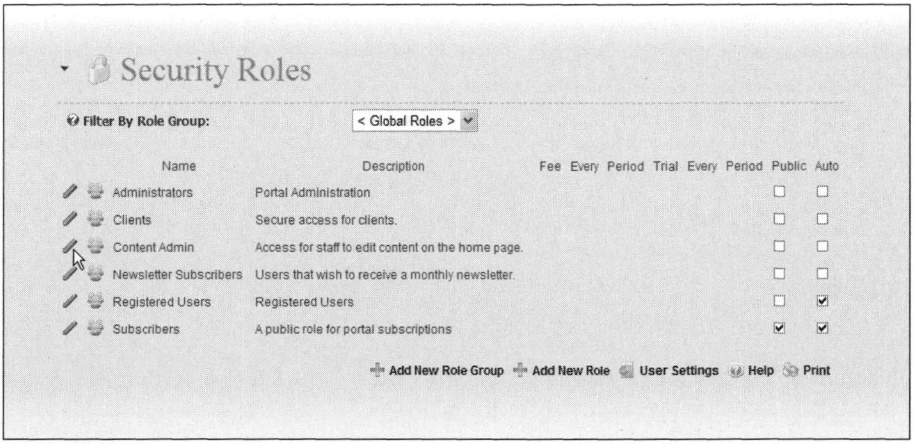

Figure 9-24

This opens the Edit Security Roles page for the Content Admin Security role, shown in Figure 9-25.

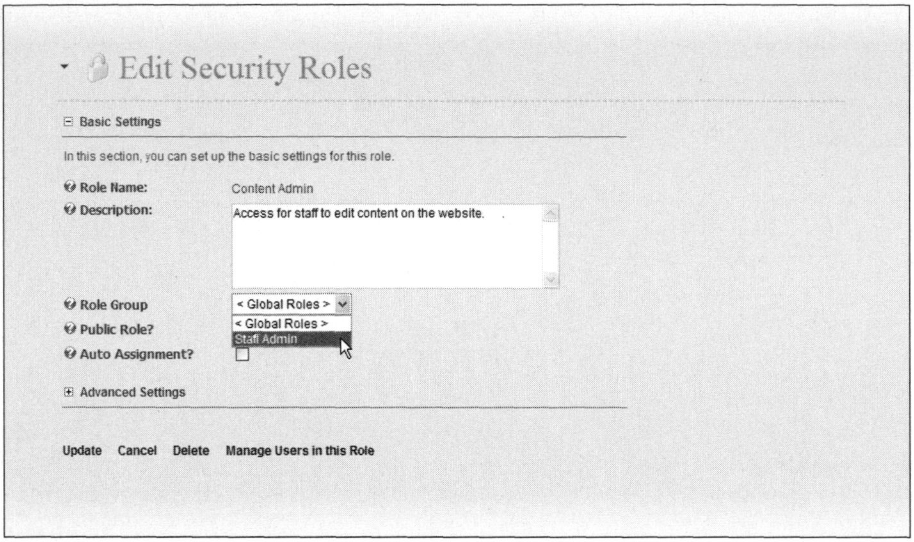

Figure 9-25

To add the Content Admin Role to the Staff Admin Role Group, select Staff Admin from the Role Group drop-down list, as shown in Figure 9-25, and then click Update to return to the Security Roles page shown in Figure 9-26.

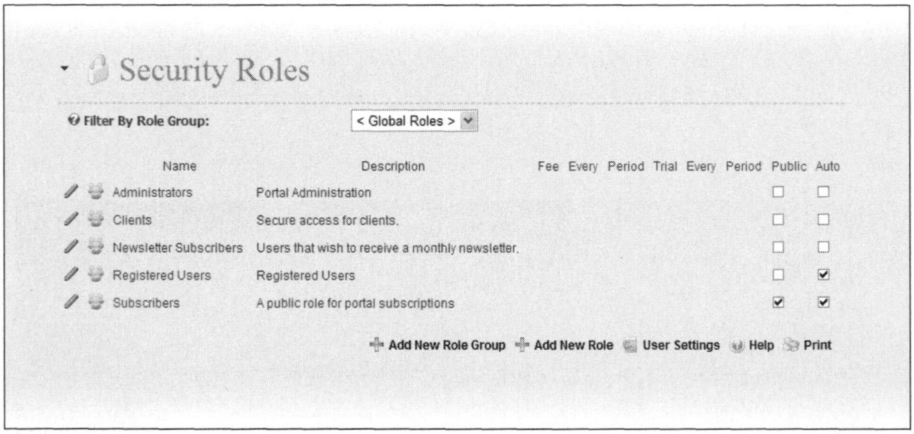

Figure 9-26

You'll notice something new on the Security Roles page now — the Filter By Role Group drop-down list, which is now being displayed because you've added a new Role Group. Also notice that the Content Admin Role is no longer displayed in the list of Security Roles because the list is currently being filtered by Global Roles. If you select Staff Admin from the Filter By Role Group drop-down list, you will see that the Content Admin Role has been added to it, as shown in Figure 9-27.

Figure 9-27

So you've successfully added the new Staff Admin Role Group and assigned the Content Admin Role to it. To edit the details of the Staff Admin Role Group, select the edit pencil icon next to the Staff Admin item in the Filter By Role Group drop-down list.

Role Groups provide a very useful function for categorizing the Security Roles on your DNN website — especially if you need to create a large number of Security Roles for different content administrators to edit different areas of a website, or if you are using roles as subscription services and have a large number of services available.

Assigning Security Roles to User Accounts

Security Roles can be assigned to User Accounts by using a couple of different methods. The first method allows website administrators to assign Security Roles on a user-by-user basis via the following steps:

1. Log in with Admin or Host access and navigate to Admin ⇨ User Accounts, as shown in Figure 9-28.

Figure 9-28

2. Select a User Account to edit. In this case, you're going to assign the Content Admin Security Role to the Staff1 User Account. Therefore, you click on the edit pencil icon next to the Staff1 Username, as shown in Figure 9-29.

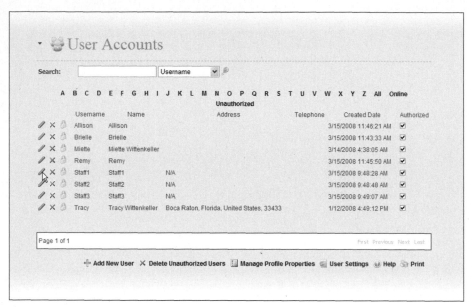

Figure 9-29

Before moving on to the next step, I want to point out that you have some options to select the User Account you want to edit. As you can see in Figure 9-29, you can type a Username in the Search field to find a user. This can be very helpful when many user accounts have been created on your DNN website. You also have the option to search by the first letter of a username by clicking on one of the letters (A through Z) below the Search field. This will list all of the User Accounts with a username that starts with the letter clicked. You can also click on the Online link to see a list of users currently logged in. And last, as I have done in Figure 9-29, you can simply click on the All link to list all of the User Accounts available on your DNN website. If there are more than ten User Accounts, DNN automatically gives you the option to page through them.

3. Clicking the edit pencil next to the Staff1 Username opens the Edit User Accounts page for the Staff1 user, as shown in Figure 9-30.

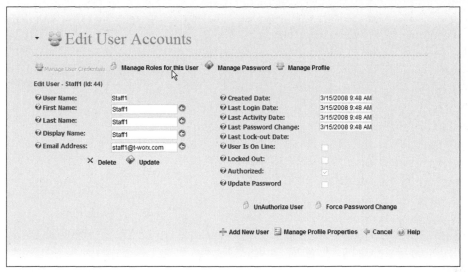

Figure 9-30

4. Select Manage Roles for this user, also shown in Figure 9-30. This will open the screen shown in Figure 9-31 and allows you to assign the appropriate Security Role(s) to the Staff1 User Account. Clicking the padlock icon next to a User Account name takes you straight to the User Roles page. However, we're going to take a long approach and see some of the other features along the way.

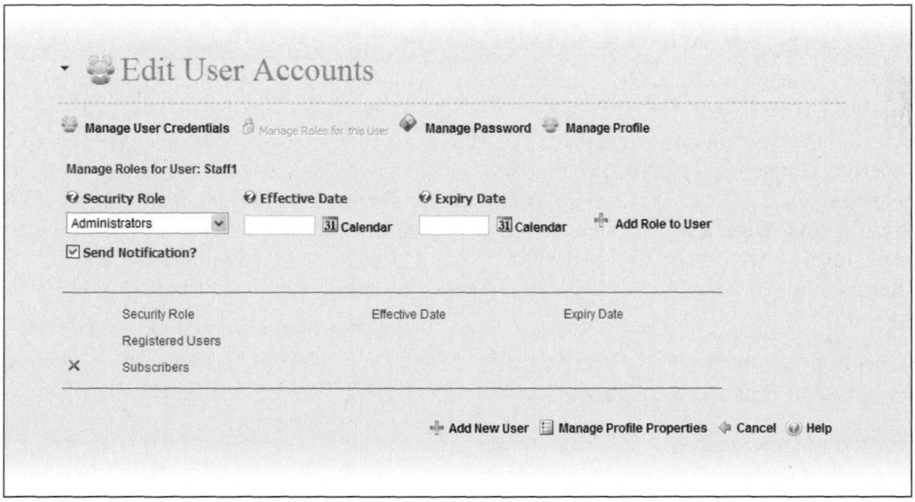

Figure 9-31

5. You want to add the Staff1 User Account to the Content Admin Security Role. Therefore, you have to select the Content Admin Security Role from the Security Role drop-down list, as shown in Figure 9-32.

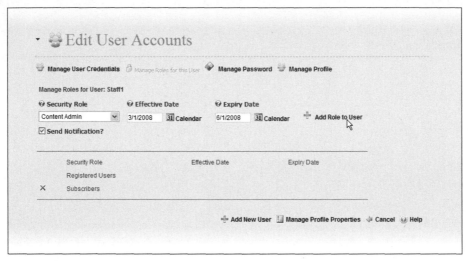

Figure 9-32

Also notice in Figure 9-32, you have the option to select an Effective Date and an Expiry Date for the assignment of this Role. If you do not enter an Effective Date, the assignment of the Role will start immediately. If you do not enter an Expiry Date, the assignment of the Role will not expire.

6. Clicking the Add Role to User link, as shown in Figure 9-32 will assign the Content Admin Role to the Staff1 User Account, as indicated in Figure 9-33.

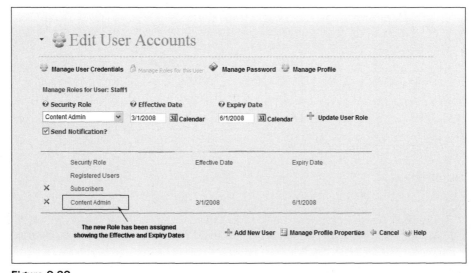

Figure 9-33

As you can see, the Content Admin Security Role has been added showing the Effective Date and expiry Date of the Role Expiry.

The other method to assign Security roles is much more efficient. To demonstrate this method, you'll also assign the Staff2 and Staff3 User Accounts to the Content Admin Security Role using the following steps:

1. Navigate to Admin ⇨ Security Roles (refer to Figure 9-19). This opens the Security Roles page once again, as shown in Figure 9-34.

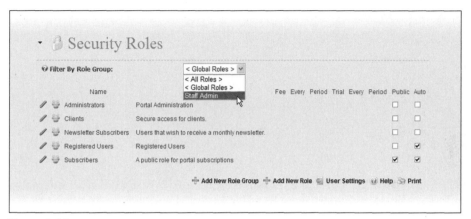

Figure 9-34

2. Because you have previously added the Content Admin Security Role to the Staff Admin Role Group, you need to select Staff Admin from the Filter By Role Group drop-down list, also shown in Figure 9-34, to view the Content Admin Security Role shown in Figure 9-35.

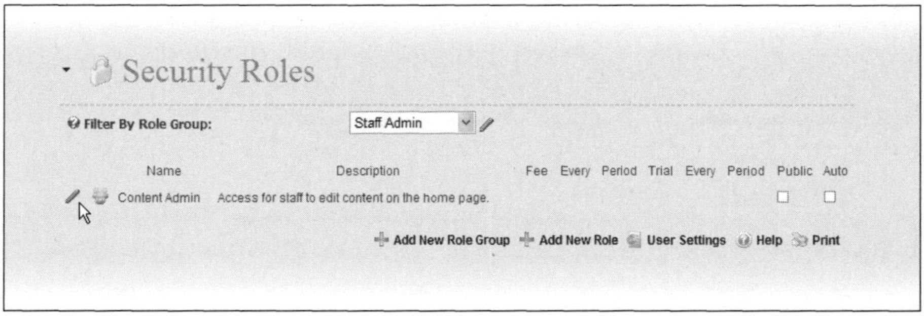

Figure 9-35

3. Click the edit pencil icon next to the Content Admin Role Name, shown in Figure 9-35. This opens the Edit Security Roles page for the Content Admin Security Role shown in Figure 9-36.

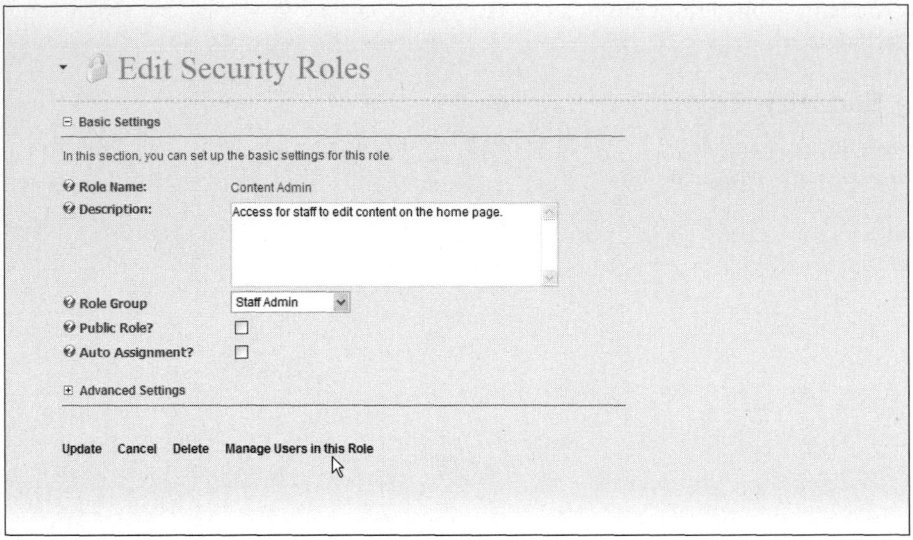

Figure 9-36

4. Click Manage Users in this Role, as shown in Figure 9-36. This will load the User Roles page, shown in Figure 9-37, and allow you to add Users to the Content Admin Security Role from a drop-down list of all available User Accounts.

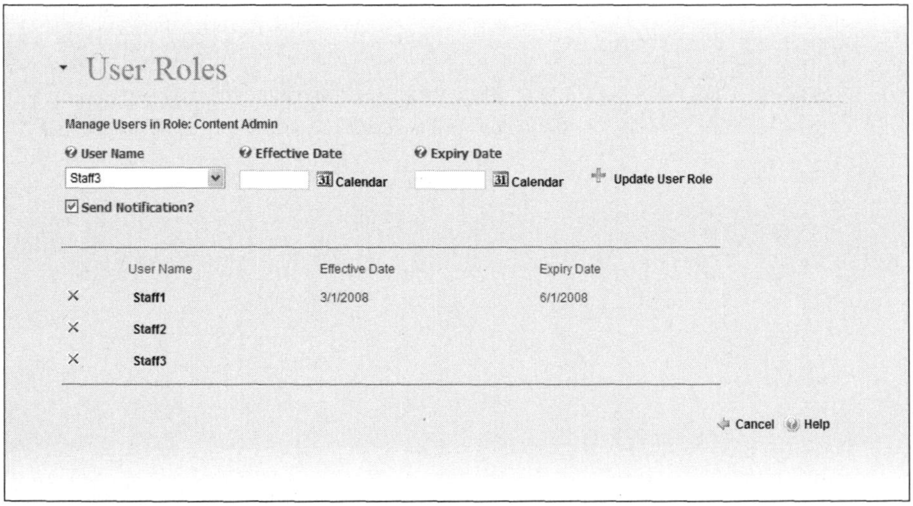

Figure 9-37

As you can see, the Content Admin Security Role has been assigned to the Staff 2 and Staff3 User Accounts. This was easily accomplished by selecting Staff2 from the User Name drop-down list and clicking Update User Role. The same was done for the Staff3 User Account. Effective and Expiry Dates were not defined for either User Account; therefore no Effective or Expiry Date is displayed for them.

Now that you have applied the appropriate Security Roles to User Accounts, let's assign Security Roles to pages and modules and see DNN's roles-based security in action.

Assigning Security Roles to Modules

You're now going to assign Security Roles to allow registered users to edit content depending on the Role(s) that have been assigned to them.

The modules you're initially going to work with are on the home page. Therefore, you need to go to the home page and log in as an Administrator, as shown in Figure 9-38.

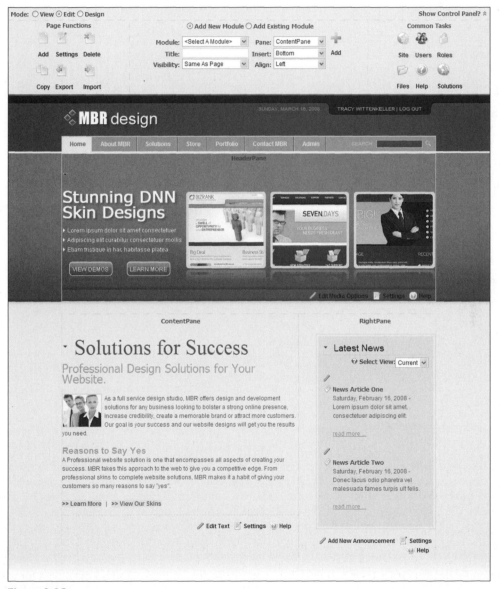

Figure 9-38

As you can see, there are three modules on the page. You want to give staff members the ability to edit all content on this page except the content in the Latest News module. You want to keep content in this module editable only by the website Administrator. So you have to define permissions appropriately for these modules. But first, take a look at the security settings assigned to the home page by clicking Settings under Page Functions within the Control Panel, as shown in Figure 9-39.

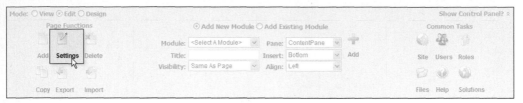

Figure 9-39

When the Page Management page opens, scroll down to view the Permissions area shown in Figure 9-40.

Figure 9-40

You can see the now familiar Filter By Group drop-down list for Role Groups. You can also see, the Permissions area displays all of the Security Roles available on the website that are not part of a Role Group. Notice that two new Roles have been created — the Homepage Content Edit Role (assigned to the Staff1 User Account) and the Homepage Header Edit Role (assigned to the Staff2 User Account). Also notice that only Administrators have the permissions to edit this page, and All Users can currently view this page. I'll explain the significance of this in a moment. For now, scroll down to the bottom of the page and click Cancel. This will take you back to the home page.

Next, hover over the Action Menu of the Latest News Module in the RightPane and select Settings, as shown in Figure 9-41.

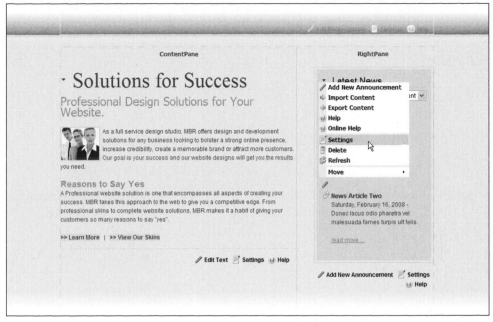

Figure 9-41

If we scroll down on the Module page, you see the Permissions area of the module, as shown in Figure 9-42.

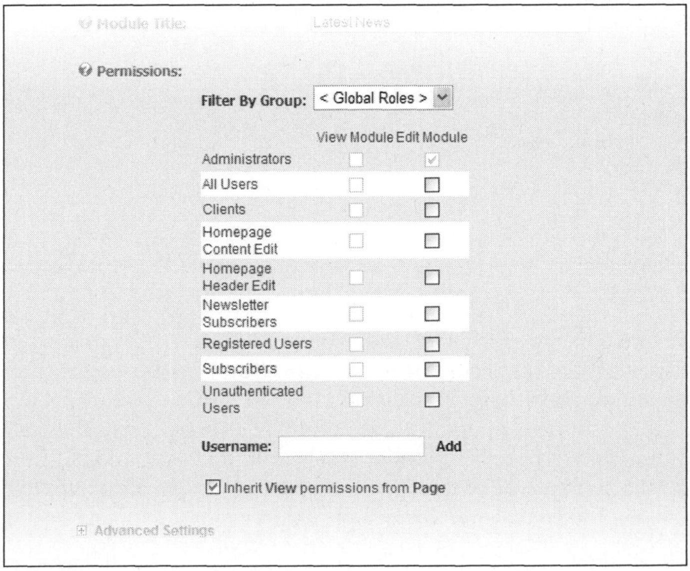

Figure 9-42

Notice below the list of Roles, the Inherit View permissions from the Page checkbox is selected. This box is checked as a default when adding modules. So the module has inherited the same permissions as the page. These are exactly the permissions you want for this module because you want only Administrators to have edit rights for this module, but you want all website visitors to be able to view the module. Once again, scroll down and click Cancel to go back to the home page.

Next, select Settings from the Stunning DNN Skin Designs module Action menu in the HeaderPane, as shown in Figure 9-43.

Figure 9-43

You can view the Permissions in Figure 9-44.

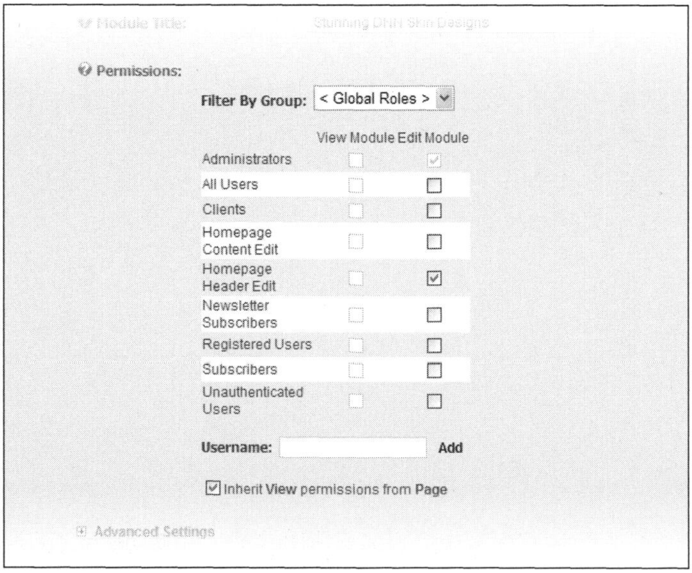

Figure 9-44

Because you want to assign edit rights only to users within the Homepage Header Edit Role, you simply select the Edit Module checkbox next to the Home Header Edit Role, also shown in Figure 9-44. This time, you scroll down and click Update to accept these settings.

Next, assign the correct permissions to the Solutions for Success module on the home page by selecting Settings from the Action menu and viewing its permissions, as shown in Figure 9-45.

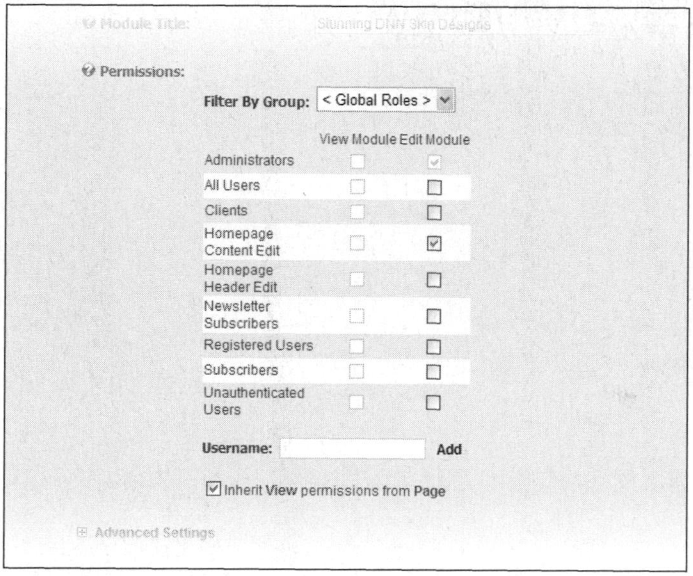

Figure 9-45

For this module, you want only those users that have been assigned the Homepage Content Edit Role to have the permissions to edit this module. Therefore, you'll assign the permissions shown in Figure 9-45 and click Update to accept these settings.

Now you are ready to see the permissions you have applied in action. To do so, first log out and log back in as Staff1 to see the results in Figure 9-46.

Figure 9-46

Because the Staff1 user was assigned the Homepage Header Edit Role, notice that this user can edit only the content of the Stunning DNN Skin Designs module in the HeaderPane (the only module on the page assigned the Homepage Header Edit Role). Also notice that the Staff1 user does not have access to add additional pages or modules. Because they do not have Administrator access privileges, neither the Control Panel nor the Admin menu is displayed for this user.

Now let's log out and log back in as the Staff2 user, who has been assigned the Homepage Content Edit Role. These results are shown in Figure 9-47.

Figure 9-47

Because the Staff2 user has been assigned the Homepage Content Edit Role, this user can edit only the content of the Solutions for Success module in the ContentPane (the only module on the page assigned the Homepage Content Edit Role). And just like the Staff1 user, the Staff2 user does not have access to the Control Panel or the Admin menu because the Staff2 user does not have Administrator privileges.

As an option to assigning edit rights to the Stunning DNN Skin Designs and Solutions for Success modules to the Staff1 and Staff2 User Accounts separately, you can easily assign the Content Admin Role that you created earlier to these modules. This would give anyone in the Content Admin Role the appropriate permissions to edit these modules when logged in.

Let's initiate the update process of the Stunning DNN Skin Designs module first by logging in as an Administrator and selecting Settings from the Action menu to display the permissions in Figure 9-48.

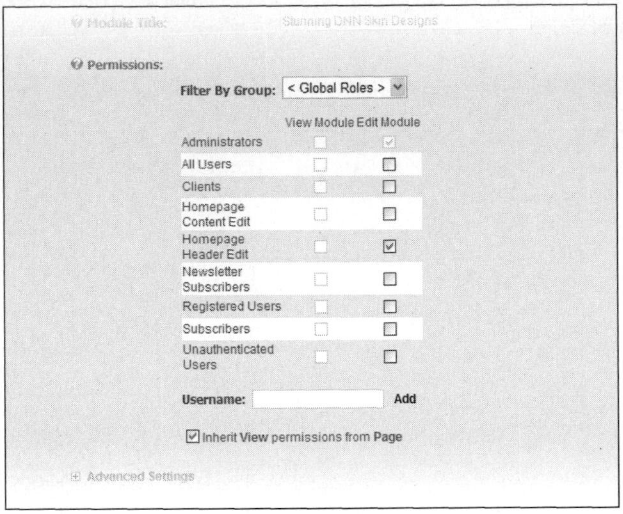

Figure 9-48

If you recall, you assigned the Content Admin Security Role to the Staff Admin Role Group. Therefore, if you select All Roles from the Filter By Group drop-down list, as shown in Figure 9-49, the Content Admin Role will be added to the Permissions list.

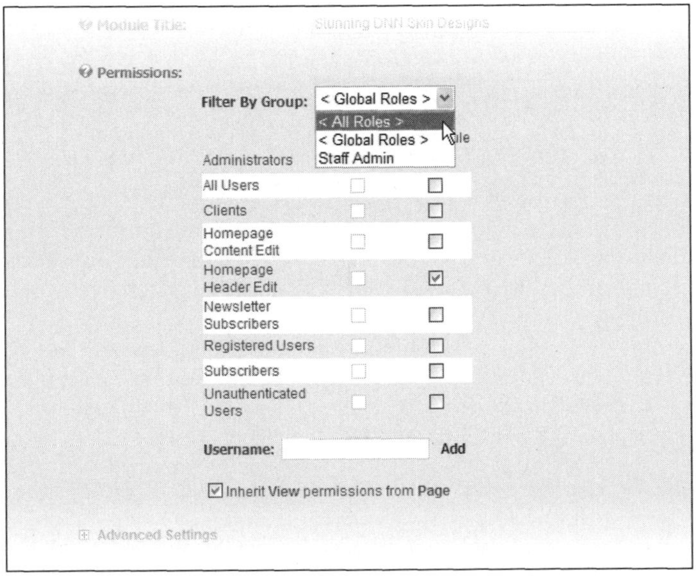

Figure 9-49

After All Roles is selected, as shown in Figure 9-50, you can now see that the Content Admin Role has been added to the list of Permissions.

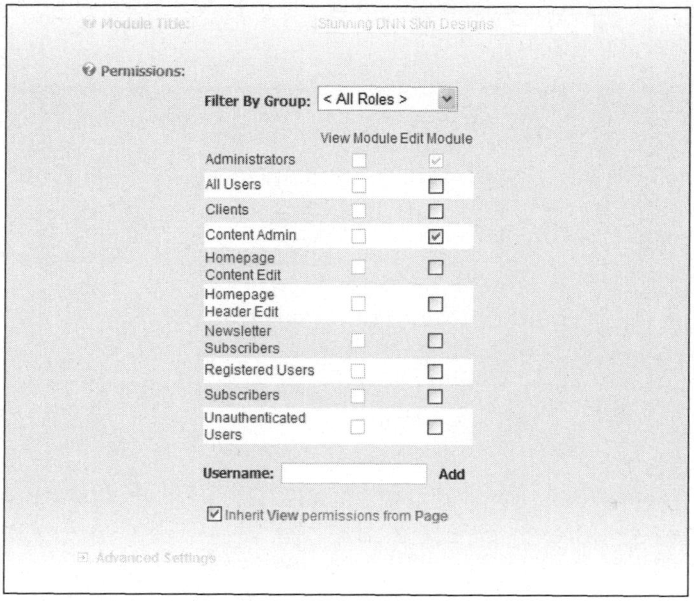

Figure 9-50

Now, you just need to select the View and Edit Module checkboxes and scroll down and click Update to save your changes.

Make these same changes to the Solution for Success module. Then, log out and log back in as the Staff1 user to see the results in Figure 9-51.

Figure 9-51

Notice that the Stunning DNN Skin Designs and Solutions for Success modules are now editable by the Staff1 user (and Staff2 and Staff3 users) because the Content Admin Security Role has been assigned.

Assigning Security Roles to Pages

You're now going to create two secure pages on the website — a Downloads page, visible to all users, so registered users of the site can download files — and a Clients page, visible only to clients, so clients can download documents.

First, add the Downloads page after logging is as an Administrator, as shown in Figure 9-52.

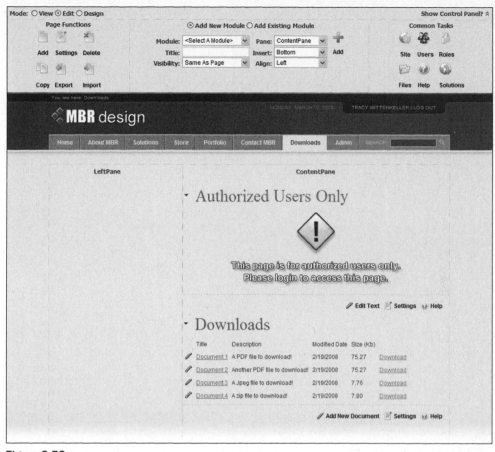

Figure 9-52

As you can see, the Downloads page has been added as a top-level menu item. Also notice that the Downloads page contains two modules — one that is displayed to users who are not registered (unauthenticated), and one that displays downloads that are available to registered users (authenticated). Let's log out and see the page as it is displayed to general website visitors, shown in Figure 9-53.

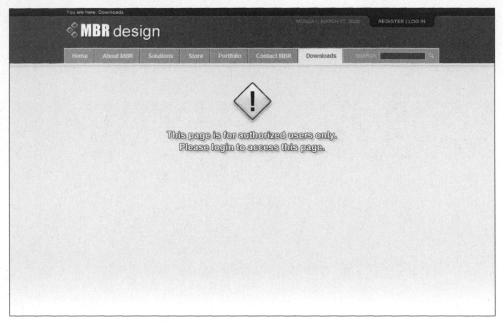

Figure 9-53

The message in Figure 9-53 is displayed to visitors to let them know that they must log in to access the Downloads. You could register at this time and create a new User Account. But for now, just log in as the existing user Brielle, as shown in Figure 9-54.

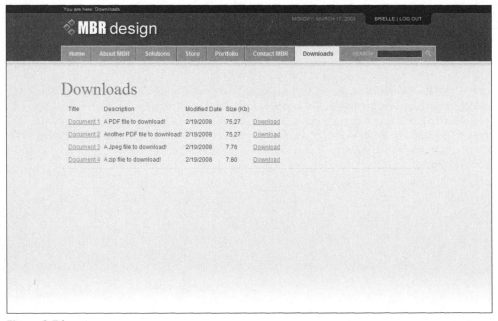

Figure 9-54

As you can see, because Brielle is a registered user, she is not shown the message reminding her that she has to log in. And because she is logged in as a registered user, she has access to the downloads.

Creating this specific access is accomplished in two steps. First, assign the Downloads page Permissions (select Settings under Page Functions in the Control Panel), as shown in Figure 9-55.

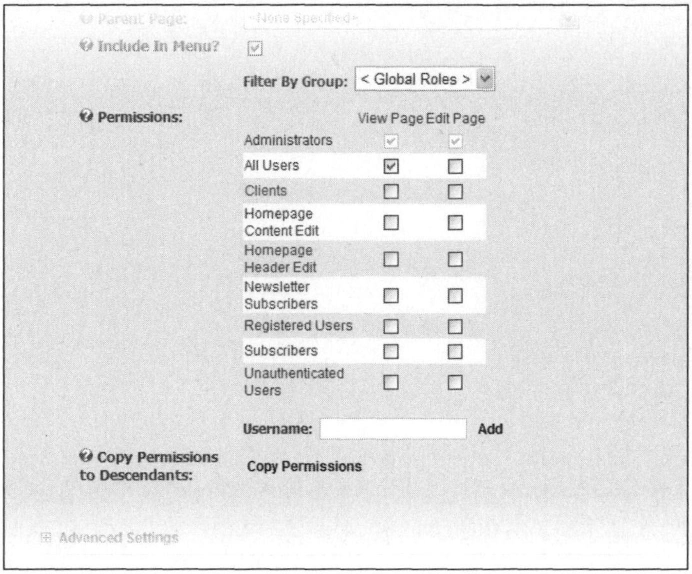

Figure 9-55

As you can see, the Permissions have been set so only Administrators can edit the Downloads page. But, because you may want to include content on the Downloads page to entice general visitors to become registered users, the Permissions have also been set so all users can view the Downloads page.

The next step to complete the secure Downloads page access is to assign the correct Permissions to the modules that have been added to the Downloads page.

Figure 9-56 displays the Permissions for the module titled Authorized Users Only. This is a Text/HTML module that was added to display the reminder message that the Downloads page is for authorized (registered) users only.

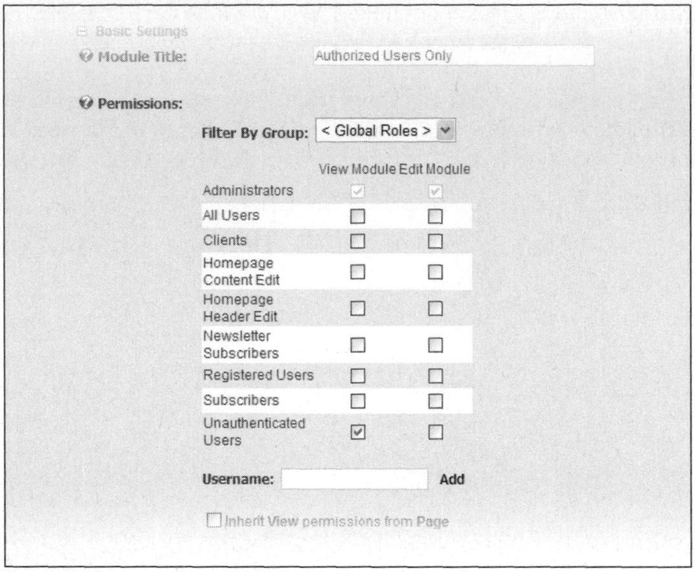

Figure 9-56

Notice that this module is set to be viewed by Administrators and Unauthenticated Users only. Therefore, the login reminder message is viewed by the general public only. So when a Registered User is logged in and views this page, the login reminder message is not displayed.

Figure 9-57 shows how the Permissions were assigned to the Downloads module. This is the Documents module that was added that shows a list of files that can be downloaded by Registered Users.

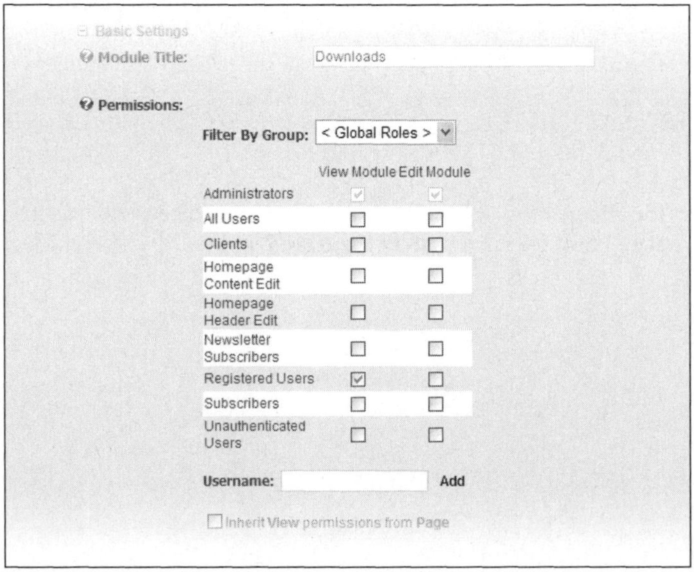

Figure 9-57

To ensure that only Registered Users can download files, the Registered Users Security Role is the only role that has been selected to view this module. Therefore, only when a user is logged in do they have access to download files from the Downloads page.

You've just learned how to create access to pages on your site that are secure but viewable by all users. Now, I'm going to show you another typical method of creating secure access to pages that are viewable only to users when logged in.

As you can see in Figure 9-58, the Clients page has been added and includes a Documents module that allows Clients to download files.

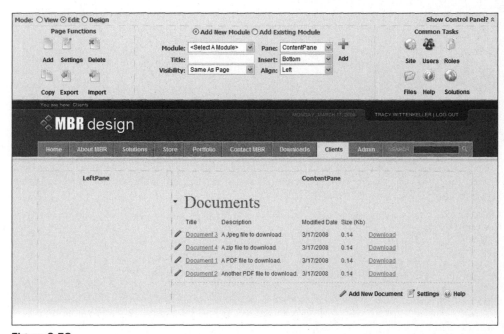

Figure 9-58

Before you log out from the Administrator Account and view your live pages, let's take a look under the hood at the Clients page Permissions shown in Figure 9-59.

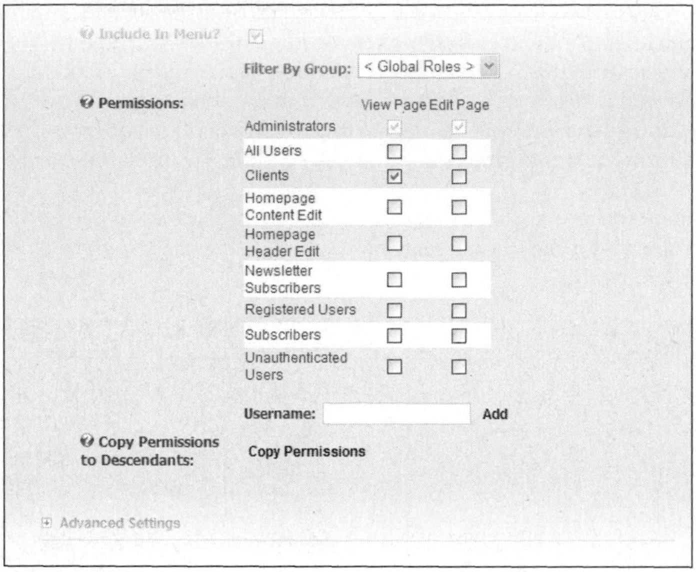

Figure 9-59

As you can see, we enabled only the Clients Role to view this page by selecting the View Page checkbox next to the Clients Security Role.

Now let's look at the Documents module Permissions on the Clients page shown in Figure 9-60.

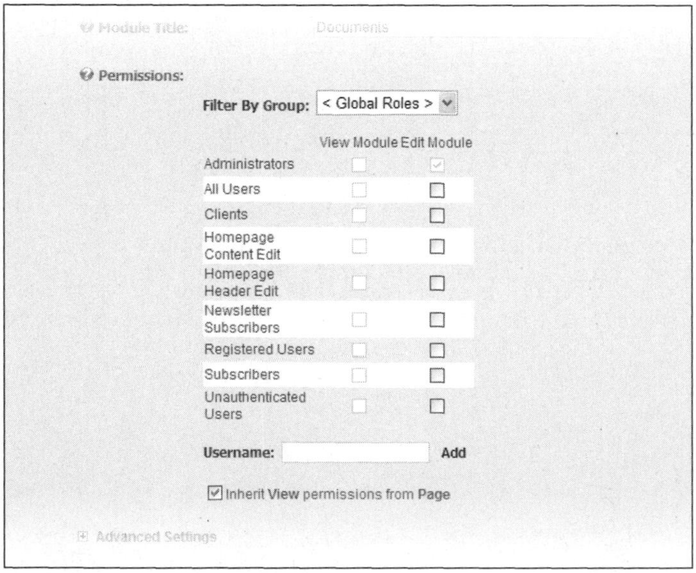

Figure 9-60

Notice that the Documents module does not require a special Security Role Assignment. You have taken care of that at the page level. Remember that when a module is added to a page, the default Permissions setting is to Inherit View permissions from Page. Therefore, because you defined the Permissions of the Clients page to be viewable only to users that are logged in as Clients, and because the Documents module is inheriting those same Permissions you assigned to the Clients page, no other Security Role Assignments are required for the module.

Let's see the results of your Permissions settings for the Clients page. Figure 9-61 displays the home page as it is seen by general website visitors.

Figure 9-61

As you can see, the new Clients page is not visible by general website visitors. However, when a user that has been assigned to the Clients Security Role logs in, in this case Remy, the client's page is clearly visible as a top-level menu item, with access to the Clients downloads, as shown in Figure 9-62.

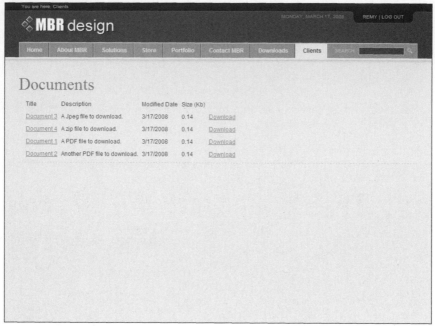

Figure 9-62

Summary

This chapter introduced some important concepts that are vital to most modern websites. First, you learned how to define the type of registration for your DNN site and customize the fields available to users at the time of registration. You also learned how to create and edit Users Accounts.

This chapter is also very important as it highlighted one of the most powerful features of the DNN framework: Roles-Based Security. As you have learned, DNN's Roles-Based Security offers an out-of-the-box robust method for dealing with permissions and controlling the tasks users are allowed to perform, by empowering you to assign roles to pages and modules that determine the access extended to users within your website.

Because of its overall importance, let me recap the concept of Roles-Based Security from a high-level view. Basically, to implement Roles-Based Security, you simply need to create the appropriate Security Roles and assign permissions based on those Roles, to users and/or groups of users, at the module and/ or page level. This allows very granular control over the actions of users within your DNN website.

It takes a little work to fully grasp the concept of Roles-Based Security. But I hope that I've shown you that it's really not that difficult, if you take a systematic approach to the entire process of creating Security Roles and defining permissions based on them. With the right combination of module and page permissions, you truly can create just about any type of security levels you desire for your DNN website. I trust the knowledge you have gained in this chapter has taken your DNN website to a whole new level of power and dimension.

In the next chapter, I focus on another important topic with most modern-day websites — e-commerce. You learn how to turn visitors into customers by setting up your own simple store, populating it with products, and allowing customers to make purchases via Paypal.

10

Tips, Tricks, and Additional Resources

Throughout this book I've offered real-world examples from my experience using DNN every day for the last four to five years. The methods contained in this book are by no means the be-all and end-all of designing and implementing sites with DNN. But taking advantage of the experience I have shared should give you a jumpstart at building your own professional DNN website solutions.

In this book, I have taken a systematic approach to detailing many techniques that have helped me become successful with DNN. My goal was to offer you real-world examples, while presenting key aspects of DNN that will help you in your day-to-day usage of the application. Ultimately, I hope the information in this book enables you to "hit the ground running" and considerably reduce the amount of time required for you to implement your own DNN solutions.

I want to finish with a chapter that provides you with additional techniques and resources that will help to make your DNN website implementations successful. The tips in this chapter, cover a wide range of topics and are offered in no particular order. At the end of the chapter, I provide some excellent resources that will offer a lot of value to your DNN endeavors. Therefore, without further ado . . . let's bring on the tips!

Skinning

This first tip is one I touched upon in Chapter 4, but it's worth noting again. When creating skins, make it a standard practice to ensure they expand seamlessly, if necessary, for wider content. It doesn't even have to be obvious to the client/website administrators.

Take it from experience, there's nothing worse than a skin "breaking" when you start applying content or when logged in as Admin or Host (adding additional menu items). If you take the extra time coding your HTML properly, you mitigate the possibility of your clients freaking out when the skin you have designed for them "blows up."

There's a simple way to do this if you are using tables-based code, although it requires a bit of nesting. The first step is to create an underlying table and apply the minimum width of your skin to it via a single CSS style. (I typically name this CSS style something like MainTable.) Here's a simple HTML code example:

```
<table border="0" cellpadding="0" cellspacing="0" class="MainTable">
    <tr>
      <td></td>
    </tr>
    <tr>
      <td></td>
    </tr>
    <tr>
      <td></td>
    </tr>
</table>
```

Then you nest tables that have a width of 100 percent, applied via another CSS style, inside the appropriate cells of the MainTable like this:

```
<table border="0" cellpadding="0" cellspacing="0" class="MainTable">
    <tr>
      <td><table border="0" cellpadding="0" cellspacing="0" class="InnerTable"
id="NestedTable1">
        <tr>
          <td>NestedTable1 Cell</td>
        </tr>
      </table></td>
    </tr>
    <tr>
      <td><table border="0" cellpadding="0" cellspacing="0" class="InnerTable"
id="NestedTable1">
        <tr>
          <td>NestedTable2 Cell</td>
        </tr>
      </table></td>
    </tr>
    <tr>
      <td><table border="0" cellpadding="0" cellspacing="0" class="InnerTable"
id="NestedTable1">
        <tr>
          <td>NestedTable3 Cell</td>
        </tr>
      </table></td>
    </tr>
</table>
```

The appropriate CSS code is as follows:

```
/* Width of Skin */
.MainTable {width: 700px;}

/* Width of Inner Tables */
.InnerTable {width: 100%;}
```

As you can see, the underlying table has a width of 700 pixels applied to it via the MainTable CSS style. This is the minimum width of the skins. Also notice that the inner tables have a width of 100 percent defined via the InnerTable CSS style.

Figures 10-1 and 10-2 illustrate this example.

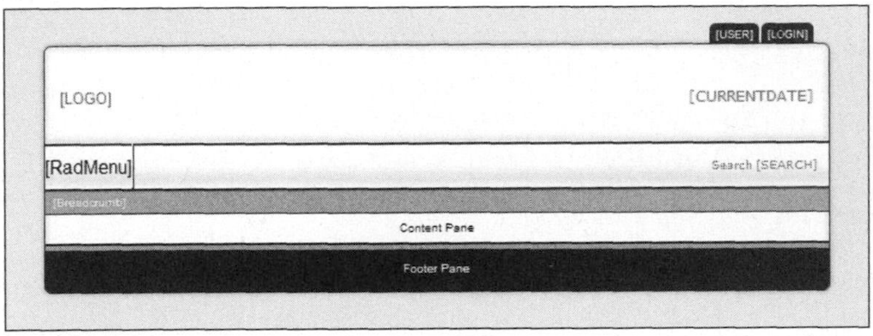

Figure 10-1

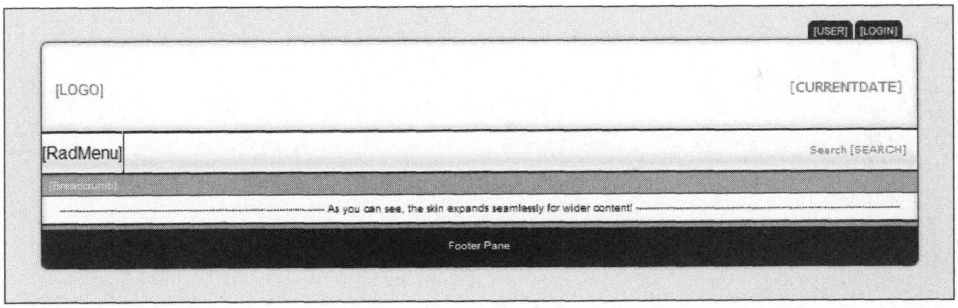

Figure 10-2

Figure 10-1 shows a preview of a skin in a browser with an underlying table and nested tables applied. Figure 10-2 shows how the skin expands seamlessly when content forces the skins wider.

This method ensures that when content forces the MainTable wider, the nested tables, with defined widths of 100 percent, will also stretch to the full width of your underlying table. If your skin is coded properly, when any content is applied, your graphics will maintain their appearance no matter how wide your web pages expand. And you'll never get a call from a stressed-out client panicking because his website has just exploded.

To Div or Not to Div . . .

You probably have heard the buzz term "web standards." "Web standards" is a general term for the formal standards and other technical specifications that define and describe aspects of the World Wide Web. In recent years, the term has been more frequently associated with the trend of endorsing a set of standardized best practices for building websites, and a philosophy of web design and development that includes those methods.

Many interdependent standards and specifications, some of which govern aspects of the Internet, not just the World Wide Web, directly or indirectly affect the development and administration of websites and web services. While any of these may be called "web standards," advocates within the web standards movement tend to focus on the higher-level standards that most directly affect the accessibility and usability of websites.

When a website is described as complying with web standards, it usually means that the site or page has valid or nearly valid HTML, CSS, and JavaScript. Web standards–compliant HTML typically also meets accessibility and semantic guidelines set forth by the World Wide Web Consortium (WC3), which develops web standards and guidelines. "Web accessibility" refers to the practice of making websites usable by people of all abilities and disabilities. When sites are correctly designed, developed, and edited, all users can have equal access to information and functionality.

Coding for web standards requires the use of pure CSS code (divs), with no tables whatsoever, because tables-based code does not work well with certain devices like screen readers for users that have specific accessibility needs. This poses some issues when creating standards-based DNN skins (and websites), mainly because you lose some control over how skins react to content. For example, when coding with divs, you cannot use the preceding method to create skins with a minimum width that adjusts for wider content. Instead, you have to build several skins with varying widths and apply the appropriate skin to your pages. This may not seem like a big issue until you consider the dynamic nature of content within a DNN website. For example, sometimes you cannot predict when a page displays content that isn't planned for a fixed-width, div-based design.

Another issue simply comes down to dollars and cents. Creating DNN skins with divs instead of tables requires approximately 1.5–2 times more development time than creating skins with tables. Is the extra time worth it? That's a question only the developer/designer can answer.

If you take this a step further, there is a larger issue with trying to get DNN websites to abide by web standards. Creating div-based skins and applying them to a basic DNN website, thereby making the skins compliant with web standards, is certainly doable . However, many DNN modules are coded with tables. And as soon as you start inserting modules that are coded with tables, you very rapidly lose validation as defined by the WC3. This means that creating compliant, standards-based DNN websites is difficult, simply because validation is almost impossible to maintain.

So what level of importance is placed on web standards as they relate to DNN skins and DNN websites? In the U.K., where they have laws governing web standards, it is important, but not in the U.S. and most other countries. So it really comes down to a matter of personal choice, either on the part of the designer/developer, or the client who dictates that choice, based perhaps on the geographic location of her web audience.

As a designer, I prefer to use tables-based code because I have a good level of control over how DNN skins react to content, which from experience, I've come to know is very important to clients and website administrators. And as far as speed goes, in today's world of high-speed Internet access, the difference between tables-based and div-based page load times is hardly noticeable if your HTML is coded properly. True, the amount of markup for a div-based skin is considerably less, but the user typically will not notice it, given the content that gets loaded anyway. So, for me, the choice is tables-based code, unless a client specifically requests div-based code.

So for me, while it's true you can do some really cool things with divs and pure CSS that you can't with tables, tables-based code works very well for DNN websites. You have to look at what is important to every solution and the bottom line. What works for one solution may not be right for another. You have to ask yourself if there is a valid reason to achieve standards-based compliance. If there isn't, why complicate your life and your website?

Use Content Panes Wherever Possible

Try to make as many areas of your skins editable (via content panes) as possible to make it easy for administrators to have as much control over their pages as possible. I see many skins that have hard-coded header images fixed in their skins, with a content pane to the right or left of the image like the image shown in Figure 10-3.

Figure 10-3

This is acceptable if you want to use the same image on several pages. But this isn't following good practice with the overall dynamic spirit of DNN. What if you want to change the image without applying a different skin each time? In this case, the image would have to be changed at the skin level. Why not just create a header pane for this area so the image and text can be changed very quickly using a module?

This method offers at least two important advantages. First, it gives complete control to the client/website administrator to update all of the content in the header. Second, it creates more flexibility in the skin because the header pane can collapse if no content is applied to it, which provides more real estate for interior pages using the same skin.

Don't get me wrong. Sometimes, based on specific design requirements mandated by a project, it is necessary to hard-code images in the skin HTML. However, I have seen fewer and fewer cases where this is a requirement. In fact, you will find that, given the choice, clients and/or site administrators would rather have the capability to change as much content as they can via content panes. This kind of flexibility puts the power squarely in the hands of clients and administrators, which is exactly where it should be with DNN website solutions.

Content

Anyone can create a great-looking skin (well, not quite). But that doesn't guarantee great-looking content, or content that is as easily manageable as it should be. In fact, many DNN users find it difficult to get a handle on formatting their content without digging into HTML. But the good news is that a little out-of-the-box thinking can go a long way.

To illustrate what I mean, let's take a look at Figure 10-4.

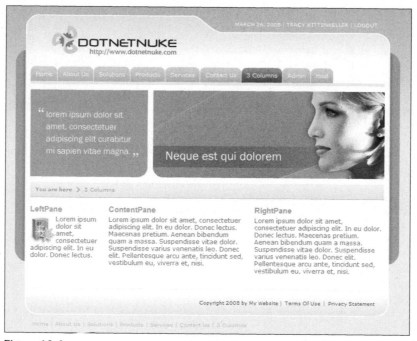

Figure 10-4

As you can see, the skin in Figure 10-4 has a three-column format, but the columns do not have an equal width by virtue of text alone. However, you can use a sneaky little trick to get the columns to display with the same width and add a little polish to the content layout, as shown in Figure 10-5.

Figure 10-5

The trick is not obvious . . . and that's the sneaky part and the beauty of it. All I did was insert a 1 × 1 pixel transparent spacer.gif at the bottom of all three Text/HTML modules. In this case, I specified the width of the spacer.gif as 200 pixels. The 1 pixel height makes virtually no difference on the page, and the 200 pixel width is consistent in all three modules, thus making them the same width. The beginning code looks like this:

```
<p>Lorem ipsum dolor sit amet, consectetuer adipiscing elit. In eu dolor. Donec
lectus. Maecenas pretium. Aenean bibendum quam a massa. Suspendisse vitae dolor.
Suspendisse varius venenatis leo. Donec elit. Pellentesque arcu ante, tincidunt
sed, vestibulum eu, viverra et, nisi. </p>
```

As you can see above, only text is in the Text/HTML module. The code that follows shows the addition of the spacer.gif that was inserted in all three modules to create the consistent width.

```
<p>Lorem ipsum dolor sit amet, consectetuer adipiscing elit. In eu dolor. Donec
lectus. Maecenas pretium. Aenean bibendum quam a massa. Suspendisse vitae dolor.
Suspendisse varius venenatis leo. Donec elit. Pellentesque arcu ante, tincidunt
sed, vestibulum eu, viverra et, nisi.<br /><img height="1" alt="" width="200"
src="/Portals/17/spacer.gif" /></p>
```

As you can see, nothing complicated was required. But the result made a big difference in how the content is being displayed. As you can imagine, this simple method can be very useful in many different scenarios with content panes. I hope you can see that using this method is a good way to provide a little extra polish and control over your content. And no one will ever be the wiser.

Displaying Content on All Pages . . . or Not

You would be surprised how many DNN users do not take advantage of the Display Module On All Pages feature within DNN. This is a great feature to display address or other key information across many pages very quickly. Quite simply, this feature does what you would expect — it allows you to place a module on all pages of your DNN website in the same content pane from page to page. This feature is applied via Module Settings ⇨ Advanced Settings, as shown in Figure 10-6.

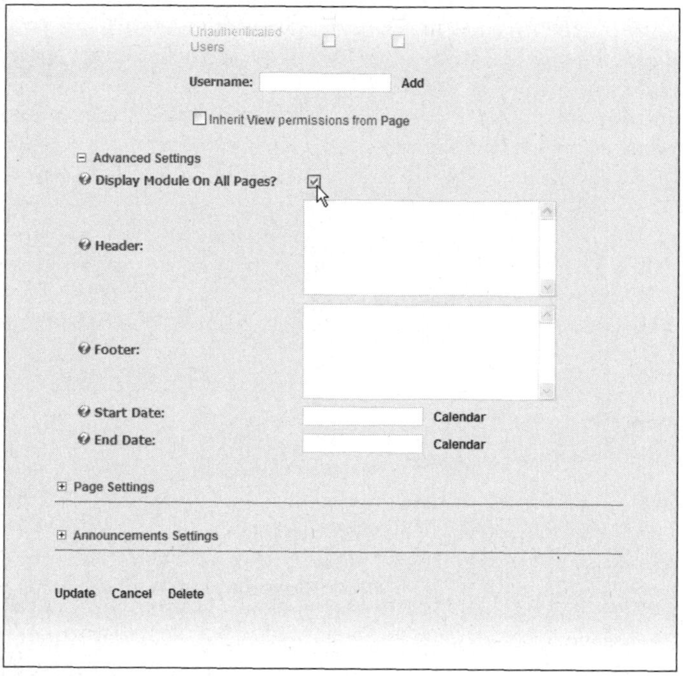

Figure 10-6

To stop a module from displaying on all pages, you simply clear the Display Module On All Pages checkbox. However, you should be aware that the page you are on, when disabling this feature, will be the only page the module will exist on, upon disabling the Display Module On All Pages feature. For example, say you insert the module and apply the Display Module On All Pages feature while on the Home page, but you disable this feature while on the Contacts page. The result will be the module displaying on the Contacts page only.

It is important to note that many users think that by simply deleting a module that is being displayed on all pages removes it from the website. But this is not the case. If you delete a module that is being displayed on all pages, you will delete only the instance of the module on the current page you are deleting it from. Because the Display Module On All Pages feature was implemented, the module will continue to be displayed on all other pages within the website.

Can you see the advantage to this? It's actually very useful when you want to display a module on all but a couple of pages within your DNN website. As an option, you could add an existing module to your pages multiple times. But why spend the extra time when you don't have to? Simply display a module on all pages, and then delete it from the pages where it is not required. This achieves the same result as adding a module as an existing module. Additionally, no matter what page you are on when you edit the module, you will see the changes site-wide.

Creating Page Templates

One very useful feature of DNN is the ability to create page templates. When you create a page Template, you duplicate the layout of an existing page to serve as a starting point for content administrators. And depending on the different layouts required for content, you could create page Templates for administrators to select from, when adding new content. This makes it easy for site administrators to manage content administrators as well, because they are fixed layouts to start the content administration process.

To create a page Template, either select an existing page on your site to serve as the basis for your page Template or create a new page, as shown in Figure 10-7. The content can even be dummy content as the page simply creates the basis for a page Template with the layout you require. If you like, you can even leave the modules blank with no content applied to them if you want content administrators to start with a clean slate.

Figure 10-7

After your page has been created, click the Export icon under Page Functions. This opens the Export Page settings shown in Figure 10-8.

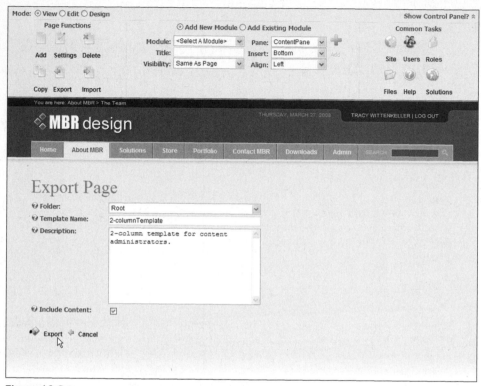

Figure 10-8

As you can see, you have a couple of options. First, select a destination folder for the template file. In this case, I chose the Root folder. Then, give the template a name and description. If you want to include the content of the modules, select the Include Content checkbox. If you don't select this option, the page Template will be created with empty modules in place. When you click Export, your new page Template will be created in the folder you have specified.

Like many features of DNN, applying a page Template is very easy (big surprise huh?). To create a new page based on a page Template, click the Import icon under Page Functions in the Control Panel. This opens the Import Page settings, as shown in Figure 10-9.

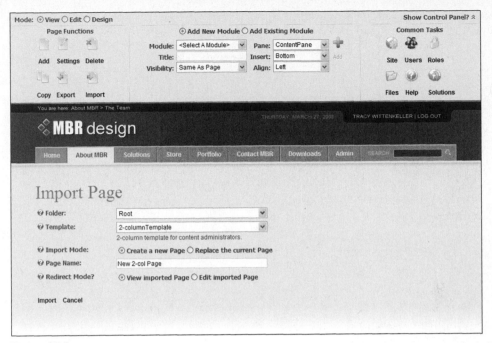

Figure 10-9

Notice that you have some options here as well. First, select the folder you exported your page Template to. Again, the Root folder is the correct selection because you just exported the page Template to the Root folder. The page will refresh, displaying Templates in the Templates drop-down list. As you select the appropriate Template from the drop-down list, you will see the description below, as shown in Figure 10-9.

Next, you need to select the Import Mode — either to Create a new page or Replace the current page you are on when selecting the Import function in the Control Panel. As you can see in Figure 10-9, if you select Create a new Page, the page will again refresh allowing you to input a new Page Name.

The last option to select is the Redirect Mode. Selecting View imported Page will take you to the actual page after clicking Import. Selecting Edit imported Page will, you guessed it, take you to the Page Management page enabling you to apply or update settings for the new page. When ready, click Import to generate your new page, as shown in Figure 10-10.

Figure 10-10

Notice that the new 2-col Page Template has been added as a top-level menu item. If you recall, when you imported the Template, there was no Parent Page menu item selection. Unfortunately, at the time of this writing, the only caveat to creating page Templates is that, upon import, they are created as top-level menu items. The good news is that you already know how to move pages to the appropriate location within a DNN site. However, depending on the Security Roles you define, certain administrators may not have the appropriate permissions to do that.

Applying a Logo

This doesn't quite seem like a tip. But you would be surprised how many people do not know how to use a simple Admin function to display a logo on a DNN website. To apply a logo, first log in as an administrator and navigate to the Admin ⇨ Site Settings page and expand the Appearance section, as shown in Figure 10-11.

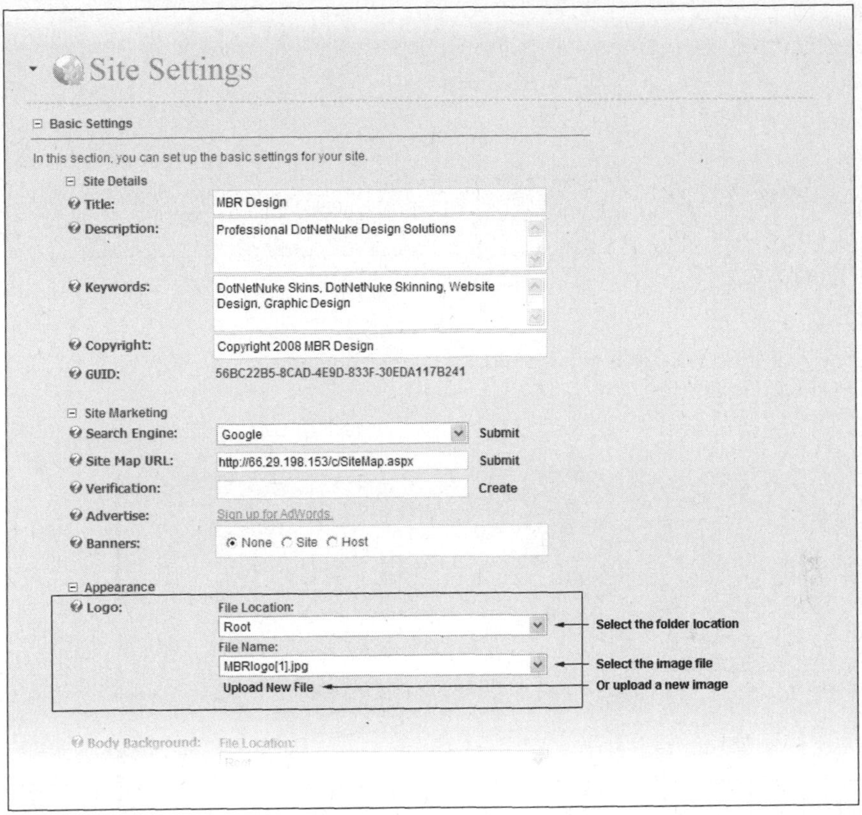

Figure 10-11

Under the Appearance section, you have the ability to select from the list of existing files, or upload a new file, to display as the logo, based on the location of the [LOGO] token that has been included at the skin level. As such, you cannot change the location of the logo here, but you can define the image you want to be displayed quite easily.

If you are using an existing file, as shown in Figure 10-11, first select the folder from the File Location drop-down list that contains the image. Next, select the image from the File Name drop-down list. Then just scroll down to the bottom of the Site Settings page and click the Update link to apply your new logo image.

If you want to upload a new logo file, again, first select the folder from the File Location drop-down list. This will be the folder you upload your new image into. Next, click the Upload New File link below the File Name drop-down list. Your page will refresh displaying the options shown in Figure 10-12.

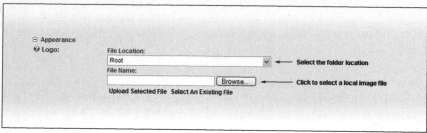

Figure 10-12

Click the Browse button to open a pop-up window, which enables you to select a local file from your computer, as shown in Figure 10-13.

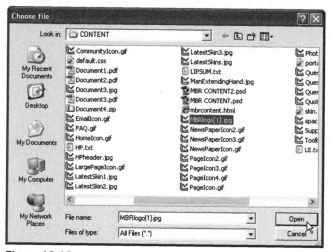

Figure 10-13

After you select your local image and click Open, the path to your image will be displayed in the File Name field, as shown in Figure 10-14.

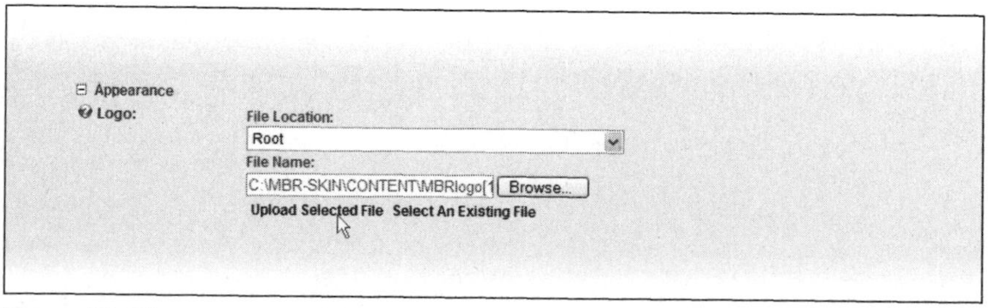

Figure 10-14

Next, click the Upload Selected File link to upload your file, also shown in Figure 10-14. After you upload your file, and after a brief refresh, it will be selected in the File Name drop-down list. Now all you have to do is scroll down to the bottom of the Site Settings page and click the Update link to apply your new logo . . . *voila*!

Changing Your Password

In the previous chapter, you learned about user accounts. But do you know how to quickly edit your account settings without having to contact a website admin? After you log in to a DNN website, simply click on your username, typically located next to the Login/Logout link, illustrated in Figure 10-15.

Figure 10-15

This opens the Manage Profile page for Allison, as illustrated in Figure 10-16.

Figure 10-16

As you can see, from this page, Allison can edit some of her User Credentials, including her First Name, Last Name, Display Name (the name displayed when she is logged in), and her Email Address.

If Allison wanted to change her password periodically, she could easily do so by clicking the Manage Password link, which loads the page displayed in Figure 10-17.

Figure 10-17

She would simply type in her Current Password, and then the New Password of her choice, confirm it, and click Change Password. A confirmation of the password change appears, and an e-mail is sent to the address Allison has included as part of her User Credentials.

If she likes, Allison could also update her profile properties by clicking Manage Profile, which opens the page shown in Figure 10-18.

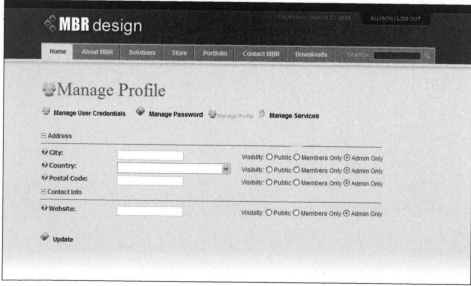

Figure 10-18

Allison could also manage her subscriptions to the site by clicking the Manage Services link, which opens the page shown in Figure 10-19.

Figure 10-19

A discussion of DNN subscriptions is beyond the scope of this book Perhaps this is fodder for my next book . . .

Editing the Terms and Privacy Statement

DNN has standard Terms Of Use and Privacy Statement language that has been developed by attorneys for everyone's benefit. If you want to change the language you certainly can. However, finding the appropriate place to do that is not intuitive whatsoever. Luckily, I'm going to show you where and how.

Log in as Host and navigate to the Host ⇨ Languages page, as shown in Figure 10-20.

Figure 10-20

This will open the Languages page shown in Figure 10-21.

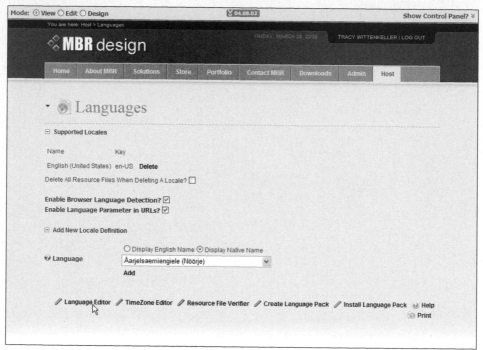

Figure 10-21

Click the Language Editor link shown in Figure 10-21 to open the Language Editor page shown in Figure 10-22.

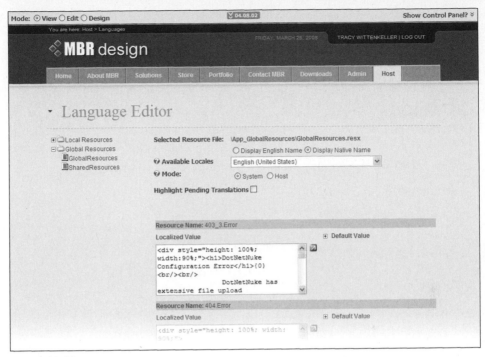

Figure 10-22

Scroll down to **Resource Name:** MESSAGE_PORTAL_PRIVACY.Text and **Resource Name:** MESSAGE_PORTAL_TERMS.Text, as shown in Figure 10-23.

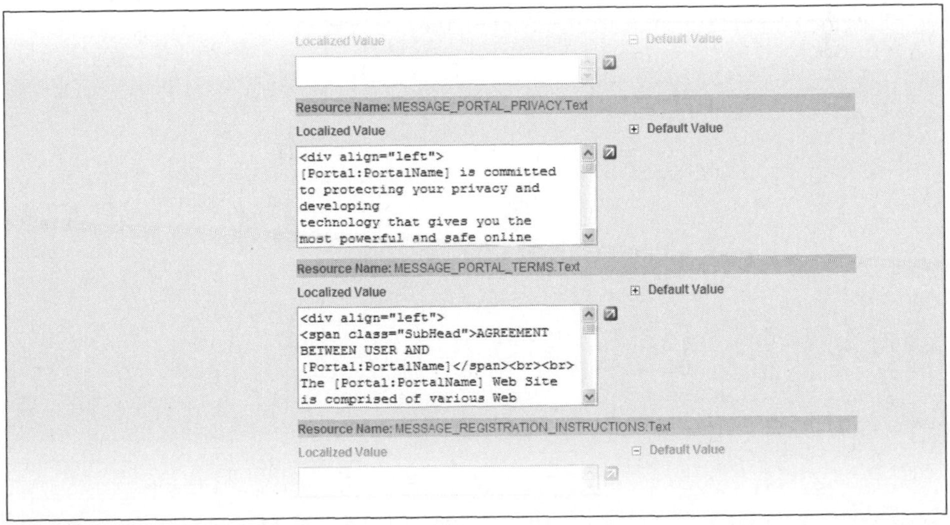

Figure 10-23

As you can see, the Localized Value fields contain the actual code that displays the content on the Privacy Statement and Terms Of Use pages. You can change this however you like. But notice the [Portal:PortalName] tokens in the code. This value dynamically displays the title of your portal as defined in Admin ⇨ Site Settings in the Title field. So be sure to leave this token in the code wherever you want the name of your site to be displayed. Also notice that expanding the Default Value icon shows you a preview of the content in the Localized Value fields, as shown in Figure 10-24.

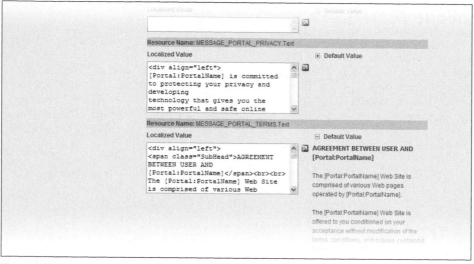

Figure 10-24

To apply any updates, scroll down to the bottom of the Language Editor page and click Update.

As you can see, the Language Editor screen displays the code for all system messages, text, and labels. While you can certainly customize these to your heart's content, be careful, so you get the desired results you're looking for. As a safety precaution, I highly recommend making a backup copy of any Localized Value content before making updates.

Although I've outlined how to update the Language Editor at the Host level, it is important to note that the Language Editor can also be changed at the Admin level, thus allowing multiple portals within the same DNN instance to define their own Privacy Statements and Terms and Conditions.

Resources for DNN Products

Snowcovered (www.snowcovered.com) is a thriving online marketplace for DNN modules, skins, and other applications. This is typically the first place most DNN users go to find additional functionality to add to their DNN websites because there are many, many products listed for sale. I particularly like the way product types are separated into categories such as New Releases and Most Popular on the home page. The Top Developers category on the home page is helpful because it shows you who the top ten sellers are. Chances are, if you purchase a module or skin product from one of the Top Developers, you'll be getting a good product that is well-supported.

Snowcovered.com is really a facilitator of sales from developer to developer, or developer to end user. Anyone can post a product for sale, and all product support is handled through Snowcovered directly between buyers and sellers. Snowcovered takes a whopping 25 percent of transactions, but when you consider that posting products costs you nothing, and the fact that all product support is handled through their system and policed by Snowcovered, it's really a pretty good deal if you don't want the headache of setting up your own e-commerce solution. And getting paid is easy as Snowcovered uses Paypal to pay vendors once each month.

DotNetNuke Marketplace

The DotNetNuke Marketplace (http://marketplace.dotnetnuke.com) is another marketplace offered directly through DNN, where modules and skins are sold. The thing I like about the DotNetNuke Marketplace is that you can submit your products to be reviewed by the DNN Core Team for a small fee. And if your products pass the Core Team's approval, you receive a Reviewed by DotNetNuke stamp of approval that you can display next to them, wherever you decide to sell them. This shows potential customers that your products meet high standards set forth by the Core Team. If I had to choose between a product that was reviewed and endorsed by DNN and one that wasn't, I think I know which one I would go with.

Similar to snowcovered.com, the DotNetNuke Marketplace pays vendors once per month via Paypal.

Summary

DNN is a phenomenal framework for building professional website solutions being used by companies large and small. And the fact that it is open source makes it even better.

When Shaun Walker originally offered the first version as IBuySpy Portal about five years ago, I don't think he could have possibly fathomed how quickly it would evolve and gain such widespread adoption. I believe DNN's increasing popularity over the past few years is attributable to a number of factors.

First, because DNN is open source, it is easy for users and/or companies to test it for viability with their own projects because no monetary cost is involved.

Second, the wide variety of built-in features provides a great deal of flexibility to apply different types of content and functionality. This is attractive for many companies that have various requirements and needs.

Third, the fact that additional functionality can be found and implemented very cost-effectively and efficiently makes DNN extremely extensible and customizable.

Fourth, DNN is built on the Microsoft ASP.NETframework and has a very strong, passionate, and committed developer community providing great support for the framework. In my humble opinion, this is the leading factor in the overall success of the DNN project and a testament to the hundreds of developers that contribute to it on a daily basis.

Over the past few years I have seen larger and larger companies discover and adopt DNN for their use. I have also seen the size of my own DNN projects increase in size and frequency. If you compare DNN's number of downloads to other open source CMS frameworks, you'll see that DNN is ahead of the curve and still picking up steam. With the upcoming impending release of Cambrian, the next major DNN release, DNN is raising the bar even more.

DNN isn't just an open source project. Rather, it's a movement — a movement that is steadily growing organically from a modest beginning. Clearly something is happening that is very exciting. I mean, heck, if it can take a hardcore, engrained Mac guru for over 17 years like myself and bring me to the other side virtually overnight, think what it can potentially do for you.

While I've only scratched the surface, I sincerely hope the information I've provided in this book gives you a glimpse of what can be accomplished with DNN. I am, by no means, an expert in every aspect of the DNN framework, as there is a lot more to it than meets the eye. I'm just someone who has discovered a great tool that has allowed me to achieve a high level of success using it and enjoy what I'm doing 110 percent. I hope DNN does the same for you.

Index

passwords, changing of, 319–321
Security Roles assigned to, 281–287
user controls. *See* **dynamic controls; tokens**
user credentials, 4, 262, 275, 319, 320
user interface (UI), 2, 72, 73
user profiles, registration fields for, 265–273
User Settings, 266
[USER] token, 81, 84, 106, 110
Username option, 160

V

Verified (registration option), 263, 265
vertical relationship, of modules, 90
vertical/horizontal orientation, of menu, 126
visibility snippet, 80, 83, 114, 129
[VISIBILITY] token, 128, 129, 131
Visible column, 268, 270
visible="false" attribute, 80, 83, 114, 129
Vista
DNN installation and, 37–56
Home Premium, 37
UAC, 39, 41, 43
Visual Web Developer (VWD), 10
download/installation, 11–14
website creation with, 16–18
VWD. *See* **Visual Web Developer**

W

Walker, Shaun, 325
WC3 (World Wide Web Consortium), 308
web accessibility, 74–75, 308–309
web application, DNN as, 7
web development tools (Microsoft), 8, 10
web pages, static, 8, 58, 74, 89, 90, 91, 92, 155.
See also **pages**
web server, file-based, 8, 10
web standards, 308–309

web.config file, 58, 62, 63
modification, 58
password length in, 58, 63
Website, MBR Design (mbrdesigncorp.com).
See **MBR Design Website**
websites (DNN), 72–78
accessibility, 74–75, 308–309
appearance, importance of, 72
content. *See* content
content-based, 2–3
CSS files and, 76
customizing, 233–259. *See also* CSS
hierarchy, 155–175. *See also* pages
registration. *See* registration
UI, 2, 72, 73
Why MBR Design? page, 157, 161, 162
widths
column, 310–311
fluid, 249
skin
expansion, 88, 92, 305–307
fixed, 88–89, 92
minimum, 88–89, 106
Windows Features window, 39
Windows operating systems. *See* **Vista; XP Home;**
XP Professional
Windows Server 2003, 10
production web server on, DNN install and, 56–69
Windows Update, 14
World Wide Web Consortium (WC3), 308
wrappers. *See* **containers**

X

XML files, 76–77. *See also* **attributes**
XML Objects, container, 131–132
XP Home, 10
DNN installation and, 10–20
XP Professional, 20
DNN installation and, 20–37